This story is inspired by and dedicated in loving memory
to my darling wife Ginny.

www.mascotbooks.com

Our Journey, My Path Home

For more information, please contact:
Mascot Books
560 Herndon Parkway #120
Herndon, VA 20170
info@mascotbooks.com

Library of Congress Control Number: 2015916816

CPSIA Code: PBANG1115A
ISBN-13: 978-1-63177-436-2

Printed in the United States

our journey

MY PATH HOME

by Jim Yake

Table of Contents

Acknowledgements

The fact is I never set out to write this book…it just sort of happened. It was a difficult endeavor emotionally, something I couldn't have considered undertaking last year. Yet doing so has been both cathartic and intrinsically rewarding for it gave forum to enable me to convey my thoughts and feelings. It is my hope others can and will benefit from reading this story.

There are several individuals who played key roles in order for this writing to come to fruition. Like in the book I will only use nicknames or first names but each of them knows the role they played.

Jan, your unending support and encouragement throughout the entire writing process helped me immeasurably. Several times during the course of the effort I felt like giving up, of abandoning the notion to share this personal story. Long ago Ginny told me she'd love to be my muse. While she was in fact the inspiration for this effort, she was not here to lend her thoughts and encouragement. I am so very thankful you helped fill that void. You are a true friend and I thank you for all your assistance.

Naren, this began as a project to share some of the thoughts contained in the many letters I'd written to a friend who happens to be a priest. It was your suggestion to provide greater background in the form of personal stories that gave rise to what became part one. Upon completion of those anecdotes, it became clear to me what I needed to do. The deeply personal story contained in part two would never have taken shape had you not quietly yet effectively coached me along. Perhaps it was serendipity that brought us together but whatever it was, I am and will always be grateful.

Lastly there are three friends whom I asked to read an early draft of my writing: Mary, Michael, and Jim. Each of you gave me heartfelt feedback that helped me temper the tone and tenor of this writing. You each made the effort purely out of the desire to help me. I am very fortunate to count you each as dear friends.

Prologue

The following is a true story of two people. The incidents, events, struggles, successes, and failures all took place as depicted.

My purpose for writing this lies in a desire to share the story in order to serve as a caution to those who, as I did, may lose their way along life's path. Yet just as important, perhaps the story may serve to provide comfort and solace to any who have suffered the loss of a loved one.

I am not a particularly unique or special person. Like most of you I've lived a fairly normal life. Both my wife and I were raised in large loving families. This gave us a significant leg up on many whose start in life isn't seasoned by such care and compassion. What makes me perhaps a little different is that I've had a special partner on this journey; a truly incredible person. She has been my girlfriend, my wife, my best friend, my teacher, and my very foundation.

There are facets of this writing that speak to matters of spirituality and of religion. I don't purport to have all the answers; or even know all the questions. I am not a theologian, a scholar, or any sort of expert in the realms of human interactions or social science. But I am a person whose own life experiences may provide insight useful to others. The path I have followed and the one I follow today may not be right for all. Your choices may be different. The key is to choose wisely once you find the one that best fits your needs and desires. Life offers us many choices and there is no single best path, no "one size fits all."

No one's life is a panacea for happiness, no less mere contentment or satisfaction. Yet each of us has within us the ability to find purpose and meaning. Most often this is found beyond our own self interests, beyond the little worlds we tend to create.

It is my hope that this writing will affect you in some profound way. That it may awaken in you the need to reassess your choices and priorities.

Part I

Part I consists of a series of anecdotes; true stories of two people who met, fell in love, and lived a life together. These provide some insight into their shared experiences from the perspective of one of them, me. It is my intent to give you this background so you can both understand this couple and perhaps see some similarities they share with that of your own life. While this is a first-person account, I made every effort to be both objective and accurate in depicting the various events and occasions.

How We Met

It was an early afternoon in August of '74 as I walked to lunch. The talk I'd had the night before with my parents still echoed in my mind. My dad had said that if I wasn't going to be attending college again this fall, I'd have to start paying rent…$25 a week. Knowing that, I figured I'd have to sell a lot more shoes to boost my commission base or go out less frequently. I wasn't keen on cutting back the latter so I'd decided to work the entire day instead of leaving at 3:00 PM as originally scheduled.

I was heading up to Amiel's, a local chain of sub shops that made a sub called a steak Napoli. It was my favorite and I was hungry, having had nothing to eat for breakfast. I almost never ate breakfast; cereal was a staple in our house. I wasn't a fan of "mixed milk," a term we used for mixing whole milk with powdered milk and water. Being one of seven kids we always had mixed milk…and I really didn't like it. As I walked into Amiel's there was this gal behind the counter who took my order. She was perhaps the most beautiful girl I'd ever seen—and I'd seen some pretty girls. She was so quiet, really shy. Not the usual quality I'd observed in girls as attractive as she. I sensed an innocence and vulnerability in those brief moments I'd placed my order. As she began to turn away to put in my order I looked to see if she had a name tag. I couldn't see one. The following week I returned in hopes of perhaps striking up a conversation with her; she'd left quite an impression on me, but she wasn't there. Same held true the next week too. I'd felt perhaps I'd lost my chance to meet her. I was sort of mad at myself for not having gone back that first day and introducing myself.

On September 4th I went down to the Reunion Inn; my most frequented tavern. It was highly unusual for me to go out on a Wednesday night but I got a call from a friend and wanted to get out of my parents' house. I didn't have much money on me. Those days I was spending most all I made, and with "rent" in the offing, something had to give. I was meeting up with my pal Gary. My two closest friends (Paul & Gary) had no interest in going out midweek…Fridays & Saturdays were our norm. Gary and I often went out, but mostly to other bars. I had been going out a lot at the time, in part since my old girlfriend had broken up with me back in May. It wasn't the toughest break up or the best. It convinced me to "play the field" as Gary would say. Around 9:30 PM I was talking to a gal (Suzy) I'd seen many times down at the Reunion. As we were chatting near the jukebox, that girl from Amiel's walked up to Suzy to say goodnight. I couldn't believe my luck. I asked Suzy if she'd introduce me, and Suzy initially said no in jest. She said if she did, she knew I would totally ignore her as my attention would be on her friend. Suzy quickly relented and introduced me to her good friend Ginny.

I spoke to Suzy and Ginny for only a couple of minutes before Ginny said she had to leave. I asked her to stay, to just talk, but she insisted it was time for her to leave. Without going into details, she told me she had had a terrible day but needed to get out of the house for a bit so she had come down to the Reunion. She insisted it was time for her to leave. I offered her a ride home (I was driving my parents' car, the '74 Pinto). Ginny said she would not get into any car with a stranger and besides, she lived fairly close by…she'd walked down that evening so was more than capable of walking home alone. Doing my best to salvage the moment, I asked her if I might walk her home, and she accepted. I turned to Suzy to say goodnight when out the door went Ginny. I ditched the beers I had in my hand; my friend Gary had just bought me another.

As we walked through the parking lot I pointed to the car I'd driven down, saying, "you sure you don't want me to drive you home?" Ginny just kept walking. We talked all the way to her home; with me of course doing most the talking (one of my well-known traits). Our chat was light, nothing too serious. I remember telling her I'd seen her working at Amiel's back in August. Told her I'd returned several times to see if she was there as I hoped to introduce myself. She stopped walking and gave me a curious look. I was afraid she might think me odd for having said anything. Instead she explained she'd only worked there a couple of weeks. She said she had a tough time standing for a long time as she was afflicted with some sort of problem that gave her severe leg pains. Anyway, the day I'd spied her at work was the last or second-to-last day she'd worked there. I told her I had graduated from Bishop Kearney High School a year before but had been working as the assistant manager at the shoe store in a nearby plaza. I explained that I wasn't supposed to be at home, but had decided just a few weeks before to further delay my college plans.

Ginny noted that she'd just graduated from Eastridge High School that year. I mentioned that my best friends (Paul & Gary) had just graduated from there as well. Over the years I'd attended a number of events at her school but had never seen her. She commented that she wasn't much into sports but had gone to a few school dances. Ah, common ground…I'd been to a few there too. She asked if I was seeing anyone steady. I recall telling her that I was seeing several girls but no one on a steady basis. After about fifteen minutes we arrived at what turned out to be her house, opposite the volunteer fire department. It was sort of an awkward moment—I knew I wanted to kiss her goodnight—but I'd yet to get her number. I blurted out, "can you give me your phone number?" She paused…not a good sign, I thought. She said she wasn't sure that was a good idea, as she only recently ended a relationship with some guy. Undaunted, I pressed forward, telling her I wasn't asking for a date but just for her phone number so that we might chat again. I reminded her that she seemed to enjoy our talk as we'd walked…felt perhaps we could talk some more. I said, "I'm a much better talker than a listener, but you seemed to enjoy listening." At that, she smiled. Her smile was absolutely captivating. She fumbled in her purse, commenting that she had no pen or paper to write down her phone number. Hearing that, I stated "That's okay. I have a thing for numbers, I won't forget it." She gave me her number, thanked me for the walk home, then turned and ran up to the side porch door. I waited until I saw her go into the house before walking back to the bar.

The next day I was dying to call Ginny but I knew I best not. I didn't want to come across as over-anxious or desperate…so I'd play it cool. I had plans to go out again, this time to the Varsity Inn, aka "the V.I."; a bar about fifteen miles from home. It being Thursday, there was a $2 cover. For that you could drink all the draft beer you want, meet girls, and even do some dancing. I remember I had a good time…almost too good. I had no idea how I made it home. Guess all I can say is that things were different then. The legal drinking age was eighteen and cops seldom bothered to nail us by hanging out near places like the VI.

On Friday I had to work but only until 4:00 PM. I had plans to get together with my best friends down at the Reunion Inn; the "big R" we called it. But more importantly, I planned to make that important call to Ginny. As I walked home from work I thought about what I'd say to her. Even though I was rather outgoing, I must admit I was a little nervous about calling. Maybe she wouldn't remember me? Maybe she wouldn't be home...out on a date perhaps? Lots of things went through my head as I walked that mile home.

It was five o'clock sharp as I began to dial her number. The phone rang twice, then a woman answered, I figured it must be her mom. I asked to speak to Ginny, and the woman asked who was calling. I almost lost it...should I say Jim, Jimmy, or simply say "a friend?" I opted with "Jimmy, the boy she met the other night." I could tell her mom sort of covered the phone and called out, "Ginny, the phone's for you!" At that, I could hear an extension being picked up and her mom hanging up. I learned later that Ginny's bedroom was in the basement and that she had a phone in it. I began by reintroducing myself, "It's Jimmy, remember me, the guy that walked you home the other night?" Ginny replied "Of course I remember you, you walked me home." Gathering my nerve, I then asked if she could go out that night. She could not. I then asked about the next night (Saturday) but she told me her parents were going out on a late afternoon boat trip on the lake so she couldn't. She wasn't allowed to go out with a guy her parents hadn't met.

This was not what I'd anticipated. Sunday was no good for me as I had to work soon after church. In what may have been a feeble attempt to salvage the situation, I asked if there was any way possible I might meet them before they went out? Ginny paused for what seemed like forever, and then told me to call in an hour. Now I don't know what was in her mind, but I was willing to do anything she asked just to get a chance to go on a date. Fifty-seven minutes later I called her back. Ginny said she'd spoken to both her mom and dad...that under the circumstances they would have her best friend's parents (Mr. & Mrs. Kirtchner) act as their surrogates in meeting me. But only under the stipulation that

Ginny and I would go on a double date with Kathy and her boyfriend John. I immediately agreed. I asked what a good time would be to meet her; "Is 7:30 PM good for you?" She said that sounded good to her…at that I told her I looked forward to seeing her.

So, later that night I went down to the Reunion to meet up with my two buddies, Paul and Gary. They were already there when I arrived. I can remember like it was yesterday. They greeted me, then I turned to Paul and said: "You're going to think I'm nuts but I think I've met the gal I'm going to marry." At that he sort of laughed and said, "Who is she?" I told them of my meeting her on Wednesday, of walking her home and about our phone call earlier that evening. Paul was a bit skeptical, saying to me, "Jimmy you just met her…you haven't even been on a date yet, how can you say you're going to marry her?" But I reiterated, "I just feel it, she's the one… I just know it."

It was many months later when I learned that Ginny had been saddened that I'd not called her sooner than I had. But once I did call that Friday, she was on the phone for most of the evening talking to her friends…she'd told them all how happy she was because "he called." Not Jimmy Yake, but just "he." It turned out she had been on the phone that Thursday after our walk telling them all about this new boy she'd met the night before.

Three years later, as Ginny and I were walking up to church to attend one of our pre-Cana sessions (November 1977), I bragged to Ginny that I knew on Sept 6th that she was the woman I'd marry. I tend to be rather competitive. Guess I was gloating a bit; rather "proud" of the fact that I knew she was the one so soon after having met. But then Ginny turned to me as we approached the church and said, "well, that wasn't the case for me…I knew if I was ever going to marry, it would be you, and I knew it the night you walked me home."

(Refer to Pictures section, pictures 01 and 02)

Her 19th Birthday

I'd begun college at the University of Buffalo in January 1975, four months after having met Ginny. Her birthday was on March 28th, but I wasn't sure what to give her. I'd given her a few gifts so far, including one that was rather unusual; the blue suede winter coat with the Maja lamb collar. She'd seen it when we were at a mall in November 1974, she loved it but she said it was too expensive. I said I'd get it for her but she refused, saying I needed to save up for college. She was often that way, postponing or denying herself things. I don't listen too well at times. A few days later I went back and bought it for her as a Christmas gift but I gave it to her beforehand. She looked stunning in it and it was her favorite color; blue.

In February '75 I was over at her parents' house, home from college for the weekend. She and I had been up in the attic looking for something for her mom. It was then I first saw this old beaten up small wood chest. Ginny told me it had come from her grandma's home; originally all the way from Sweden. To hear her tell of it, the chest was made back in the mid-1800s. Over the years it had become quite beaten up and was covered in many coats of paint. Its last use was as a garage tool bin at her grandparents'. I remember having gone to that house soon after we'd met to help her dad with moving some stuff. Her grandma passed away just weeks after we'd met in '74. Some thought it strange that I attended the wake and burial, but she'd asked me to stay with her, and I was more than willing to comply. Seeing the chest that day gave me an idea.

I had done a little furniture refinishing—restoration really. Ginny seemed to really like the chest despite its poor condition. She figured one day she'd fix it up. That evening I'd been invited to stay for dinner. Afterwards, when her dad went into the living room to have his af-ter-dinner cigar, I asked him if he'd mind if I fixed the chest up for Ginny for her birthday present. He liked the idea. In the next few days he and I arranged a time for me to pick it up. I'd come over without them telling Ginny I was there, as she often spent time in her bedroom late in the afternoon listening to 45s on her old turntable. I snuck in—quietly—went upstairs in the attic with her dad and then took it out to the car. I closed the hatchback, drove it to my parents', and stuck it in the basement where I would work on it over the coming weeks. I learned later that evening when I returned to see Ginny that she thought she heard the Pinto earlier, but her dad said it was just someone turning around in their driveway; a white lie for a just cause.

I didn't have a lot of time to do the work since I was at college during the week. That left me only the weekends, which was tough since Ginny and I spent most of the time together when I was home. I can recall us chatting the next week when I got home late Friday via a bus from Buffalo. She asked me what time I was coming over to see her in the morning. I told her I had chores to do and some "homework," so I wouldn't get over until later in the afternoon. She sounded disappointed but she said she understood. I'd planned to begin work on the chest, having already picked up some supplies Friday evening before going down to see her.

Saturday morning I was down in my parents' basement lathering on "Strip-Ease," a rather toxic paint stripper. It took me hours to get off the many coats of paint. By 3:00 PM I'd removed most of it but still had a lot of work to do…sanding was going to be a real chore. I didn't have a mechanical sander, so this effort was truly going to be a "labor of love." Over the next several weekends I spent many hours on this project. I'd selected a "Danish walnut" (dark) stain, and porcelain hardware with antiqued back plates. More than once my mom sort of balked at the smell that was filling the house as I used the paint stripper, stain, and finally the polyurethane finish. I put three coats of poly on it to give it a durable finish, sanding each coat with steel wool to get the finish smooth. By the third week in March it was done. I liked it…but the question was, would she?

In 1975, her birthday was on a Friday. I wanted to give her the chest that day but I had classes to attend before I could get the early afternoon bus to Rochester. I went to all three of my Friday classes then took the Trailways bus to downtown Rochester. From there I'd have to take a city bus out to the suburbs which would leave me off about a mile from my parents' home. As I walked that mile home I was anxious, as I wasn't sure she'd like the chest. It had come out fairly well, though I wished I'd gotten the finish even smoother. She and I were going out that night to celebrate her birthday…I believe we went to the "big R," as we so often did. We were supposed to meet up with some of our friends, including some of Ginny's high school girlfriends. I remember taking a quick shower, then loading the "Sweden Chest" into the Pinto. I had an old sheet draped around it to prevent any scratches, and to ensure she didn't see beforehand.

Her mom and dad knew I was bringing the chest. They too had kept it a secret. When I got down to her house, Ginny's dad had called her down to the basement as a diversionary ploy. He told her he could not find one of his tools he needed to adjust the water connection on her mom's portable dishwasher. Her parents had five girls, no boys. Still, Ginny was the only one of the kids who knew anything about hand tools or working on a car. She and her dad had a special bond, in part because she had always shown interest in helping him on home projects. Well, the diversion worked long enough to enable me to get the chest into the living room where I kept it covered up with that old sheet. It wouldn't be hard to tell what it was, so when Ginny came upstairs to the kitchen, we'd closed the door into the rest of the house. Her parents then went into the other room—her dad taking my camera which I'd left atop the chest. When he called my name it meant he was ready so I could bring her in. I made her close her eyes…walked her to a point beside the gift. I was excited for her to see it.

Her dad took a picture with my old Kodak X30 instamatic camera just as I lifted the sheet up and away; the picture captured her surprise. Her look is so very precious…she truly was surprised. She gave me several big hugs and kisses and then insisted on moving some things around in her bedroom to accommodate her new piece of furniture. As a result, we went out a little later than planned. That night she told me how special she felt knowing how much time and thought I'd put into her birthday gift.

Though they never said much about it, I always felt that it was this gift that really sold her parents on me. The gift, it seemed, had really impressed them, for they knew how much work was involved in restoring it. At that point she and I had been dating six-and-a-half months. No doubt in my mind that her parents knew how very much I loved her. But it was the gift of the chest and all the work involved which I think made them see that this guy Jimmy was likely to be around for quite some time. A "keeper," as Ginny would say in jest at times.

(Refer to Pictures section, picture 03)

Summerfest 1975

Ginny and I both love music. Though my tastes back then were a bit eclectic, ranging from Led Zeppelin to the Carpenters, we both loved certain groups. One of those was the Beach Boys. There were so many of their tunes we liked: "Surfer Girl," "Wouldn't It Be Nice," "Don't Worry Baby," etc.

Shortly after meeting Ginny we were down at the Reunion. I asked her what songs she'd like me to play in their jukebox. She replied, "You pick." The first song I selected was "Surfer Girl." When it came on I put my arms around her waist and mimicked the lyrics as it played. Now Ginny's not from California, she doesn't have blond hair…but those lyrics somehow seem to fit her to a tee: "Little surfer, little one…Made my heart come all undone…Do you love me, do you, surfer girl?"

In the summer of 1975 we learned that the Beach Boys were going to be the featured group at the Summerfest music festival being held at the New York State fairgrounds in Syracuse, NY. This was a concert we couldn't miss.

The concert date was Tuesday, September 2nd, the week before the un-official end of summer and my return to college. There were a total of six of us going, including my brother Michael, my good friend Gary, Ginny, myself, and two gals my brother knew. Gary had offered to drive since he had a van with plenty of room.

The weather was questionable with possible showers expected. As con-cert day approached I got antsy about the forecast. This was the last "event" of my summer so I wanted everything to be perfect.

We took the thruway to Syracuse, exiting as several billboards instruct-ed. We had a great time goofing off and talking all the way there. As we tooled down the thruway, I loaded my camera with film, then popped a flashcube on in time to take a picture of Ginny just as she was about to tell me to put my camera away. The camera loved her, and so did I.

(Refer to Pictures section, picture 04)

As we'd driven east, the weather seemed to get better. The concert had been declared a "rain or shine event," so we knew we'd be in for a show one way or the other. I don't know why I had such angst about the weather other than I wanted it to be a fun and memorable day. Aside from the two other gals going with us, no one but me seemed particularly concerned about the likelihood of rain. Gary's rather easy-going, laid back, so little seemed to faze him. Ginny, she seemed to revel in the moment.

We got to the fairgrounds in plenty of time. Aside from ourselves, we'd brought a full cooler of beer for the concert. As we approached the turnstiles to enter, we were told that although beer was permitted, no bottles or cans were allowed. Seems the organizers had had some bad experience with people tossing beverage containers. They did give us two plastic gallon jugs that we could fill with the ice cold beer; not even our cooler was permitted. Guess people must have thrown those too. I hated the idea of lukewarm beer, not to mention backwash.

We got to our seats ahead of the first group's appearance. I think it was Jefferson Starship; a retread of the old group Jefferson Airplane. No sooner had they begun to play when a thunder crack echoed through the stands, followed by torrential rain. It rained for fifteen or twenty minutes, and thanks to the sheet of plastic we'd brought, we hadn't gotten too wet. Perhaps that was it and the sun would come out?

As the afternoon grew into early evening, it continued to rain on and off. A new group would perform, only to be driven off the stage by heavy rains. The longest intermission lasted about thirty minutes; they were falling behind schedule. I began to get concerned that if the rains persisted, the Beach Boys might not show. But show they did, arriving by helicopter in the early evening. By this point all the jugged beer was flat and we were all drenched, but I put it aside once the Beach Boys got on stage. They were the only one of the six acts that day that didn't get driven from the stage by rain. They'd played all our favorites, performing longer than any of the other groups.

The concert ended a bit later than planned. Since I had stopped drinking hours before (I hate flat beer), I drove Gary's van back to Rochester. The drive was nerve-racking, as thick fog blanketed the thruway, but eventually we made it home safely. Upon dropping her off, I asked Ginny if she'd had a good time. Her answer was simple but telling: "I always have a good time whenever I'm with you."

Odd as it may sound; I now fondly look back upon that day, though at the time I recall how unhappy I'd been about the lousy weather. The Friday night following the concert a bunch of us had met up. The Summerfest concert was a central topic that evening. From the way Ginny and Gary spoke about it and laughed at the challenges we had that day, you'd think they'd gone to a different event. That says something about living in the moment and making the best of a bad situation; both lessons which I just didn't see at the time. Some of us are slow learners. Yet to this day whenever I hear a Beach Boys song, I remember that day and I think of my own little "surfer girl."

The Proposal of Marriage

I've always been the kind of guy who plans things out ahead and adjusts for contingencies. When I was planning my proposal to her in December 1975, I decided to ask Ginny's parents for their daughter's hand in marriage. I'd sought support from one of her friends to get her out of her house so that I might have some time to speak to her parents. It was a Saturday morning when my unannounced visit to her parents took place. It was the first week in December 1975, if I recall correctly.

I went to the side porch door, rapping gently. Her mom answered, told me Ginny was out for a bit but was expected back in a couple of hours. I asked if she had a little time that I might talk with her and her husband about Ginny and me. We went into the living room, she made no move to bring her husband into the room; so rather than go get him, I simply began. Rather nervously I expressed my intention to ask Ginny to marry me. Her mom was quiet for a moment before she spoke. She told me that with me in college, Ginny being very young (just 19), and with our history of having a rather intense relationship (read as vocal and passionate) that she thought it best for us to wait a few years. She went on to cite a recent example. I had called Ginny very late a week or two prior, after we'd been out. I'd come home to find my pet hamster (Chubs) had died. Ginny answered the call, and both of us ending up crying…enough beer coupled with a sad event tends to have such an effect. Well, her mom ended up picking up the phone upon hearing Ginny crying on the phone. This day I proposed she said, "Jimmy, you and Ginny are too young…why just the other week you both were crying on the phone over the death of pet hamster of all things. Life gets much harder, you both have growing up to do." I had not anticipated such a reply; I was in trouble. (Picture a fighter plane being shot down, flames streaming from the wings…I had to do something fast.)

Undaunted, and armed with single-mindedness and unmitigated gall, I proceeded to go into her parents' bedroom where her dad was reading on their bed. I had the very same conversation with him while her mom was still in the living room. His reaction was quite different. He told me how pleased he was with the idea of having me in their family. He came out and announced as he walked into the living room, "Ruthie isn't that great that the kids plan to marry?" Her mom gave me "that look," or perhaps more like the evil eye. Her dad said to us, "I know it's only morning, but I'm going to fix us each a drink so we can toast to this great news." He then left the room, leaving me to Ginny's mom's wrath. Utter silenced ensued; you could hear a pin drop. But her mom relented and told me it would be okay, yet we still had a lot of growing up to do. Talk about side-stepping a bullet.

A week or two later I planned on surprising Ginny with my proposal at what used to be the Shakespeare restaurant situated at the base of the downtown Xerox tower. Right before I left, my parents told me that in order to take the car I had to drop off a number of packaged Christmas gifts at the downtown post office. It being December 20th, I was a little put out, but it was their car. Further, my mom wasn't done wrapping and addressing them, so I would have to first go pick up Ginny then bring her back to my house to get the packages. I drove down to Ginny's just as it had begun to snow big puffy flakes.

After returning home to get the parcels I held the car door to get Ginny safely into the car. As I walked in front of the car I disappeared. Normally sure-footed, I slipped on the wet snow, falling flat on my behind. I got quickly up and made my way around to the driver's side. As I opened the door, there was a strange silence. Ginny had this funny quirk; she always laughed when she saw someone fall down as soon as she knew they were okay, just a bruised ego. Well this time she was laughing so hard that she could not breathe. My pride was a bit ruffled but I have to admit it must have looked funny. Ginny kept laughing… and then saying, "one second you were there, then whoops, you were gone!" This was followed by more excessive laughing. Tears were streaming down her face. It wasn't that funny…at least to me.

The snow was coming down heavier as we made our way downtown. I could not find a place to park outside the main post office so I ended up parking with the flashers on…right in a bus lane. Though I was gone only five minutes, when I came out Ginny told me to take her home. She said multiple buses came along blaring their horns at her in the car. "Just take me home, I don't want to go to dinner." I finally convinced her to go with me to dinner after repeatedly apologizing for having left her in such a predicament. We got to the restaurant at about 7:30 PM. As soon as we walked into the Shakespeare and the waiter took us to our booth, Ginny saw the bottle of champagne, flowers, and even a plant with a stick figure Christmas mouse. She looked at me and said, "What's this all about?" I replied, "Oh nothing, I just wanted this to be a special night." We sat, ordered our dinners and a drink. When the drinks came, that was my cue to pop the question. Reaching across the table, I handed her a wrapped little box. She took it, but with a rather disconcerting look. She opened the box, and then closed it while pushing the ring back to me saying, "I'm not good enough to marry you." At that, I took the ring/box back, got out of my seat, and stood beside her before going down on one knee. "Ginny, you would make me the happiest guy in the world if you would accept my proposal of marriage, I love you so." She began to cry as I slipped the ring on her finger. People and staff within earshot began to clap when they heard her say the word "yes." The rest of the time at the restaurant was a blur. I was so very happy and she was too.

After we'd eaten dinner and despite the snowfall, I told her we were going to go to the Reunion Inn to celebrate…that's where we'd met. But Ginny said, "I'm not wearing this dress down to the big R." (She had made the dress herself.) So we stopped at her parents' so she could change. I suspected it was really so she could show her mom and dad her engagement ring. We got down to the tavern at around 10:00 PM. Many of our friends, as well as my three brothers, were down there to greet us. She said to me, "How did you know I would say yes? I guess you were pretty confident in yourself." I simply replied, "I love you with all my heart and thought you felt likewise." At that she gave me a big hug and kiss. It was one of the happiest days of our lives.

I will never understand how she could have ever felt that she "wasn't good enough" for me. After all these years it is I that truly believes I got the better of the deal. She was, is, and always will be the love of my life.

Changes (College Years)

It was late afternoon on January 12th, 1975. I stood in the rain wondering how everything had just changed…again. It's not often at this time of year in Upstate New York that it rains, but it did on this day, as I can recall my face was wet.

In just four short months, Ginny and I had become inseparable. Our parents had commented on that fact more times than I care to remember. Since our chance meeting in early September, my life revolved around her, and to my great surprise the feeling was reciprocated. Though I was only a young man of twenty, I'd never felt this way before about anything or anyone.

Today my parents had dropped me off at college; of course she'd come along as well. They helped me get situated and get my few things moved into my assigned dorm room in McDonald Hall. We'd met my roommate, Raj. Turns out he was a graduate student in biochemistry who had come all the way from India to attend the specialty graduate program the college offered. This was my first campus visit since I'd blown off the opportunity to see it the prior week. Everything was new to me, including the emotions that welled up within.

I recall those last moments together like it was yesterday. My dad had driven the family station wagon; a 1972 Ford Suburban complete with faux wood grain along its sides. Ginny and I had sat together the way there…not talking aloud a whole heck of a lot, though we whispered to each other how everything was going to be okay. As if our saying such would make it so. But I knew better, as did she. The dread of that day had been on my mind for quite some time. As a child I had always dreaded the start of school in the fall. That reality had always sort of ruined my mid-August birthday celebration as I grew up. Seeing ads on TV or in the paper for "start of school" sales had always cast a pall on the idea of turning a year older. Yet this wasn't August or even September, it was January. But it was my fault, for I'd been scheduled to begin college the prior semester but decided rather late in the game to change my start date. Little did I know at the time how critical to my life that change would become.

Had I not "chickened out" of beginning college in the fall, she and I would never have met. Still, I remember how disappointed my dad was that I'd postponed my start date. You see, I'd also initially signed up to join the college's NROTC program. My dad had done so some twenty plus years before at his college. He'd told me what a great difference having joined the Navy had made in his life. I guess my backing out was sort of a shot against the path he'd chosen, though that's not why I'd backed out. I just wasn't ready; call it immaturity or a desire to enjoy the initial fruits of "independence" while still living at home. I'd had a job and enough money to frequently go out; what more could a guy need? Between May and September of 1974, I went out a lot and saved almost nothing.

Yet as this January afternoon began to draw to a close, I felt I knew what it would mean…or at least I thought I did. My dad and mom seemed thrilled that I was finally committing to college. I'd "taken off" the last year and a half since high school to live in the "real world"…or so I thought. I'd been an assistant manager at the nearby Endicott Johnson shoe store. That job taught me that there was no way I wanted to slave away in retailing my whole life; I needed to get a degree. My brother had gone to the local community college but then ended up in a factory job…and I didn't want that either. My two closest friends had taken different paths. One worked in a factory, the other had begun college in the fall. So I had to do something or I knew my opportunities would be quite limited. I didn't have any real aptitude for a trade-related job or any particular inclination for such. I didn't know what I wanted to do or be. That is, until I met Ginny. She was the main reason I knew in my heart I had to go to college. She had just graduated high school the year before and she had no desire to go to college. She didn't see herself as the "college type." Ginny would say she wasn't "book smart," but over time I learned how wise she was in so many ways; especially when it came to the most important things in life.

Shortly after my parents, Ginny, and I returned from a late lunch at the Red Barn, my dad noted it was time for them to leave. I said my good-byes to my parents; Dad was smiling but Mom seemed to be fighting back the tears. It was time for Ginny and I to say our goodbyes. I remember looking into her face, and her eyes were tearing up. I held her in my arms and assured her everything was going to be just fine.

So there I stood watching as they drove away, she in the back seat with the palm of her hand pressed to the window, a final wave. It hit me like a ton of bricks. How was I going to do this? All I wanted, all we wanted, was to be together. I knew I had to do this or I'd never amount to anything and we'd always have to struggle financially. I was no Einstein but I knew money, or rather the lack of it, was often the cause of so many failed relationships.

Time seemed to sort of stand still. I just continued to look in the direction they'd left and wondered how this was the right solution. I was never what you'd call stoic, but I also didn't often wear my heart on my sleeve. But that was before, as now everything had changed. I turned around, then walked up to my room to write her a letter—the first of many during that first semester.

You have to remember; have to have been around back then to understand. In those days there was no Internet. Long distance phone calls were expensive. No one uses that phrase anymore, but it was a harsh reality back then. We found that out in short order. What was it, something like ninety cents for three minutes of talking? That first week I'd called her twice. I spent more on those calls than I did food for that day. So writing letters became our only weekday means of communication, and we both did so religiously. I learned a long time later that she'd saved every one of my letters...just as I'd saved hers. Matter of fact, as I write this story I know where all of them are, safe and secure. Perhaps sometime in the future I'll read them again, but not now—not for a long time.

I had no problem getting back into the swing of college. Having gone to a parochial high school I was used to a full course load. That first week I recall signing up to seven courses my first semester; twenty-two credit hours. That was a learning experience. In subsequent semesters I never signed up for more than six courses.

It was the plan that I'd take a bus back home that first weekend, and so I did. I didn't even bother to eat dinner at home, but raced down in my parents' second car as soon as they'd let me borrow it. I'd called her as soon as I'd gotten home. I don't even think I asked, just told her we were going out, but that I'd be down to see her in just a few minutes. You'd think I'd been away a month by the reception I got when I arrived at her house that Friday night. Fortunately, her mom had invited me for dinner. I'd not eaten a thing that entire day. I was so focused on getting back to Rochester, getting home to her.

Now, eating at Ginny's home was a bit different from how it was at my parents'. My parents had seven kids: four boys, then three girls. Ginny though, was one of five girls. None of them were "big eaters." But when you're one of seven, or maybe one of four boys, you learn to eat fast and as much as you're allowed. At Ginny's, they served the food somewhat sparingly from my perspective. Worse yet, her younger sister had a habit of taking a lot of food but then not eating it—an unheard-of action in my experience. By the time this day arrived, her mom knew my voracious eating habits. That meal, she made me two burgers to start. Funny, but they often had hamburgers along with spaghetti and meat sauce. To me the two were different meals…you either had one or the other, but never both. That night I was glad we were having both.

By eight o'clock that evening, Ginny and I were down at the bar. Uncharacteristically, we'd sat at a small table and not along the bar itself. I wanted to see her face…her beautiful eyes, her wondrous smile, her angelic face. I'd only been away for five days and couldn't quite figure how I could miss her so…but I did. And she, well, she seemed to mirror my own sense of the matter too. We had a great night. That first Saturday back we spent the whole day together. But then came Sunday…a day I'd learn to dread, for it was time to go back. Before I left my dad had a talk with me. He told me that while it was nice to see me come home, he expected me to limit my visits to every two or three weeks. We'd never discussed it before, but he made it clear I needed to stay at college the next weekend or I would never get the "full college experience." I didn't like the notion one bit and even though I was paying for college with my own savings and loans, it's not like I could dismiss his expectations without ramifications.

That Sunday night I wrote her, and among other things told her what my dad had said about not coming home every week. It wasn't until Wednesday that I got her initial reply. She seemed to take it well…said she understood what he meant. She also wrote that I had to understand that what I was doing was important to "us," not just her or me. Like most all her letters, it was so good to hear from her. I always read her letters over and over.

The following Friday rolled around, as it's prone to do. I planned to get some reading done then perhaps I'd go down to the Ratskeller later that evening for some drinks with a couple new friends. That's just what I did. But come Saturday morning, I was miserable. I'd walked into town, just sort of occupied myself trying to fill the day. By late Saturday evening I just had to call her. I called at 6:00 PM; her mom answered but then called down to Ginny to pick up. She did immediately. We spoke for at least fifteen minutes; damn the cost. I told her I couldn't do this. It got quiet...she asked, "What do you mean?" I told her I couldn't stay away on weekends no matter what my parents thought. What worked or didn't work for them wasn't going to work for me, for us. Then all I could hear was her crying. She told me when I said I couldn't do this, she thought I meant have a long-distance relationship, but when I told her "it" was being away from her...well, that made her cry for a different reason. She told me she had been miserable. She was asked to go out the night before with her girlfriends but declined. Instead, she had spent the day cleaning her room and reading over the letters I'd already sent her.

It was at this point that I learned the meaning of two words that would remain with me most of my life. Those words were "miss" and "sacrifice." The word "miss" has several meanings. For the first time in my life, the word took on a whole new level of intensity. The sense of longing, of yearning for another the way I felt about Ginny was new to me. I knew it no longer as a word but as an intense emotion. We both understood that sacrifice was necessary, giving up something now for the future. That's what this was all about. In time that meaning would also have deep-seated implications. But now, that day, I told her she'd see me the following Friday, hell or high water I was coming home to her.

By the third week in college I also learned an economics lesson. I had had jobs since I was eleven years old (paperboy), so most always had some money. I'd never paid a lot of attention to how quickly I could spend it. I hadn't signed up to the student food plan, so initially I didn't pay a lot of attention to how much I was spending on food. But a quick calculation told me at my current rate, I'd spend all my funds by mid-May. I had to do something. Since I was taking twenty-two credit hours my first semester, finding even a part-time job wasn't going to work. So my plan was simple; I would eat but one meal a day—a late lunch. Beginning in March that year that's what I did, ate one meal a day. Anything can be done if there's a will to do it—that's where forming habits comes in. I can recall making "cup-of-soup" using hot water right out of the dorm's tap. I also learned where and when the local places ran dinner specials. I would go to Woolworth's one day, Pizza Hut another, and so forth. I got to the point where from Monday to Thursday I knew exactly what and where I'd be eating. Now even forty years later, I still most often just eat one big meal each day. It reminds me what my dad once said: "It's good to be hungry sometimes, as it makes us appreciate the food we do get." He also noted that many folks go hungry as a normal course of their lives— adults and kids. I never forgot that, even though it hasn't been an issue of economics for me for so many years.

Perhaps my most memorable time during my first semester of college came at the end of February of that year. Beyond my wildest hopes, Ginny had convinced her parents to allow her to visit me at college. She'd told me their decision the weekend before; I thought she was kidding me but she wasn't. She told her parents about my dorm, about my roommate, and that as such we'd not really be alone. Her parents said that they knew they'd raised her right and that they also knew how much the two of us cared for each other. So they told her yes they'd allow a short visit, Friday out, returning Sunday afternoon. The idea was like a dream come true. Aside from the fact we two were very much in love, there wasn't a whole lot of time we were ever truly alone. The date got set and I prayed that the winter weather wouldn't throw a wrench in the works.

I can recall going down to the bus station to await her arrival. I was so excited; it was like a holiday. Sure enough, she got there more or less on time. We'd worked out our meeting at the downtown main bus depot. I'd gotten there a half-hour early, just in case. As the bus from Rochester pulled in, I spied her sitting beside one of the windows near the front. I got such a wonderful greeting. We took a "city" bus to campus, arriving mid-afternoon. She hadn't eaten at all that day; said she was so nervous figuring something would happen to ruin our plans. For my part, I'd made sure my roommate knew she was coming and was okay with that, which he was. After dropping off her overnight bag in my room, we caught a bite to eat at the Ratskeller along with a couple of drinks. The weather was unseasonably nice so we went on a walk through the campus. Around 7:00 PM we headed back to my dorm where I introduced her to a number of the folks I'd met over the last few weeks, including the RA. We watched a little TV in the common area before heading upstairs to my room. I expected to see Raj but he wasn't there. He'd left me a note that said he'd not be coming back that night as he had other plans. Now I tell you, I read that note two or three times before I said anything to her. Things don't normally pan out better than I'd hoped, at least from my experience. Usually something comes along to mess them up; but not this time.

Had there been any doubt in my mind or hers in terms of how we felt about each other, none remained come Sunday. The fact that Sunday would bring us back to reality didn't have the effect I'd anticipated. Yes, there was a tearful goodbye at the downtown bus depot, but things were different now…and would always be. She did come to visit me again that first semester, in April. That visit was special too. We both absolutely believed we were made for each other—soul mates.

During that semester I continued to go home each weekend. I never again stayed at college to take "a break from each other" or to get "the complete college experience," as my dad had suggested. I had no regrets about the decision to spend weekends with Ginny or the commitment it implied; nor did she.

Though it's now been over forty years since her February visit, the memory of that weekend has stayed with me. That night, and Saturday night too, brought the most peaceful sleep I think I'd ever had. On Saturday we spent the day going to a starving artists show on campus, talking to new friends, and just enjoying each other's company. Sometimes in life our plans fall short of our expectations. That weekend just the opposite occurred. The truth be known, that weekend wasn't the first time we'd been "together," but it was different...it was special in ways hard to explain in words. In looking back, the best word I could use to describe that time is "magical." I know it may sound trite, but for us it was the case.

Weedsport Weekend

It was late summer of 1976 when Ginny and I were invited to visit the Weedsport Speedway. We'd spend the weekend of Sept 4th and 5th with two friends, Bob and Charlene. The raceway was owned by our friend Bob and his family. Bob's parents lived next door to my parents. His dad and brothers ran the residential construction firm that built all the homes in our neighborhood.

By the time Ginny met Bob he'd already been married a few years and left the building trade. One night while Ginny and I were down at the Reunion we ran into Bob. He had the "great idea" to take us back to his home afterwards for some eats and to meet his wife Charlene. At least we three thought it was a great idea; Charlene, who'd been fast asleep, didn't agree. That had been a number of weeks prior. Nonetheless, we all hit it off right away. I can take some getting used to but Ginny, everyone gets along with her. She hasn't a pompous or pretentious bone in her body, or as Charlene commented, "She's such a sweet kid."

Bob, along with his dad and his brothers, had long been heavy into stockcar racing. They'd work on their racer right next door to my parents, sometimes late into the night. Their avocation eventually led them to purchase a dirt track speedway. That's where Ginny and I were headed on a sunny late summer Saturday morning.

We'd been instructed to "just bring yourselves," so that's just what we did. Usually I'd have brought iced beer and something for Ginny to drink too, but Bob assured us that they had all sorts of stuff; a full concession set up, including food and drinks plus a small bar in the clubhouse.

Very few know the story of that weekend. In part, this is because I don't like to advertise my bone-headedness. On this particular Saturday morning we drove down to the Speedway with the idea of spending the day with Bob and Charlene then watching the scheduled races that evening. They had sleeping accommodations too, so we'd not head back to Rochester until Sunday. I was thrilled with that idea in part because Ginny had a green light from her parents. Guess I was growing on them. By this time, we'd been engaged for a while, though our wedding date was still over a year away. Still, they knew how very much in love we two were.

The Weedsport speedway was built as a dirt track stockcar raceway; situated in the southern tier area of Central New York. We arrived early afternoon. Upon entering, Ginny spied a small building that she said looked like a big chicken coop. Turns out it was the place we'd stay that night. It did sort of look like a big chicken coop with the front roof line lower than the back. But we didn't care; this was sort of an adventure for us so we just took it all in stride.

Within one minute of our arrival, calamity hit. Ginny sprained her ankle as she caught her foot in a rut just a few feet from our parked car. Though I wasn't trained in first aid, I was right there to help Ginny. I'd sprained my ankle before, so I gave her the same advice I'd been given by my high school gym teacher; best thing to do was just "walk it off." Perhaps in hindsight that wasn't such a good suggestion. Nonetheless, we made our way over to the track area, meeting up with Charlene, who was doing some pre-race preparations in the clubhouse. Char could see Ginny was limping, and suggested we ice her ankle, but Ginny explained my idea of just ignoring it. Char wasn't keen on that, but Ginny was game to try. To make matters worse, I also suggested she continue to walk around rather than sit or lie down. It began to swell but as Ginny would attest, she was prone to both ankle sprains accompanied by some degree of swelling.

The fact she'd sprained her ankle was going to put a bit of a crimp in our plans, as we had intended to take long walks around the raceway and general environs, sort of take in the sights. Yet I figured we should save the walk for later when her ankle felt better. I left Ginny with Charlene in the clubhouse as I went out to find Bob and see what he was up to. I found him on a tractor, grading the track in preparation for the night's races. After climbing aboard we spent the next half- hour going round and round the track and just shooting the breeze. Afterwards, we joined the gals, who I suspected were still back in the clubhouse.

I'd told Bob about Ginny's ankle, so it came as no surprise when we found them at the bar drinking some soft drinks. Only then did I take a close look at her "minor sprain." Her ankle had swelled up to twice its normal size and was already black and blue. Even though Char had given her some aspirin, she said it hurt to even flex her foot, no less walk on it (nice move Jim). It was then I was open to suggestions. I was very sure she hadn't broken it but she needed something. Seeing her swollen ankle, Bob said, "I have just the thing for that." He came back a couple minutes later with a big drink—he said it was called a "dirty mother." When Ginny asked what was in it, Bob told her almost everything. Ginny drank that first one in about thirty minutes—said her ankle felt a little better—so Bob brought her another. That seemed to help too.

We watched the races that began at 7:00 PM and finished at 9:00 PM. During that time Ginny had a third drink as we watched the races; or was it two more? When the races were done, we all went into the club-house for drinks and snacks. It was at this point I'd wished I brought beer since the only kind they had was Schafer. I never drank Schafer beer before that trip, and never have since. Ginny had another couple of drinks over the next hour or so. She'd kept to drinking dirty mothers, not wanting to switch, figuring that might make her sick. At around 11:00 PM we all headed to the "chicken coop," which is where she and I would spend the night. It was really not bad. Bob and Charlene joined us soon after for a nightcap.

I took a picture of Ginny right before she "shot-gunned" a cigar (inserting the lit end into your mouth then blowing smoke out the other end). She'd seen Bob shot-gun his cigar just moments before, then said to him, "Where's mine?" You can readily see from the picture that, true to my word, Ginny was feeling no pain. I hadn't thought of this story in so many years. I knew enough not to bring it up, for it always elicited a dirty look from Ginny as she doesn't recall it with quite the same fondness as I. We had such a good time that weekend, though when I got her home, her mom was none too happy. I remember her mom saying to her, "Jeanette, what have you done?" She only got called Jeanette when her mom was upset. Ginny explained the incident, along with my valuable advice about walking it off. Her mom gave me a look I wouldn't soon forget. At least I made sure she was anesthetized most of the evening. Ginny of course doesn't remember the details of the story; good thing I was there, huh? As an aside, she never did get sick…but had a headache to beat the band come that next morning. Must have been from the lack of food I bet. There wasn't a lot of talking on the drive home as I didn't want to worsen her headache, seeing I had a little bit to do with it.

(Refer to Pictures section, picture 05)

We had a great time that weekend despite Ginny's sprained ankle. She'd tell you the same. Though my 'doctoring' skills were sorely lacking, I very much wanted to help her, to relieve the pain of her injury. There's literally nothing I wouldn't do for Ginny.

The Plan Forward

Since that first semester in college I'd worked out a plan that would have me graduate in less than three years. After speaking with my assigned college counselor, I made a decision that would accomplish two goals. It would get me finished with college sooner and enable Ginny and I to get married sooner too. However, it committed me to going to college year-round by taking accredited elective courses during the summers at the local community college (MCC) and it meant I had to take a minimum of twenty credit hours per full semester. This was an aggressive plan that cost me, among other things, two summers of my life. I literally would be in college from early morning to late evening from June through August.

After a full summer of college in 1975, I found I had to enroll in another college for the fall semester. This was the only way to make my plan work, as my initial college (University of Buffalo) required I take all my primary courses there. The State University College of Brockport offered greater flexibility. I'd still live at school in the fall of 1975, but now

I was only thirty-five miles from home. However this was still long distance when it came to phone calls, and I had no car to get home. In time however, I hooked up with another student (Teresa) who commuted daily from Rochester. Teresa and I became good friends. I'd pay for her gas and she'd get me home on weekends that fall. She and Ginny got along quite well too.

My parents didn't like my plan from the start. I suppose the reason had more to do with the fact that by the spring of 1976 I was going to use my parents' home as my base and not a college dorm or off-campus housing. To their credit, they agreed to let me try. My dad told me I was biting off too much too soon. Not only was I foregoing the matter of "truly experiencing the college life," but I was placing too much emphasis upon time. If I failed or had to withdraw from even one core course, I'd not graduate until the end of 1977.

When I look back, one thing that I can recall more than anything else was that I had no break from college of more than a couple of weeks. I remember being at either the community college or other local college offering a key course throughout those two summers. I found full-time summer college was quite tough. My friends were home—they'd go boating and have get-togethers, but if I wasn't at college, I was working on completing the reading and written requirements. I understood the old adage; all work and no play makes Jack a dull boy. Well, I almost gave up that first summer—came close a time or two. In hindsight perhaps I'd become overly focused on getting done ASAP; but what drove me, what inspired me to continue even on those toughest days was Ginny. She'd never push me—never insisted I stay to the plan. What she would do is remind me to think about why I was doing it. Those days I remember playing the 1966 Beach Boys tune down at our favorite tavern. That song, "Wouldn't it be Nice," summed it up…it became sort of our "anthem." I can recall on a number of occasions that as the song played, she'd quietly whisper those lyrics to me, "Wouldn't it be nice if we could wake up…in the morning when the day is new… and after having spent the day together…hold each other close the whole night through." We all have our own sense of motivation and inspiration—one day being married to "my Punkin" was mine.

In May 1977 I graduated from college. My parents, my brother Ron and sister Susan, along with Ginny (my fiancée), all attended the ceremony. Back then as well as now, they don't give you your actual diploma that day, just a certificate that indicates the degree you've earned. But that day in May I was surprised when I walked up to the podium to receive my certificate. They announced I'd been named the Business Department Scholar.

The seating was such that we sat with our families, not our classmates. As I made my way back to my seat, Ginny was smiling ear-to-ear, talking to my parents. As I sat back down she gave me a big hug as she said, "that's my Jimmy…I love you so." What is that, just seven words but they were the sweetest words I'd ever heard.

If someone tells me that I missed out on the full college experience or reminds me of the great times that were sacrificed during the summers of 1975 and 1976, all I do is smile. I know what I did, what we did, was worth it. Faced with doing it again, I'd change very little that took place during my college years. My only regret from that time is that I should have told Ginny more often that she was my inspiration to doing well and getting done as quickly as possible. Too often I simply assumed she knew.

That First "Real" Job

Even before I graduated in May of 1977, my greatest concern had been to find a good job. I recall that just a few days after graduation I'd taken a trip to New York City to be interviewed at several different firms. The trip was memorable for several reasons. I had a full four days of interviews all set up. All involved some facet of financial planning or analysis. I remember most of the firms; Bank of America, USG Comptroller of Currency, Standard & Poor's, and Arthur Anderson. Two of the interviews included taking tests geared at determining my financial aptitude. I hadn't expected such, but felt I'd done well on them. After the first couple of days, several things weighed heavily on me. Did I really want to live in such a large metro area? Did I need to move so far away right away? Perhaps it was better to wait to make a move via a future job change where the employer would pick up the cost of relocation? By the middle of the third day I had convinced myself I wasn't up to relocating to the New York City area as yet. I had been scheduled to return to S&P for part two of the interview so I called my contact to say I'd not be returning. He wasn't upset, but felt they could really use a guy like me. But, I felt the fit just wasn't right. Though my flight home was set for Friday evening I decided to try to get an earlier departure time.

I got to the airport in plenty of time but made one small mistake. While I'd flown in to LaGuardia, my flight out was departing from Kennedy. Fortunately, I'd found my mistake in plenty of time so I hustled over to Kennedy via the shuttle they run between the airports. I arrived better than two hours before departure. Since I had time to kill I headed over to one of the many little bars they had to grab a drink. Even though I was but a young guy, I had no issue striking up a conversation with strangers. I'd been an extroverted person since around fifth or sixth grade.

While in the bar at Kennedy, I met a fellow on his way back home after being abroad the last six months in Saudi Arabia. He worked for a large oil company, though I can't recall which one. The guy was busting at the seams being back in the States. He was headed for Texas, no surprise there. He and I talked and talked. He spoke of his adventures, of the big money draw for anyone interested in working long hours in a far-away land. I remember showing him a picture of Ginny, the same one I've carried in my wallet now for over forty years. Upon seeing it, he said no wonder I was in a hurry to get back. Before I knew it he'd bought me a few beers on top of the one I'd purchased. I guess you could say all the drinking had left me a bit buzzed, as I'd not eaten a thing that day. I didn't miss my flight, though I barely recall how I got to the departure gate, no less much about the trip back home. I do recall how beautiful New York City looks at night with the thousands of lights all aglow. It was June 9th; I was headed home.

While I think I may have once again disappointed my dad who'd grown up in the northern New Jersey area and attended high school in New York City, I knew living down there at that time in my life wasn't the right thing for me; or for us. So as I returned, I sort of felt like I'd failed. But after I went to see Ginny the next day, she was overjoyed that I'd decided to stay local. I still didn't have a job but she told me not to worry. She was sure that a "smart guy" like me would find a job without too much trouble, even in a sluggish economy. I wasn't so sure, but she always made me feel better about the decisions I'd made.

The following Monday I went to an area job placement firm. My placement specialist was an older fellow who I liked almost immediately. He wasn't the least bit condescending and seemed to have my interests at heart as opposed to just the agency's. I asked him who normally paid for placement. A rather naïve question perhaps, but I was a real neophyte about a lot of things. I was glad to hear him say, "Normally the hiring firm pays it." After looking at my resume—which largely was just a summary of my college experience—he suggested that I consider letting him help me potentially get a scholarship to his alumni university, Harvard. He told me that even with the fact that I'd graduated from the SUNY system, my GPA was outstanding. He was certain that I could get a substantial—if not full—scholarship to grad school. When he said that, I think the blood drained from my face, because he asked me what was wrong. I answered by giving him an analogy. I told him that for most students, college was like a marathon race. But for me, I'd run it as a sprinter. I couldn't possibly delay finding a job. I absolutely didn't want to go to graduate school. All I wanted was a decent job so that we could be married.

Within a couple of weeks of my meeting with the placement agency, I landed a job with a local engineering & manufacturing firm. I remember that my new boss, Doug, asked if I wanted to start that Wednesday (June 29th) or wait until after the upcoming July 4th holiday. "The sooner the better" is what I told him.

As I drove home on the 27th, I stopped at my parents' to let the agency know I'd accepted the job. Heading down to Ginny's home, I was so excited. This is what we'd been hoping for, a job right in town. Though the starting pay wasn't going to set any records ($11,480 per year), it was fair. I was confident I could rise in the organization over time. As I pulled into her parents' driveway I got to thinking, maybe I should have called first. Nah, I said to myself, I would spill the beans on the phone or she'd see right through my calm demeanor; I'm almost never calm. I rang the bell and Ginny answered. I didn't even have to open my mouth, she just knew by the look on my face. She looked as happy as I felt. It was a good day for us. One of many more I hoped.

Landing the job just a month after graduating completed a key part of the plan that she and I had drawn up some two-and-a-half years prior. I can only imagine how tough it is for so many college grads today that go many months without finding their first job. No doubt about it, we were both lucky; perhaps blessed is the better term for it. A couple of months into my new job I received a job offer from the Comptroller of Currency; said they'd start me as a GS7 level employee, whatever that meant. Still I was very happy where I was; stayed there twenty-three years.

The Best Day Ever

I will tell you that the best day of my life beyond any doubt, was the day my fiancée became my wife. That day was December 17, 1977. We had initially planned a September wedding that would have more or less coincided with the anniversary of when we'd met. But as I recall, we just couldn't get the scheduling to work.

While it may sound odd to many, both she and I absolutely loved the Christmas season. So it seemed a natural default when September fell through, she asked if December was okay by me. She chose the date of Saturday the 17th. She also loved the idea of the two of us coming back from our honeymoon right before Christmas. December weather in the Northeast is generally highly unpredictable, but we were young and rather impetuous.

Even now as I look back, the fact is I never understood what a woman as beautiful as Ginny, both inside and out, ever saw in guy like me. At least when I was young, I'd admit I wasn't a homely guy, but she—she was radiant all the time. I knew, not thought, that I was the luckiest guy in the world to have such a person fall in love with me. You don't hear it said often these days, but in my case the adage is so true… she is my better half. Not a doubt in my mind…or that of others who know us well.

The day of our wedding was fast approaching. She and one of her sisters had made all the bridal party dresses. Considering there were ten or eleven bridesmaids that was some feat. I wore a tux, rather outdated if you were to see it today. It was cream and brown in color. The grooms-men wore light blue tuxes to match the bridesmaids' gowns. Her bridal gown was traditional white. As was customary, I hadn't seen her dress ahead of time, but I knew she'd look spectacular in it.

We had attended the requisite Pre-Cana sessions in order to be mar-ried in the Catholic Church. The priest, Father Jim, was a great guy. He was young and that enabled us to better relate to him, and he to us. I have to admit that in hindsight what I recall most about these sessions was not the talk with the priest but the talks Ginny and I had as we walked to and from the church. Our talks were heartfelt; dealt with all the plans and dreams we had for our future.

We had a rehearsal dinner on the 16th. I remember this because my dad and two of my brothers missed it, as they had to attend to the out-of-state death of my grandfather. While it put a bit of a dampener on that evening, it didn't affect the excitement of our wedding day. My grandfather had been ill for some time. His health had started to wane upon the loss of his wife. In many ways he never recovered. I remem-ber he shied away from having visitors after her death. Now it may strike you…why all this talk about death as I relay to you the story of our "best day ever?" I guess it depends upon what death represents. In time I've come to believe it isn't an end, just a new beginning. It's all a matter of perspective.

The wedding wasn't until 11:30 AM but I tend to be an early riser, so I'd been ready quite early. I'd awakened in our new apartment, where I'd lived since the start of the month. Ginny had actually made our first "home-cooked" meal together just two weeks before. The 17th began as a sunny day, just the sort of day we'd hoped for when we'd committed to the date months before. By 9:00 AM, I headed over to my parents' to kill some time. I planned to change into my rented tux there as well.

Two of my brothers had come in from out of town just the evening before. I thought I'd raze them before they did the same to me. It was a bit before 11:00 AM that my best man, Paul and I showed up at the church, Saint Salome's. Father had put us in the sacristy. Guess they used it as a sort of groom's waiting room. We'd snuck a couple of cold beers in with us, just to take the edge off. I know, many would say bringing beers into a church is highly inappropriate, but we were young and a bit free-spirited. Father Jim caught us in the act. He simply said my name sternly; we got the point, and had just one can each. I recall the photographer taking a few shots of Paul and me. You know the "escaping groom" trying to exit the rear door. But I wasn't going anywhere, for this was the day Ginny and I had been waiting on for years.

The next thing I can remember is watching the horde of bridesmaids and groomsmen come down the aisle as most folks had already been seated. I remember how happy both sets of parents were…they knew how much we loved one another. The music preceding the bride's entry began…my mouth was so dry and I was nervous despite all our preparations. I was not prepared for my own reaction when I spied her as she made her way aside her dad up to the altar. That moment when I saw her I couldn't believe my eyes…to me she was absolutely radiant… she looked like an angel. Emotions roiled within me…utter joy and happiness coupled with such pride and relief that our day had finally arrived. I have forgotten many things in my life but that day is etched forever on my heart and in my soul.

While the ceremony proceeded—I have to be honest—I was still so thunderstruck, I don't remember much. I remember the exchange of rings, our first marital kiss, and then being introduced by Father Jim as man and wife. No matter what life would bring, I can say without equivocation, that moment was the happiest of my entire life. It truly doesn't get better than this.

Since our reception wasn't due to begin until 3:00 PM or so, we had time to kill between the wedding and that event. Ginny and I had talked about what we'd do and where we'd go. We made our way down to the Reunion Inn tavern where we'd met three years before. The owners were thrilled we came, even brought out a bottle of champagne for us to make a first toast as man and wife. I know many might question the idea of going to a bar on such a day, but then anyone who knew us, knew it was exactly the right thing for us to do. We didn't stay very long; though I remember when we went to leave I was hesitant. I wanted the time to slow so that we could savor it.

The reception was held at the Heritage House. It was very nice but not what you'd call "high end" by any means. That made no difference to us. Standing in the receiving line was actually a lot of fun. We had a large refrigerated cooler located right behind us with both soft drinks and ice-cold beer. I proudly stood beside my new wife. It was like I wanted to just tell everyone, look at the amazing woman who has just become my wife. Better yet, she felt exactly the same way. Dinner was typical wedding fare, not all that memorable; though I'm sure it was good. We danced, we laughed, we talked, and we drank to so many toasts. The time seemed to move faster and faster. Of course, we had the requisite wedding cake but there were ice sculptures too. The music was handled by a DJ playing our many favorite tunes. Three special tunes that just had to be played were: Barry Manilow's "Mandy" (this was "our song"), and of course the Beach Boys' "Wouldn't It Be Nice" and "Surfer Girl." Our day had arrived but I just couldn't get it to slow down. Neither of us wanted it to end.

(Refer to Pictures section, pictures 08 and 09)

As the reception ended we had to make our way to a hotel where we'd spend the night before heading off to a Pocono Mountains honeymoon resort the next morning. Now I know a lot of folks so look forward to their wedding night. The truth is we both were so exhausted from the day's events. I do recall I went to sleep holding her in my arms, as content as any two could be. If the world was to end at that moment it would have been just fine, for we were together, "snuggling" as she called it. No, in fact, it doesn't get better than that; I might as well have been in heaven.

While the weather cooperated on our wedding day, not so much on Sunday as we drove to our honeymoon resort. That drive was epic. It took us over seven hours to drive the roughly two hundred miles; the last half in a storm which included freezing rain followed by heavy snow. Our "new" car, a '74 red VW Beetle that Ginny named "Herbie," made it through places where many rear-wheeled vehicles could not. There were cars off the road all over the place in Pennsylvania. In the end, we got there and that week together was wonderful.

Even if it were the case, few guys would ever admit that their wedding day topped their list of great days. In our male-dominated society, weddings are viewed as the purview of the woman—that she has successfully snared her man. That somehow the man gives up more and thereby loses his freedom. Not me; December 17th was my best day ever! I'd love to go back and do it all again.

Apartment Living

In the first few years of our marriage we lived in an apartment. Those were the lean years in terms of our finances. But hindsight now yields mostly fond recollections. Our rent started off at a mere $185 per month. A pittance compared to prices today. I can still recall some of the installment payments we made. My student loan was $50.03 each month and the inexpensive luggage set purchased for our honeymoon via mail order was $8.13.

(Refer to Pictures section, picture 07)

I understood from early on that Ginny's dream was to be a great wife and stay-at-home-mom. This did not conflict with my career or life aspirations. However, it was a source of some criticism on the part of others who believed a two-wage-earner income was the way things should be. At times Ginny's feelings were hurt when an off-hand comment was made by a friend or family member. Most were not being critical of her, yet indirectly I could see how she took a comment as criticism. However, there were a few times when, perhaps due to envy, a person would blatantly give us their unabashed opinion of a "non-working" spouse. It made me mad that others felt a need to tell us how we should live when they weren't models of proficiency themselves. Ginny would say she felt she'd be more at home if she'd been born at an earlier time when dual incomes weren't the norm. Me, I was fine with anything she wanted and found in time that creating a home had more to do with love than it had to do with money. Ginny was endowed with so many fine attributes that I knew early on she was a very special gal and I was one lucky guy.

Like most young couples, we had to scrimp to save for an eventual down payment on a home. Though money was tight, we found ways to stretch our money. Yet more importantly, we didn't place a lot of emphasis on accumulating things. I recall that for the first few months at least, the "curtains" in our small apartment consisted of cheap carpet protector runners that her dad had given us; akin to foam packing material. They looked cheesy for sure but they served the immediate purpose of giving us some sense of privacy. We did have one credo we always used: Better to buy higher quality items that would last than the cheaper variety that would have to be replaced.

Initially, much of our furniture consisted of borrowed pieces we took from our childhood bedrooms. However, we had purchased a dining room table & chairs along with an oak cabinet for $750. That money came from a bequest Ginny received from her grandmother. My dad had found this furniture that had survived a warehouse fire and minor water damage about a year before. The dining room set was well made—the style (French provincial) wasn't particularly my taste—but Ginny liked it a lot. I recall also that our stereo was from a Western Auto store. I'd purchased it at a sidewalk sale back when I worked at the shoe store before we met. Though the faux marble top of the coffee table was cracked, the stereo worked well...AM, FM, plus a turntable. One brand new item we'd purchased before our wedding was a queen-sized mattress and box spring. It turned out to be a big part of the solution to a chronic health problem.

When I met Ginny she'd been under a doctor's care for undiagnosed leg pains that she'd suffered for several years. At the time, she was on all sorts of prescription meds, including some rather potent pain-killers. Many times during our dating years she'd get an unexpected onset of terrible leg pains. Despite numerous hospital and doctor visits before we'd met, they never found a definitive cause. She did however have what doctors termed a "minor case of scoliosis" (curvature of the spine). Some of the doctors believed this was the issue; however some of them felt otherwise. While I lacked any medical background, I recall the first time I sat on the mattress she used in her old room. That old mattress she'd slept on provided next to no support...either it was all worn out or defective. I recall briefly falling asleep on it one time, and waking up with a really sore back. Now telling her parents I'd fallen asleep on her bed was just not something we were prepared to convey, no less that I felt it was the cause of her chronic pains. However, when she and I went shopping for our own mattress in October 1977, I told her we needed to buy an extra firm one. She balked. She wanted a soft cushioned one like she had at home.

Normally compromise is the best path toward solving any disagreement. Yet I was so sure, without any proof mind you, that I was right about the type of mattress she needed. Most married or almost married couples might be thinking about or considering other issues when it came to choosing a mattress. In the end I asked her to trust me… told her she'd get used to and come to enjoy sleeping on a bed that gave her back more support. She finally agreed. While her chronic leg pains never completely disappeared, they were never again as bad as they'd been. As far as the meds she'd been on, she was off all of them months before our wedding. Generally, doctors try their best to diagnose and remedy a medical issue but in Ginny's case I think they opted for the medication route too soon and with too many types. Like I said, I'm not a doctor, just a guy who loved someone and didn't want to see her suffering in pain.

Sometime in 1978 we replaced our "curtains" we had with real curtains. These too were hand-me-downs, but they were a great improvement for us. Now we could actually open the curtains to let the sun in versus undo the masking tape that held the foam carpet runners against our windows.

As is the case with most young women, Ginny came to the marriage with limited, yet more than adequate cooking skills. Most of us develop our taste for certain types of foods in part based upon how we're used to having them cooked. The early years of our marriage saw more than a few tears shed when her meal plans fell short of her (or my) expectations. We generally ate foods commensurate with our modest means (hamburger and chicken), but every so often we'd splurge by buying a beef roast or "family" steak. On one particular occasion I recall how nervous Ginny was in preparing a roast beef dinner…complete with mashed potatoes and homemade gravy. She made the best gravy! She had grown up using a gas range but was relegated to making do with the cheap electric range we had in the apartment. On this particular Sunday, she had used her new meat thermometer to ensure she didn't over or undercook the roast. She wanted everything to be perfect. That day we both learned a few lessons. Lesson one…a roast will continue to cook even after you remove it from the oven. Faint praise means little when you find yourself chewing on leather that was supposed to be a special dinner. As I was carving the roast, Ginny could tell by the look on my face that rather than medium-rare, it had come out well-done and then some. Didn't matter what I said, for she could see the disappointment on my face. Ginny would say it was "gray meat," a term her dad used to describe over-cooked beef. Despite her best efforts that day, the meat was a disappointment. As we sat down to eat she tearfully commented that she couldn't even chew it. "It's like leather!" At that, she jumped up from the table, and ran off to our bedroom.

The bedroom door had one of those cheap locks on it, but I knew better than to go barging in to tell her not to cry. I felt terrible for having reacted as I had. While I told her it was no big deal, she knew from my facial expressions that I was disappointed with the outcome of her efforts. I called in that the mashed potatoes and gravy were fantastic… but got no reply. After about ten minutes the sound of her weeping subsided. I knew I had to make up for my reaction—had to tell her that it didn't matter—not really. Sometimes in life things don't work out as we'd planned. How we act and react in those cases will largely determine how the event will be remembered. While Ginny will always remember she'd overcooked the roast, I will remember that I didn't respond with understanding and empathy. In the end, we both would retell this story to friends and family with some fondness. I learned that day to be appreciative of an effort, regardless of a result. Like a gift, it is true that it's the thought that matters most. *She never again served "gray meat." Over the years she'd say, "We can always put it back in for more cooking if it's too rare."*

In those early years we had quite a few parties in our apartment, like the Halloween party in 1978 when all the guys dressed up as gals. The idea started out as a dare but ended up being a surefire recipe for laughter. That year Ginny dressed up as a witch, complete with green skin and a hooked nose. Green costume make-up created quite the convincing look, but it turns out it doesn't come off as easy as you might think. I remember laughing at her the next day as she tried various creams and solutions to remove the pigment.

Halloween of '78 went down as one of the best parties we ever had. We had so many friends who came over to the apartment that night. Everyone not only came in costume, but remained that way throughout the evening. And while the guys all "looked cute" in their wigs and female garb, it was the women whose costumes were so clever and stunning. In my eyes "Ginny, the Wicked Witch of the East" was the best, but then I'm biased; she'd stolen my heart long ago.

(Refer to Pictures section, pictures 10 and 11)

Initially, most all our closest friends had lived in an apartment when they were first married. After a couple of years though, they had either upgraded to a first home or moved into a larger place. Ginny and I were trying to save money for a down payment on a home but in the late 1970s and early 1980s, it seemed no matter how much you saved, the prices of new homes was rising faster and faster. Though we had plans to eventually be first time home-buyers, they ended up being accelerated by a couple of events at the apartment complex.

When Christmas 1980 rolled around, as we were putting ornaments on our tree Ginny noticed that some of them had mold on them… including her favorite hand-painted Bambi ornament. The storage areas in the basement of the apartment suffered from high humidity during the summers. A couple of months later as I was putting garbage in our trash bin located in the basement, I had my first experience with seeing a rat. It surprised me. I stamped my foot, only to have it respond by standing up on its hind legs. While I took the garbage down most the time, on occasion Ginny did. When I went back upstairs I figured I best tell her…bad move. Ginny would not set foot in the basement thereafter. She "suggested" (read insisted) that we needed to either find ourselves a small house or another apartment. We began house hunting in earnest the following week.

I look back upon those three and a half years in the apartment with generally fond memories. Like most young couples, we struggled financially yet were so rich in terms of the love we shared. Things were simpler then, less hectic, more carefree.

Some suggest that not every man and woman should get married. I'd agree, but Ginny and I didn't fit into that group. Married life was ideally suited to us. In those early years Ginny would sometimes say a phrase that reflected just this sentiment. "Hi, my name is Ginny Yake, what would you like?" In that one little statement, she showed how happy she was to be married to me. I can't tell you how good this made me feel and how lucky I knew I was to have captured her love. And the best part, she felt the same.

Our First House

On May 4th of 1981 we—with the help of a realtor—found our first house. It was located on the outskirts of the city in a quiet neighborhood that was undergoing a generational turn-over. The original owners still lived in a bit over half the homes built back in the early 1940s. All were single family and most of the homes were on the smallish side as compared to new homes. That meant we had many neighbors who were much older than us—often in the range of seventy-five to eighty years old. To them we were kids, for I was twenty-seven, and Ginny was twenty-five.

The Sunday we found "the home" was a beautiful day. It was not the first home we'd seen but right away it struck both of us as having great potential. It was a small Cape Cod with a detached garage. It needed painting badly, inside and out, as well as considerable work on the lawn and in the gardens. The price was within our budget ($44,500) assuming we could get a small loan from each of our parents to help with the 20% down payment requirement. The realtor warned us that the home had just been listed—that the price was firm—and that if we really wanted it we had to act quickly. Now I don't think any realtor, then or now, has ever used other words than these…but we did believe she was right, we had to act.

(Refer to Pictures section, picture 12)

The place we found was only about a mile or so from my work…that had its good and bad points. It was about 1,100 square feet, located on a tiny parcel of land in the Northeast part of the city—Mildorf Street. It was built in 1940 and had its original copper plumbing (unlike many homes built a bit later with lead pipes). The house had real plaster walls—hard as nails as they say. The windows were all original double-hung style with rope-drawn counter weights. The kitchen was outdated, best described as being typical of those from the 1950s. The heating system was natural gas via a converted coal boiler system, complete with asbestos-wrapped heat ducts. The interior, similar to the exterior, hadn't seen a fresh coat of paint in years. Overall, it was what many would term "a good fixer-upper." But it had going for it something no other place had…it was going to be our new home.

After we first saw the house we spoke to both Ginny's parents and my own about the idea of borrowing some money. I remember the talks well. My parents still had two kids in college and three more living at home. They weren't going to be able to help a lot, but they did loan us $2,500. By this time Ginny's mom and dad were "empty nesters." We hoped that perhaps they could loan us a bit more…we needed at least an additional $4,000 to make the down payment and cover closing costs. I recall her dad told us he was impressed that we had been able to save as much as we had on my still rather meager salary…by then I think I was making about $15,000 per year. Her parents agreed to loan us the money, her dad insisting upon making it $5,000 as he was sure we'd underestimated some of the costs we'd incur. By day's end we were back at the realtor's office to confirm we wanted to make an offer on the home.

Aside…over the next five years the loans to both sets of parents were paid back in full along with interest compounded at 5% per annum. I can still see the loan payment schedules I created which showed amounts due and the portion that was interest vs principle. We never missed a payment or were late. Payments were mailed just like those to other creditors. When we made the final payment to her parents, her dad made a point of telling us how impressed he was that we not only kept to the schedule but even accelerated it over time. The old axiom of never lending to family or friends didn't apply to us.

Since it was our first home and we had limited credit history, we had to get preapproved for a mortgage. We didn't know this until our realtor told us. We were neophytes to the home buying business. We later understood the requisite of getting such pre-approval in order to speed the offer and acceptance process. Today, few folks would understand that back in the early 1980s inflation was a big deal. The company I worked for since graduating had gone to semiannual salary raises. They did this not because they wanted to be magnanimous but because inflation was running double-digit. They had to offer twice-annual increases in order to stay competitive with the hiring market and prevent the loss of key workers who were often being enticed to change jobs by other area firms. What this meant in terms of buying our first home was this… our mortgage rate would be a three year, 15¼% balloon mortgage plus two points up front (2% of the mortgage as prepaid interest). We were qualified for an amount up to $37,500. Even these many years later I can readily recall the facts of this purchase quite well. In 2009, three homes later, we paid considerably more to replace a slate roof on our NJ home than the purchase price of our first home. But in 1981, the finance terms were very difficult on any person trying to buy their first home.

We closed on that first home on June 26th, 1981. We moved out of the apartment on the 27th with some fanfare and a lot of help from family and friends. We even had a theme song from a TV show. Ginny christened it as our official moving song…the show was called *The Greatest American Hero*. The lyrics to the song "Believe It Or Not" include these words which Ginny felt was so fitting: "Just like the light of a new day, it hit me from out of the blue…breaking me out of the spell I was in, making all my wishes come true."

Our "new" home was modest by most every measure, yet it would be our first true home. The day we moved, that song played no less than three times on the local radio station; perhaps an omen of good tidings. All I knew is that the house represented a sense of permanence to both Ginny and I that was sorely lacking in our apartment. It's true that we look back through rose-colored glasses. Yet like that silly television show, that time in our life was one of innocence and discovery. I'd yet to grow cynical of the world; life was still full of the idealism of our youth.

My advice to any young person today would be, don't ever lose your awe of life or your belief in others. As it turns out, having the right perspective is largely a matter of choice, not circumstance.

Moving day was all planned out…but our plans didn't quite go as expected. In hindsight, although we had all the help we needed from family and friends, we didn't quite get all our things out in one load as we hoped. I remember that my brother Rick had driven our 'new' car (1980 Dodge Omni 024) in part because I'd opted to sit in the back of the U-Haul van to ensure stuff didn't crash down and break. In hindsight that wasn't a particularly smart move on my part, for it was pitch dark in that closed van. If something fell the best I could do was act as a cushion. Note to self, the human body isn't a good substitute for packing blankets/cushions. Nonetheless, by the end of the day, we were completely out of the apartment and more or less situated in our new place.

In the fall of '82 I had a closely guarded secret. We were due to go to a baby shower for one of her cousins or something like that. I wasn't thrilled with the idea, though joint baby showers had come into vogue around that time. I had other plans already set in motion. Ginny had been dropping hints that she'd really like to get a pet dog. Me, I'd grown up with the typical fare of hamsters, birds, turtles, and one cat, Snoopy. We'd never had a dog so the idea of getting one didn't really appeal to me. But I understood her attraction to the idea, as her family had had several dogs over the years. Her specific desire was to get a female miniature Dachshund, a short-haired red. Since Ginny was a housewife in the traditional sense, she was often home alone most of the day. At that time in our lives, I didn't work particularly long hours, but I could see her point.

On this sunny Sunday morning I remember our trip to the breeder. The shower was being held on the west side of town yet as we began to drive Ginny could see we were headed southeast of Rochester towards Fairport. She commented we were going in the wrong direction: "where are you taking us?" So I told her that we were going to look at some Dachshund puppies that I saw advertised in the paper.

She was ecstatic. The whole shower commitment melted away. Two birds with one stone I guess.

The breeder's home was not as far away as I expected, so we were a bit earlier than the time I'd relayed to them. Once inside, they had to take the mom into another area, as she was naturally very protective of her pups. Straight away we asked about females—they had three. They told us that the puppies were all in good health and had had their initial shots as well as AKC papers. The only question I asked was which one of the females was more active, perhaps a bit mischievous? The breeder replied that would be the little one chewing on a sock toy. They told us that earlier that day the pup in question had gotten into the bathroom. She'd then proceeded to empty an entire roll of toilet paper, leaving pieces all over the place. I looked at Ginny, told her it was up to her. They'd given that particular pup a name (Edelweiss) that we used as her middle name. However, this little pup would be named Schatze; a German nickname that more or less translates to "girlfriend." Our neighbor Paula, an older German immigrant, told us that "mistress" was the more apt translation.

Schatze came home with us that day. Though we were basically ill-prepared to house a little puppy of just seven weeks old, we managed with the help of Ginny's parents. Her mom and dad had a next-to-new wicker dog basket. That, along with some old blankets and a new food and water dish got us started. Now for a guy who never wanted a dog, she quickly found a way into my heart. Ginny was listed on the papers as the owner, but it wasn't long before we ended up defaulting to the use of the words "mom" and "dad." Ginny was so very happy having that little pup in our home. I sort of felt guilty not having found her a pet sooner. When I told her that, she said that we couldn't have gotten one sooner, or it wouldn't have been "our Schatze." No matter what, Ginny had a way of looking at things in the most positive light. That quality in her I always so admired.

Over the next few years, Ginny and I initiated many home improve-ment projects. In most cases, we'd do them together as a team. There were a couple of exceptions…like the re-grouting of the bathroom tiles and the drainage ditch I dug around the detached garage. Yet overall, any project we did on the home was a joint project…she was always there, working with me right by my side. In hindsight, I didn't appreci-ate that fact enough at the time, but I do today.

Some projects turned out to be bigger than we could do ourselves; like putting in the new front bay window. (Our friend Bob and his brother Steve did the work in October '83.) Yet another big job begun in the summer of '83 was quite telling. We had a two-week "vacation" plan that hardly qualified as restful. I would spend it painting the exterior of our home. I recall beginning the work of sanding the exterior of the house on Monday morning, July 18th. The existing paint had "alli-gatored" over the years; not uncommon for older shingled houses. I figured I would use most of my two weeks' vacation to sand and paint it. Its condition was that bad. After a couple of days using scrapers and power sanders it occurred to me that at this rate I'd only get done one side of the house this "vacation." That meant I would end up painting just one side of the house each year. Given the years of neglect, in all likelihood as soon as the fourth year was complete, the following year I might have to start the process all over again. That prospect was more than a bit disheartening. So at the end of that second full day, I went in to take a shower; I was covered with dust and paint flecks. After my shower I walked into the living room to talk to Ginny. I suggested that perhaps we needed to get the house sided in vinyl just as her dad had done a few years before. Ginny looked up at me and simply said, "I was wondering how long it would take you to come to that conclusion."

Though Ginny hadn't tossed water on my ambitious house painting plans, she knew how stubborn I could be at times. Therefore, she'd made no effort to try to talk me out of my initial plan. Instead, she let me come to my senses, to figure out the right solution. We made contact with the same siding contractor her dad had employed. He did a fabulous job; it didn't even look like the same place. We were both thrilled.

Painting the house's exterior points out an issue that plagued me for most my life. My problem all too often is that I would define a task and come up with what I thought was the best solution. On the surface this sounds okay, however I didn't always ask Ginny what she thought. This indicates not only a single-mindedness but also stubbornness and a lack of being solicitous; either in asking or listening. Where she would often reserve comment, thereby allowing a degree of self-discovery, I seldom did. She was a very wise woman in many ways. I should have given her more credit in that regard. Too often I was quick to criticize, yet not to compliment.

The next big project we had planned showed I'd learned something from the house painting decision process. This project was near and dear to Ginny's heart; the kitchen renovation. The work was done exclusively by our friend Bob. He, Ginny, and I discussed at length what Ginny most wanted and where. He took our basic plans and though it took longer due to a delay with the cabinets, the project came out even better than either Ginny or I thought possible. On this project I did some of the more minor work, like refinishing and staining the broom closet door and all the floor molding to match our new kitchen cabinets. I also helped Bob with the brick work that served as a "counter splash" between the bottom and top cabinets (it came out great). If you were there that day—July 20th, 1985—you wouldn't even have to ask if we liked it. I was very pleased, and Ginny, well not only did she get the kitchen she'd dreamed about, but she finally got the gas stove she'd always wanted; no more electric ranges for us. Ginny was so very happy; I'll never forget the look on her face—it goes down as one of my cherished memories.

parents'; Ginny was bursting at the seams wanting to tell them. She'd changed into one of the maternity dresses at the store, a sleek light tan outfit; she looked wonderful in it.

We arrived unannounced at her parents' house in the early afternoon. Ginny's mom, who'd answered the door, seemed to sense something right away. I think she could tell something was up; perhaps she spotted the loose-fitting dress. Yet there was something else too—they say women tend to acquire a special glow when they're expecting. I never believed it myself. Yet in hindsight, that is exactly what was different... Ginny had that special glow. I'd never really seen such before, yet it was unmistakable. We went into their living room where her dad was watching some program that Saturday afternoon. Ginny and I sat down on the couch right after asking her mom to come into the room too. Their eyes lit up when she gave them the news. I recall her dad saying she should sit on the recliner since it was better for her back and she could stretch out too. Yes it was a very special day...one she and I would never forget.

(Refer to Pictures section, picture 13)

Saturday evening we ate at home. She'd made a special dinner, sort of odd I thought, as we'd not gotten home from her parents until around three o'clock but hey, I'm always into one of her delicious home-cooked meals. She also made a chocolate cake. When I asked her what the occasion was that called for a cake, she just looked at me with her beautiful smile and said, "Well, I wanted to make you something special... just think—you're finally going to be a dad." I was so very pleased, and she, well, she was beaming with pride and joy. I also thought to myself, what a lucky child this will be to have Ginny for a mom.

Over the next few days we spread the news. My brothers Michael and Ron both learned of it when we had them over for dinner. We saw

Michael on the 15th when we had him over with my mom and dad then Ron on the 29th when we had him over for his birthday. But perhaps the neatest announcement was when Ginny told her friend Jan as we visited her in the hospital on the 30th. Jan was there having given birth to their second child, Jamie, a couple days before. Jan knew how very much Ginny had wanted to be a mom. It was nice moment.

During the next few months we set to work converting our new house into a home for our new family. Our house was small by most measures, yet we felt it would be an ideal place to raise our new baby; at least for his or her first few years. In hindsight, it never bothered me to give up my den. We'd just painted it that summer and filled it with furnishings typical of a guy's den. It had an oak bookshelf, my prized leather chair, a desk, pipe stand, and floor lamp. I think Ginny felt I'd push to have the baby's room upstairs, but that made no sense to me. After all, I didn't want her having to take the steps all the time, let alone all the safety precautions that would come along with it. Deep down I must admit I was a bit wistful, for the den wasn't even in full use by the time its conversion to a nursery began that autumn.

While some women gain a lot of weight due to all the hormonal changes that occur during pregnancy, such was not the case with my wife. She honestly seemed to grow even more beautiful as time passed. If any woman was ready to begin a family, it was my Ginny. She'd always been so great with kids; cousins, nieces, nephews, as well as all our friends' children. She was "Aunt Ginny" to so many of them, like we were all one big happy family. Her patience, gentle nature, and warm heart were well known to all our family and friends.

By year's end, we had a fully equipped nursery located right next to our own bedroom. It had everything a child and new parents would need, including a new rocking chair and a nice selection of children's books. The small bed/crib was something Ginny took great care in picking out.

The funny thing is our dog, Schatze, seemed to sense a change going on. I've always felt dogs were far more perceptive than we humans give them credit for. Since shortly after Christmas, Schatze got to going in the unoccupied nursery, curling up and going to sleep under the bassinet. Her actions seemed almost maternal, though I didn't really think Schatze understood all that was about to unfold in the next two to three months

Back then, probably now too, it was typical for first-time parents to attend a number of prenatal classes. They're a smart idea, given I for one knew next to nothing about being a parent. So these classes were a godsend when it came to me, though Ginny always seemed to be several steps ahead. She'd done a lot of reading on the subject and had friends and families who either already had kids or were also were pregnant at the time. That reminds me of a picture I took of Ginny and four girlfriends around New Years 1984. Four of the five wives were pregnant at the time and the fifth had just had a baby girl that past summer…must have been something in the water.

As the date grew closer, I'd made up a special kit. In it were a number of things I needed to take with us to the hospital. It included some "new father" cigars, a six-pack of Genny beer, a few small bags of snacks, a can of beer nuts, and a list of phone numbers along with plenty of dimes for the pay phone. I was committed to be her rock when things got hectic. Yeah, we were all set.

The day finally arrived; March 1st. At the time Ginny and I were watching an episode of Miami Vice when this look came over her and she said, "It's time." Now you might think we were all synced up on our communications…but at that moment I had no idea what she meant.

Besides, the television show was just getting to the good part. She quickly dispelled any notion of me watching the last twenty minutes. In no time, I had the car packed with her suitcase and my "man kit" (can't forget that). We'd been to the hospital a number of times before so I knew exactly the best route to take. It being Friday night traffic was light and the roads were good; no late winter snow to hassle us. We got to the emergency entrance where they took her in for admittance. I parked the car and was by her side in less than five minutes. It was good that we'd gotten there as quickly as we had, for now we had plenty of time to just wait. I'd expected her doctor to be there soon after we'd arrived, but we were told he was tied up with an emergency. That sort of upset me, for him being there from the get-go was the plan; he too was supposed to stick to the plan. I know it sounds silly, but I hadn't even considered the idea the doctor would be late.

The whole birthing process, as had been explained, can take a considerable amount of time. This is particularly true in the case of the first child. Ginny was such a trooper. I knew she was in some pain but she just took things in stride. Me, well, I sort of got off on the wrong foot with the head nurse as she didn't seem the least bit inclined to be more specific about the doctor's whereabouts other than "he had an emergency." I'm a person who wants to know the specifics. Perhaps it's my way of sizing up the matter at hand. After a bit, I mentioned to Ginny that it turns out we could have watched the last twenty minutes of the program. She gave me an odd look. Perhaps she too had thought of that, perhaps she was thinking something totally different. She gave me an assignment to "go call our parents." I did so right away, seeing that she was a bit busy with other things. My parents told me to let them know as soon as the baby was born. I'd contrast that with Ginny's parents—though it was late, her dad said they'd come right up. They were there somewhere around 11:00 PM or so. Her parents were already grandparents many times over, but that didn't matter—they'd be there for us. They were great. They didn't try to horn into our special day but were there—available to talk to or not as we saw fit. I must admit I began to get nervous when midnight rolled around and still no doctor. Just when I was about to check his status once again, he arrived. However, the first thing he told us was also not something we'd planned.

It seemed that the X-Ray or sonogram taken right after our arrival indicated that the baby (sex unknown to us as we wanted it to be a surprise) had shifted inside Ginny's womb from her last doctor's visit. The doctor called it a "breech birth," but assured us many women continue to go the natural childbirth route even in such cases. This was a major issue in both Ginny's and my eyes. Though the doctor told us some parents opt to go with a C-section, he was sure everything would be fine. That was the only time that evening that Ginny got a worried look on her face. She said to me, "No, I don't want to try natural, lots can happen if the head doesn't come out first." Then and there we decided on a C-section. That possibility was discussed at the last prenatal class…the one I told her we didn't need to attend, as it was on problem births. Within a minute or two, we relayed our decision to the doctor. He seemed disappointed, but not nearly as disappointed as me. In those days, husbands weren't permitted to be in the delivery room unless it was going to be a completely natural birth process. Of all things, Ginny apologized to me for wanting the C-section, as she knew how I felt about being in there with her. I told her there was no need to apologize, this was our decision and if it meant me waiting in a separate room that was just fine. Ginny's and the baby's safety were absolutely paramount to me.

We figured they'd take her into the operating room right after we'd relayed our decision, but the doctor wanted to wait a bit longer to allow the normal cervical dilation to advance. Now I thought that was about as dumb as you can get. If you know it's going to be a C-section, why wait? Seeing how my opinion at the hospital was somewhat below that of the night janitor, I kept my thoughts to myself. Meaning I told Ginny what I thought and she told me to just go with the flow. That night at least, what she said is what I did, period.

Somewhere around 3:00 AM they came to take her. I really was a bit concerned. All our plans had me right in there with her, not in some out-of-the-way waiting room. But that's where they put me. The room was tiny—maybe ten by eight. The good thing was that it had a television in it—and I had my kit. The only thing I could find worth watching was an old rerun of the movie Bonnie and Clyde.

At about 3:25AM a nurse came out of the operating room to tell me I was the father of a healthy baby boy! To that I replied, "How's Ginny?" The nurse smiled and said, "She's doing well—the doctor is suturing her up as we speak." This was one of those moments folks talk about, that they will always remember. I was so overjoyed. Just then her parents walked out of the waiting room, hearing my excited voice. I said to them, "Now we have one of each." My mother-in-law looked at me quizzically. I said, "We have a baby boy and we have Schatze as our little girl." She replied with a touch of exasperation; "Oh Jimmy!"

It wasn't until another twenty minutes or so that they brought Ginny to her room. She was still groggy from the anesthetic but she had such a wonderful and peaceful look. I was so proud of her. We had talked often over the years about having a family—and now that's what we were—a family. I stayed with her a while but then the nurse told me it would be best for Ginny if I perhaps went home to get some rest as she needed hers. Even though she'd had a C-section, Ginny had gone through nearly the entire labor process too. I was charged with adrenaline, yet was also admittedly tired too…and I hadn't done anything but wait around aside from eating my snacks and having a couple of beers. In the ensuing excitement, I'd left most of my kit behind at the hospital. It didn't matter; besides, I figured maybe some other guy would appreciate the gift.

The next morning I was up early. I had been told I could come up any time after 7:00 AM. I was there before 7:30 AM and marched right into Ginny's room. She was wide awake and very happy to see me, in part because they told her she could not hold our little boy until I got there. It was some sort of hospital policy since she'd had a strong sedative only hours before. At that, I asked the nurse if she'd bring our little boy to us. She smiled and said, "right away"…and added that she was glad I got there, as my wife has been very anxious to hold our son. I sort of felt guilty that I was thirty minutes later than I could have been.

When they brought him in, Ginny said to me, "Jason James, this is your father." I had tears in my eyes, as did she. These were the good tears…the ones that come from rapture and joy, not sadness. Jason was fairly big; 8 lbs, 3 ounces. Her doctor came in soon after. He told us we'd made the right decision, as Jason was larger than he'd expected, so it would have been a very difficult birth had she gone natural; so much for the doctor always being right.

The hospital told us that since Ginny had a C-section, she and Jason would be kept a couple of days longer than otherwise. Friends and family visited over the next two days and then we all headed home on March 5th. I remember her parents coming to our house for the trip home. Ginny was still rather tired and hadn't had an opportunity to take a shower or change. But none of that mattered. Her dad took a picture of the three of us with me holding Jason. He took the shot just as Ginny landed a big kiss on my cheek. The look on my face was not at all typical of me. I seemed so content, so happy with everything. It's a shame we can't freeze time at moments like that.

(Refer to Pictures section, picture 14)

I can vividly remember the night she gave birth and the day she and Jason came home. Few times in our lives leave such lasting impressions. I only wish I could turn the clock back and relive it all again; unfortunately that's not how it works.

Visit to the Doctors

Though I can't recall the exact date, sometime in late April or early May 1985, Ginny and Jason each had doctor appointments. Hers was a routine postnatal visit, while his was for early vaccinations and a general exam by his pediatrician. I recall it was during the work week, so we'd made an evening appointment.

She had made the appointments with his being first—typical in that she always put others before herself. The pediatrician noted that all was well; no issues were uncovered, though I seem to recall he suggested a change in his infant formula might be prudent. We had a little time between appointments so it was decided that I'd take Jason to the car and we'd wait for Ginny rather than exposing him to others waiting in her doctor's office.

It was a clear yet cold evening; the sun had set so the temperature had begun to fall. After getting him all bundled up and into his infant car seat, I drove the short distance over to the main entrance of the doctor offices located adjacent to the hospital where we'd wait for Ginny. Jason was apparently quite tired, as he fell asleep within just a few minutes. I had the car radio tuned to our favorite oldies channel. As we waited, the song "Anticipation" by Carly Simon came on. I don't know what it was, but that day I listened carefully to the lyrics. Until that day I guess I'd never really understood them in reference to my own life. Specifically the meaning tied to two lines near the end of the song: "And tomorrow we might not be together, I'm no prophet, I don't know nature's way".

It occurred to me that Ginny and I really had everything we'd ever wanted. That while we were still so young and full of big plans and dreams for our future, time was marching on. My stare was fixed upon a peaceful little sleeping baby. His addition to our family was such a blessing. Ginny and I had never been happier.

The lyrics to the song are often interpreted to represent the dynamic nature of relationships. That while things today might seem grand, we never know how time and circumstance are going to affect the relationship. Yet right then my thoughts were focused on the life of the tiny child asleep in the back seat. While there was no doubt Ginny was and would be a great mom, I wondered, would I be a good dad? Would I find the right balance in my life? Whoever said, "it doesn't get better than this" must have had just such a moment of reflection.

I didn't even see her approach the car, for as I turned from gazing into the backseat Ginny was standing right outside my window just looking at us. She then walked around the front of the car and got in. She told me her checkup had gone well, no issues whatsoever. She then simply said to me, "Do you know how much I love you?" I smiled and said, "Yes, whole bunches."

I've thought of that moment many times over the years; of sitting in the car with a tiny baby in the back seat while waiting for my wife. At that specific point, all our hopes and aspirations seemed to have come true.

Hamlin Beach Excursion

As we had done many times over the years, we planned a Memorial Day picnic at Hamlin Beach Park along Lake Ontario. These picnics had become sort of a tradition for a whole group of us. The group most always included four couples, though at times that doubled in size. In the early years back when we were dating, the picnics were all-day affairs. These were always big events, both early on and as children began to enter the equation. All of us would bring hotdogs, burgers, and coolers full of cold beer and wine coolers. We had side dishes too, as well as snacks and deserts. Oh, and a radio was absolutely requisite as we all loved listening to tunes.

Over the years, the group continued to grow as couples became families with multiple children. In 1985 this would include one of our very own for the first time.

We'd make the Hamlin Beach trip generally twice a year...most often this included the Memorial Day and Labor Day weekends. Memorial Day was always a bit of a gamble in terms of the weather. Late May in the Northeast was unpredictable. I can remember some very warm and sunny days as well as a few cool and rainy ones as well. We seldom cancelled picnic plans unless the weather forecast called for rain all day. Still, there were some soggy outings, especially when we didn't have to worry about the kids getting wet and perhaps catching cold.

On this particular Memorial Day weekend, we'd decided to make the trek on Sunday, meeting up in our regular spot; parking lot number five. We found over the years that even on nice weekends, few park visitors would bother driving all the way to the furthest lot (number five) so we often had more or less free reign of the entire area. We'd set our meeting time as 11:00 AM to give folks time to gather all the essentials that day. Unfortunately, in 1985 the weather was going to be on the cool side but only a brief rain was in the forecast. The day started unseasonably cool but temperatures were expected to reach close to 70 by mid-afternoon. Perhaps that was a bit optimistic, since we'd be picnicking alongside the lake where the water temp was still in the upper 40s and the breeze was expected to be out of the Northwest.

It seems to me it took Ginny and I a lot longer to pack up. The Omni bought in 1980 was our first "new car." In those days, Detroit hadn't yet gotten the message on quality. Still, it was a reliable car. The hatchback was absolutely full of stuff...much of it baby-related items. We had a stroller, a small bassinet, and a diaper bag with at least two changes of clothes. In addition, we had our normal provisions including a picnic basket, cooler, portable AM/FM/cassette radio, Frisbees, ball and glove, blankets, and the like. I recall telling Ginny that I felt like a gypsy with all the stuff we'd packed; she just smiled.

The roughly thirty-mile trip to Hamlin went well. As we traveled west we could see that the sky was clearing up ahead, which was a relief. Hamlin has a number of things going for it, but unlike some local parks, it had very few covered shelters in case of rain. We got there pretty much on time. We were never the pokey ones. As couples we knew each other well. We all knew who'd be there first and who'd invariably be the last to arrive.

It took me three trips to get all the stuff from the car to the picnic site we'd chosen. Not bad, though I wasn't looking forward to trying to fit everything back into the car at the end of the day. The load would be lighter, as the beer and much of the food would be gone, but with all the bulky items things would still be tight. That would be the issue if our departure was hastened by a late afternoon shower, but I was trying to think positive.

Sometimes I set expectations fairly high, but this day I admit came off even better than I'd hoped. The weather got progressively warmer as the day wore on and the chilly breeze subsided by early afternoon. Though all our close friends had met our new baby since his birth, that day he seemed to garner more attention than the other children. He slept much of the day and when he was up, he was very attentive and not the least bit colicky. The girls had plenty of time to chat about all sorts of things and us guys took our normal long walks along the lake; taking some of the older kids with us as relief to the moms.

(Refer to Pictures section, picture 15)

Several things struck me this particular day. First, Ginny looked fantastic. No way would anyone guess she'd given birth less than three months ago. I rarely would step back and just observe her, but that day I did. My whole perspective on life had changed. I couldn't help but think how lucky I was that a woman so wonderful had decided to spend her life with me. I wish I'd told her just that but I seldom voiced such thoughts aloud. That day I also noticed how cohesive our entire group had become over the years. Invariably, someone would forget some basic item or items but with all the attendees, there was always enough food and drink and whatever to share. In some very real ways we were like one big family.

Lots of young people did what we did in those days but I dare say few of them worked to maintain the lifelong relationships the way we generally had. As the day came to a close, we packed up our "caravans" to head back home. It was a great day as it turned out, another in a series of successful Hamlin ventures.

Those trips to Hamlin Beach served as a sort of reinforcement to the many friendships. I don't really know why, but late in the 90s those biannual trips waned, and then eventually ended. Where Fridays and Saturdays had been our days to go out, these too eventually ended. Perhaps other family or personal demands took precedent. It is easy to grow apart; both friendships and marriages can suffer this fate. The key is to never lose one's sense of priority; what is and isn't important. Sometimes

1. Easter Sunday, March 30, 1975 (perhaps her favorite
early picture of us)

2. Ginny and I at a friend's wedding on June 14, 1975

3. Ginny's 19th Birthday present (the "Sweden Chest")
March 28, 1975

4. Ginny on the way to Summerfest, September 2, 1975

5. Weedsport Weekend, September 4, 1976

6. Ginny and I overlooking Niagara Falls, July 31, 1977

7. Ginny preparing our first meal in the new apartment,
December 2, 1977

8. Our Wedding Day, December 17, 1977

9. Our Wedding Day, December 17, 1977

10. Prepping for Halloween Party October 28, 1978

11. Halloween Party October 28, 1978

12. Our First Home, Mildorf Street 1982

13. Telling Her Parents July 14, 1984

14. Home from the Hospital, March 5, 1985

15. Hamlin Beach Picnic, May 26, 1985

16. Ginny and I camping at Darien Lake with friends,
September 26, 1987

17. Christmas 1999

18. Ginny's Birthday at my parents on Saturday March 29, 2003, the day our offer for the New Jersey house was accepted.

19. Ginny and I in our New Jersey home (COTL)
October 10, 2003

20. Ginny with our pet Dachshund Jesse in New
Jersey on her 1st birthday (August 2004)

21. COTL (lakeside view) before our last move (July 2013)

22. Ginny ready for our lake trip (background is our first
Webster home)

23. Ginny and I at a friend's wedding, August 26, 1995

24. Ginny and I in an Adirondack cabin, September 2, 2000

25. Ginny, pretty as a rose, October 2001

26. Ginny and I for last Thanksgiving at Appian,
November 28, 2002

27. Ginny and I at Hedges on June 6, 2009

28. Ginny with her sister's new dog 'Lucy' at
Christmas 2009

29. Ginny and I in our new Webster home,
September 9, 2013

30. Ginny and I in NYC for our 30th Anniversary
in Dec 2007

Part II

Part II is a chronology of events commencing late May 2013. The story of this couple picks up from Part I but many years later. Some detail of what took place during the intervening years is included throughout Part II using "flashback." Each time this technique is employed, the words are printed in italics.

Another Memorial Day (28 years later)

It was approaching noon on Sunday May 25th, 2013 as we drove back along Route 81S just north of Binghamton. We'd just spent a short holiday weekend visiting family and friends in the Rochester area. Typical of most of the trips we'd take back and forth from our home in Northern New Jersey to Upstate New York. The mood was tempered, a bit quiet, though not what one would term sullen. I was thinking about the great time we'd had going out with our old friends that weekend, how much we missed seeing them more often. Out of the blue I asked Ginny a question that would trigger many changes in our life. "Have you ever thought about whether you'd like to move back to Rochester?"

I pride myself on having a good sense of what she might be thinking or feeling, but the speed of her reply surprised me. She turned to me and said she'd love to go "back home." At that I asked her, "Why haven't you said anything to me about how you felt before now?" Her reply spoke volumes about the type of person she is. "This is something you needed to conclude on your own…if I'd said anything I felt it would have put pressure on you, and I know how much you love our home in New Jersey." People that know me know that I'm seldom at a loss for words…but her reply had me dumbfounded. I'm afraid that over the last few months I'd been too busy brooding about some things. She was right about how I felt about our New Jersey home, yet the fact was there was nothing preventing us from moving. It should have occurred to me that she, even more than I, might have some very strong feelings about it. My reply to her was simple, "If moving back to Rochester would make you happiest, that's what we will do."

We had plans to retire earlier than most folks but some events that transpired in the fall of 2012 sort of forced my hand. Overall, the background of what happened really wasn't important in the big picture of things. While it's important to find a career/job that is rewarding, happiness and success in life is sourced outside of work. It took me too long to really understand and appreciate this reality.

As we drove along, Ginny became rather enthusiastic. At first her reaction was tentative as she wasn't sure I really meant what I said about moving back. She looked at me and said, "Really?" "Yes really!" I replied. In those few words I'd convinced her I hadn't just agreed by way of capitulation. She immediately began to make a list of the things we'd need to do. Ginny was a "list" person. Anytime we had a project or big plan, she'd make a list of the steps or actions that needed to occur to make it happen. I always admired that about her. Right away she mentioned that we should ask a neighbor—Peggy, who lived in our lake community—to be our realtor. Just like that, the normally quiet ride back to New Jersey took on an air of adventure and excitement. More than that, I could readily see how very happy she was over the prospect of moving back to the area we'd both called home most of our lives.

This move wouldn't be our first…but right away we both agreed it would be our last. As we drove along, we played music consisting of songs of the 60s and 70s. These "records" (CDs) are normally reserved for the trips up, but all that was soon to change, for as she said, we're moving back home. I began to think of our other moves, the first from the apartment to our first house in the city. My mind shifted to another time when in '88 we'd moved from there to central Florida. I'd been asked to join a "recovery" team for one of my parent company's failing ventures. I remembered that before that move, her dad had noticed how torn she was about leaving. He was undergoing chemo and radiation treatments for cancer. They thought he'd beat it two years before, but it had come back. Ginny felt like she was abandoning her dad and mom and that they would need her more than ever. But he'd told her, "You need to go with your husband, you two have a life to lead. Don't worry about us, your mom and I, we'll be fine."

In Florida we didn't buy a house but instead rented a place. We'd agreed to do that since we didn't know if we'd like "Florida living" and due to the uncertainty of the business venture. When I'd finally accepted the new assignment, my boss and I sort of viewed it as temporary; two years. If the team I was joining turned the business around, I'd have the opportunity to either stay with that business, transfer to another Florida-based operation (the parent's headquarters resided in Florida), or transfer back to Rochester. It made a lot of sense to rent as neither Ginny nor I had any idea where in that area we'd like to live; or whether we'd ever acclimate to the area.

As it turned out, our stay in Florida lasted only about eighteen months. At the close of that assignment we had to make a decision about moving back north. I can remember talking to Ginny about it. She turned the question around, asked me what I wanted to do. I told her I'd prefer to return north. Ginny then said, "That's good because that's what Jason and I are going to do too." At that she smiled…her way of saying, "I will go where you feel we need to," but she really wanted to go back home to Rochester.

Looking back, the move to Florida prompted perhaps my first significant life regret. It had nothing to do with the business venture. It had to do with defining and weighing the impact of our life's decisions.

While her dad had assuaged her concerns before we'd left, things for him went from bad to worse over the next few months. Though I got her back to see him one more time, he lost his battle with cancer in August. I always felt I'd taken her away, denied her that additional precious time with him and of being there for her mom when she most needed Ginny.

Her dad was a great guy, the best father-in-law a guy could want. He was a product of the Great Depression and WWII, quite a man in so many ways. He had a simple philosophy on life, which served him well. His dear wife and five daughters would miss him terribly as would his countless friends and extended family. He passed away on the feast of the Assumption, a day after my birthday. Ginny said she was sure he held out to ensure my birthday wouldn't be burdened with the memory of his death. If you knew him you'd know that was just the way he was; selfless. I didn't have to wonder where my wife acquired that same trait. I never got a chance to say good-bye and I regretted that as well.

An important by-product of our Florida move ended up teaching me a valuable lesson. I'd gone down a couple of weeks earlier than my family to get living arrangements secured and to begin the new role. Ginny, Jason, and most of our possessions followed a couple of weeks later. About 7:00 PM during my second week in the new role, an exec from Corporate HQ had noticed the lights on in my building. I'd known Jack only superficially, as he had once held a key role in the Rochester operation. He stopped in to say hello and ended up giving me some sage advice. He told me that my dedication to work was admirable; yet added a "but." He asked me what sort of long-term financial plan I'd set up to ensure a secure future. I had to admit we didn't have one. His advice was simple...create a plan and stick to it. He noted that few people take the time to develop, no less implement, a financial plan for themselves and their family. Subsequently, I did just that. In time the whole subject of personal financial planning became an avocation. Over the years, we worked at our plan. I say "our" because it was both hers and mine. More often than not, Ginny would defer the investment decisions to me. That didn't bother me. What did was when she would say stuff like, "investing your money is really up to you." Didn't matter that I would correct her, telling her it was "our" money. Though during our marriage she'd not worked outside the home, she was every bit a full partner. My tendency to always plan things out was generally good, but having a plan can make us think we're in control when in fact that is just an illusion. While it may be true that failure to plan is often planning for failure, having a plan doesn't assure things will go as you expect or even imagine.

"Who should we use as a moving company?" Her question brought me back to the present. We were less than 100 miles from our New Jersey home. She turned down the radio as she asked if we could make a rest stop. "Besides, I want to show you the list I've made…we have lots to do for this move." We made our last stop soon after. I've got to tell you, I was impressed with her list. It was comprehensive and time-phased. Ginny has many good qualities; being thorough is one of them.

I was fairly confident we'd sell our New Jersey home without much trouble. I turned to ask Ginny what sort of target date she thought was doable. "You mean in selling the COTL (cottage on the lake, our term for the New Jersey home) or being in our new home?" "In our new home" I replied. She looked at me somewhat sheepishly and replied "Halloween?" To which I told her we'd beat that date, I was sure of it.

As I drove the last stretch it struck me that it was unlikely we'd recover all the monies we'd sunk into the New Jersey home. During the ten years we'd owned it, the thought of selling had never entered my mind. That got me reminiscing about the day we found the place back in 2003. I remember it so well.

I'd taken an operations role for a small firm based in Northern New Jersey back in August of 2002…commuting home to Rochester on the weekends for nearly ten months. In late March of 2003 she accompanied me back to New Jersey on Sunday the 23rd. Our plan was for her to begin house-hunting that week as I worked. I'd lined up a couple of real estate agents for her; one was recommended by a woman (Liz) that worked with me. Even though I'd lived there a few months, it turned out I was clueless in terms of real estate pricing. The $300K preliminary budget Ginny and I had initially set turned out to be woefully insufficient. She'd been down to New Jersey before for visits, but this was the first time she had such a daunting job, finding us a new home.

During this visit she stayed with me in the tiny room I'd been renting in Bloomfield, New Jersey. It was equipped with a single bed. It brought back memories of a time so many years ago when she'd come to visit me in Buffalo during my first semester in college. We'd slept together in a single bed then too, and never slept better.

The first couple of days of house-hunting Ginny spent with a more seasoned real estate agent. The woman seemed intent on getting her to consider condo living rather than a single-family home. Despite Ginny's protests to the contrary, they'd gone to see several condo complexes. Each night Ginny would tell me how the agent would tell her that condo living was the way to go and that she had to find a place suitable for a small business exec. Ginny sensed the agent had her mind made up and wasn't even listening to what Ginny wanted. By the end of the third day, Ginny dumped that agent in favor of the one Liz had suggested (Nancy). On Thursday, Ginny and this new agent went to see some single-family homes. *That evening Ginny was discouraged. She'd seen a few places but none of them were even close to the type of home she envisioned. The next day I was scheduled to go with them; it would be my first New Jersey house-hunting trip.*

As it so happens that day was March 28th, Ginny's birthday. The three of us had looked at a couple of places late that morning…neither of which impressed either of us. The realtor told us of a place just listed that was a bit out of our price range but she felt it might fit the parameters we'd set. We'd told her to focus on "different," low maintenance, 1,500 square feet, and not more than twenty miles from work.

It was early afternoon when we arrived at a house in the little town of Denville. As soon as we pulled up, I liked what I saw. At a glance I could tell Ginny did too. The house was a Cape Cod built in 1928 on the shore of a small manmade lake. Upon entering we could see right out to the backyard, which was small but the lake view was incredible. Ginny turned to me and said, "Unless we're going to buy this place you better get me out of here because I already love it." We went through every room, and Ginny kept asking, "Are you sure we could afford this?" By day's end we'd submitted an offer. The next day we drove back to our house in Webster, New York. The current owners of the New Jersey place were living in Florida but we expected to hear something from our agent before the weekend was out. That Saturday we received a call…they'd countered our initial offer, so back again we went. Our second offer, still below their asking price, included the purchase of their bedroom furniture. The bedroom furniture was a seven-piece set made of solid cherry by Harden. I really liked the set, Ginny not quite as much, but she could see how much I did so she agreed. The next day we got a call from Nancy late in the morning before I was due to head back to New Jersey. Our offer had been accepted. Ginny was ecstatic. I pointed out to her that this was the biggest birthday gift she was ever going to get. She smiled that wonderful smile of hers, gave me a big hug, and told me how much she liked the "new place" and how much she loved me. It was a special moment. Moving meant that my weekend sojourns would come to an end; the idea really appealed to me. And for Ginny it meant no more lonely nights with me in New Jersey and her in New York.

(Refer to Pictures section, pictures 18 and 19)

As we pulled into the COTL at just after 3:00 PM on May 26th, 2013 I already sensed something had changed. It was as if the house knew we'd be leaving. I know how strange that may sound. It was the same way I felt when we had decided to sell our first house, the little Cape Cod on Mildorf Street. Both these houses held very fond memories. That wasn't the case when we left our first apartment, or the Florida condo, or even the Appian Drive home in Webster. It struck me that we'd closed on the COTL almost exactly ten years earlier on the Friday before Memorial Day 2003. But today, no sooner had I unpacked the car than Ginny was on the computer looking up real estate listings in the Rochester area. I'd seen it before, once my wife sets her mind to something, either help or get out of the way. The truth was, I'd miss our New Jersey home for many reasons, but none of them could compare to the exuberance that now captured Ginny. I felt sort of guilty for not having thought of the idea a few months before. I left her to do her research on the computer while I went into the living room to watch some television. Though I turned it on, my mind wandered back to a time ten years before.

When we'd come down in 2003 there were three of us…Ginny, Jason, and myself. But Jason decided to move back to the Rochester area on his own within a year or so thereafter. Still, going back there would be three of us again. This time with Jesse, our miniature Dachshund who'd joined our family back on September 27th of 2003. I'd been very close to Schatze, our first pet Dachshund. It really affected me when we had to put her down (June 1999). I didn't want to go through losing another pet. But once Ginny was in New Jersey, she found a breeder with Dachsies on that early autumn day. I recall the day coincided with the New York City garlic festival since the breeder was not at home when we called. Fortunately though, her husband told us we were welcome to see the pups. I'd agreed to go "see" the puppies, but told Ginny we'd not be bringing one home that day; "we're just going to look." To this day I can still picture Ginny holding the little pup beside her face as she smiled at me at the breeder's. My heart melted, for I could see how happy it would make Ginny. The only thing I said to the breeder was, "how much?" That evening we named her Jessica Lynn…a name Ginny had chosen years ago for a baby girl if we'd been so lucky. But two miscarriages after Jason, we'd more or less given up on having more children. That was hard for me to accept; harder still for her, as she was such a wonderful mom. But that day in September 2003, the name she'd chosen years ago for a baby girl would be given to a little girl dachsie who quickly wormed her way into both our hearts.

(Refer to Pictures section, picture 20)

In the years we'd lived in New Jersey, we always seemed to be working on some sort of restoration project. The house was nice but had not been maintained to any great degree. Built initially as a summer cottage, it wasn't very well insulated. Our heating bills the first couple of winters bore that out. Yet slowly over the years we took on projects, often requiring outside contractors too, making our home what I considered the prettiest little house on the lake. As it turned out, we expended quite a bit of money and sweat equity to make that happen. We painted every room, working side-by-side as we'd done in the past. When it came to projects outside, that was generally my sole purview. I recall the many hours of preparation I spent repairing the exterior stucco sides. Based on the condition, my guess is that the house hadn't been painted in more than ten years. Some areas like the back porch and the garage door had to be replaced completely as the wood was too far-gone. It sounds funny to say garage door, for that's what it appears to be. But some thirty years prior, the owners at the time had built a room where the garage was placed. When you open the carriage doors you find out it was more a shed, only about twelve feet wide and six or seven feet deep. I missed having a garage but I did love that place. By the time we got back from this most recent trip north, the home had never looked better.

(Refer to Pictures section, picture 21)

That home in New Jersey was truly a good home for us. The town, well I can't say enough good things about Denville. Unlike most "towns" in New Jersey, Denville actually had a main street lined with little shops all located within walking distance of our home. Over the years, family came to visit fairly often. No visit was complete without a trip to Denville Dairy, the ice cream parlor in town. It seems these days that people like to go to the malls or buy on-line; but for us, dealing face-to-face with the owners of small businesses was the way to go. I recall that once or twice a year I went in to town to a small jewelry shop where I found all sorts of special little pieces for Ginny over the years. I miss seeing those nice folks, though Ginny would always say she already had too much jewelry. She never liked spending on herself, so I did.

One time on an Alaskan cruise, I had to beg her to let me buy a few of pieces of jewelry I'd found at a couple of the stops along the way. After the first stop and purchase she'd put her foot down and said, "No more jewelry!" In the end, she agreed to let me buy "just one last piece." I so enjoyed getting her nice things, yet no matter what they were, the pieces always looked so great on her; like the Swarovski necklace pictured in the photo shown on the back cover.

The Big Move

Our new project, the move back to Rochester, was one that would require a lot of work from both Ginny and I to pull off. Unlike most all our previous moves, this move wasn't going to be underwritten by a company; the cost would all be "out of pocket" as they say. Perhaps more pertinent, this would be my first "roll up the sleeves" engagement. In the previous moves, Ginny acted as the central point of contact and was directly involved in doing all the organizing and a fair amount of the packing. She pointed that fact out to me on more than one occasion. Like that I'd only packed my small toolbox when it came to the move to Florida. So, I was the neophyte when it came to moving a household hundreds of miles, not she.

We'd set a reasonable target in selling our current home and being in our new home: October 1st 2013. That gave us four months to make everything happen. Too big a task for some, but as Ginny would often say, "Not too tough for the Punkins."

Punkin? I remember when I first heard that word…it was back in September 1974. The first time she said it to me I thought she'd called me a pumpkin. "That's not what I called you, I called you 'punkin'"…and I replied, "What's that?" "It's not a what, it's a who" she told me.

Back then I couldn't look it up on the Internet, but you can today. The urban dictionary defines "punkin" as a nickname or pet name that some use in referring to their boyfriend or girlfriend. Over the years I couldn't count the number of times we called each other by that name. When she first began using that term she'd told me she'd never had a punkin before, though she'd had other boyfriends…she went on to say, "you see, there are millions of other guys in this world, but there will only ever be one 'punkin' for me." When she said that, I honestly never remember having felt so special. But that's just her way.

We had quite a few tasks we'd have to do in order to put our New Jersey home up for sale. Hurricane Sandy had left its mark in August 2012, having taken down two of our next-door neighbor's trees. Unfortunately, they both landed on our lakeside dock, crushing our fully restored gazebo. By end of May I'd had most of the debris cleaned up, thanks in large part to the help of neighbors and friends with chainsaws. However, we rightly noted there wouldn't be time to rebuild the gazebo, nor would we get any payback on doing so. Aside from that, I had some painting of the new stucco areas around the fall 2012 installation of a lake-facing bay window. The list of things that had to be done was long but we two were up to the task.

Our New Jersey realtor used a staging specialist who'd suggested moving out about a third of our furniture and belongings, and we agreed. That little modification to our moving contract with Allied cost us another 2,000 dollars or so. By the time everything was said and done, the move cost over 13,000 dollars; ouch. We had an open house, which attracted quite a few potential buyers. In short order, we accepted an offer just ten days after the house had been listed.

During those weeks after we decided to move back, Ginny and I continued our normal routine of going down to a nearby TGIF restaurant on Friday night. Routine is the right word too. In the ten plus years we lived in New Jersey we never did find a small tavern we liked as much as those we'd go to up North. Yet at TGIF's we'd made some friends. Some became dear friends while others turned out to be mere acquaintances. It's hard to explain why that happens, but I guess those who become true friends accept us for who we are; both the good and the not-so-good. Others get relegated to acquaintances as whatever it was that once formed the bond wanes away. I particularly remember a few of the bartenders—they were young enough that we could have been their parents—still we thought of them as friends. Steve was our favorite of them all. We met so many folks there over the years; a few I still think about to this day with fondness.

Unlike our previous moves, Ginny found us a home using online searches of the local area real estate. The fact is, our Rochester-based realtor really had little to do with our finding the new home…it was really all Ginny's doing. I remember when she first saw the home on-line in June. I tried to caution her not to get her heart set on any one place since we'd not be able to get up to see any of them until mid-July. Regardless of what I said, she felt the one she found would suit us perfectly…nice sized, one story, built in the early 90s, low maintenance, three-car garage, and perhaps best of all, it backed up to a "forever wild" woody area.

June and early July had us working long days to get things packed and completing the outside painting and pre-sell preparations. We needed quite a few specialty packing boxes (read expensive) for this move, since we planned to pack Ginny's Dickens Village collection, which was extensive.

Her Dickens Village collection had been acquired over many years. Ginny had over 100 houses and 200 accessory pieces. It was perhaps her one noted extravagance, yet was also a hobby we both enjoyed. She got her first piece from my mom back in the mid-80s. Every Christmas she was assured that under the tree would be both more Dickens Village and a piece of Lenox Holiday pattern china. The latter built upon a single piece our best man Paul had gifted us for our wedding. Boy that gift cost me a lot over the years.

The village displays Ginny would conceive and plan out were elaborate; including fountains, lighted streets, and tiered terrain. These displays eventually took her many days to set up, forcing her to begin the annual effort right after Halloween. She was a "nut" when it came to Dickens Village. I was more than happy to "feed her craving," as I could see how happy it made her. Many times I'd come home during the season and she'd be so excited to show me what she'd done that day. She even had a "music box" CD she'd play, giving it an almost mystical appeal.

It was on July 18th, 2013 when we saw in-person the house that was the favorite of the places she'd found on-line. We both were immediately sold on the idea that this should be our new home. We knew then and there it was what we wanted. I actually told her as I stood in the back yard before we even entered the house that this was "the place." That very day we submitted an offer. The offer matched the owner's asking price. We didn't want to tempt fate by having someone come in and take it from us. We got an acceptance response back the next day. We were thrilled, but it turns out the deal wasn't quite as assured as we thought.

The following week while back in New Jersey we got some unwelcome news from our realtor. Our offer was predicated on our selling our New Jersey home. The buyer had received two other non-contingent offers. I remember it well. Ginny had taken the call while I was off on errands. She called me on my cell phone in a panic. She was very concerned that we'd lose the house. I came right home from wherever I was to talk to her and address the matter. Ginny was in tears when I arrived home. In speaking to our realtor, she said we'd have to prove available funds equal to the asking price or we'd lose the house. In short, we had to remove the contingency from our offer. This was something neither of us had expected, but in the back of my mind I had a feeling things had gone too smoothly up to this point.

That lesson on personal financial planning I'd learned all those years ago was about to pay off. We had sufficient monies in a "taxable" (non-retirement) setting. By the end of that day, I emailed a scan of a recent account statement. The following day we were back on track. Ginny was both very happy yet a bit concerned that if we didn't sell our New Jersey home quickly, we'd not only have two mortgage payments to make, but we'd have lost the majority of the funds we'd plan to live on during the early years of our retirement. While we had accepted an offer on our New Jersey home, it too was a contingent offer. Ginny knew from the past that home buying and selling is fraught with last-minute issues that can try the patience of Job.

Through it all, Ginny was a driven woman. I hadn't seen her so focused and so excited about anything in years. Anyone who's gone through moves to and from out-of-state locations knows that the efforts are both tiring and stressful. We were no exception to that rule. Ginny seemed to tire quickly but mustered on nonetheless. She wasn't sleeping as soundly as in the past either, but I attributed both these things to the stress of the move. She'd get up earlier than I at times, which was surprising since I'm the morning person in this family. When I'd wake up and see her gone, Jesse and I would make our way downstairs. *Yes, Jesse slept in our bed too. For an eleven-pound dog, she sure did take a lot of space. We had to break her of the habit of sleeping horizontally, forcing both Ginny and I to cling to the sides or risk falling off.*

One morning when I went downstairs I found Ginny already hard at work on revising the list of things we had to do that day and she'd already packed a couple of boxes. I could tell how long she'd be up since my coffee was in a thermal carafe and the coffee maker was already off. I noticed the carafe was almost full, which it shouldn't have been. We both loved our morning coffee; she'd always have two big cups. When I asked her why she made so much coffee, she commented that she'd made the normal amount but had only one cup earlier. She said it didn't taste good to her today for some reason. She looked tired to me, so I asked her how she felt. She said she was fine but just couldn't sleep with so much on her mind and left to do. "By the way" she said, "you apparently haven't noticed, but I've lost ten pounds. Sort of a side benefit I guess to all the things we have going." I lied, telling her I had noticed but didn't want to say anything, fearing I'd be wrong about her losing weight which might make her feel I thought she needed to do so. I suggested perhaps she should take a nap later in the day to catch up on some sleep. She gave me that look which says, you've got to be crazy, nap, with all we have to do? At that, I decided my best move was to leave her be. As noted earlier, once she gets something in her mind to do, look out.

We struggled through the rest of June, July, and through mid-August. In the end, we got everything done on or ahead of our already accelerated target dates. Closing on the New Jersey home was set for August 28th but not without having to overcome some last-minute obstacles (delay with the buyer's bank paperwork). Regardless, we supervised the loading of our moving van on the 27th. That night, we slept on an air mattress in our once jam-packed bedroom. Since we weren't required to be at the buyer's closing, we planned to leave mid-morning on the 28th. It's a funny feeling being in an empty house that used to be your home. You start to remember all the good times you'd had as well as all the projects you'd done to bring your home to the point you'd wanted. Though there were no reservations about leaving, we both found it oddly difficult to say goodbye to the place. In a manner of speaking, at that moment we felt like gypsies with no "home" to go to until the close on the new place on September 6th. In that interim we'd be staying with my parents, something we'd most often do on our visits up North. This time it would be for nine days, which is a fairly long time to live with anyone else. I'm one who sort of agrees with the old assertion that guests and fish begin to smell after three days. Thankfully, my parents felt otherwise.

So while we would miss many aspects of our home in New Jersey and of the small town we'd grown to love, in a very real sense we were going home; again. This time we were serious; this time would be our very last move.

We got on Interstate 80 for what would be the last time in a long time. Ginny always hated Route 80. In New Jersey it is one of the busiest thoroughfares in that most densely-populated state in the nation. Now I'm a good driver; though Ginny might have a thing or two to say about that assertion. I promised her I'd stay in the far right lane— worse case briefly in the center lane—for the forty miles before we hit Pennsylvania. That Wednesday I kept my word, never shifting into the far-left lane to pass some pokey person. Ginny noticed and thanked me, adding that her nerves just couldn't take the added stress.

The mood on the car ride back got progressively better after we paid the toll at the Delaware Water Gap. Ginny excitedly waved to the sign indicating we were exiting New Jersey. I guess the old adage, "home is where the heart is" really applies. We had thought that New Jersey would be our final move. I remember discussions we'd had about that back in 2003. When her dear mom passed away in 2005 I remember how tough it was for Ginny. She told me she felt like an orphan but didn't expect me to understand since both my parents were still with us. It had been her idea to replace the tile countertops with granite using some of the inheritance from her mom. At the time it seemed she was absolutely bought into the idea that New Jersey was it, our last place. But then I got to thinking.

Years ago, even before we got married, Ginny would tell me she would live wherever we needed to, wherever made me happy. "I'd live in a box if that's what it took for us to be together." It struck me as we drove this day, what was it that I gave up? What sacrifice had I made compared to those she had? She never complained when we would make our trips up north two or three times a year. Yet every time we'd have to head back, there was a palatable sadness when it came time to leave. I had my job, my career. But what was it she was going back for? The answer was obvious…she was going back for me. Even during the time when I commuted on weekends for all those months in late 2002 and early 2003, she never complained. What hit me like a brick this day was that she was the one who'd been making all the sacrifices, not me.

I was glad that while her mom was with us, we'd always stay a portion of our time with her in the home where Ginny grew up. Unlike my parents' place, there was no central air so it got pretty uncomfortable during those summer visits. Yet in hindsight, I was so glad we'd stayed with her mom too. We'd play Euchre with these oversized playing cards that her sister Carol had bought Mom. During the last few years, her mom's vision had been failing but she could still make out the numbers and suits on those giant cards. Both of us enjoyed playing Euchre, especially with her mom. Her mom would say "Jimmy, I'm going to rooky duke you"…meaning she'd figure a way to Euchre me. I was always so competitive but not quite so much when it came to cards. We'd laugh when her mom's threat came true as she stopped me from winning my three tricks. I never realized it until after she'd gone, but those visits, all those times we'd spend with her mom; they were like an energy drink that recharged Ginny. In hindsight, on this day as we drove North, I wish we'd made more of those trips to see our family and friends. I guess sometimes we think we always have more time to do such things than perhaps we really have.

We drove on with plans to stop, as we most always did, at the rest area aside Route 81 North in Pennsylvania. That stop was about 100 miles from the COTL; about the maximum distance we could go before either Jesse's or our own bladders cried foul. On this August day the air was cool, as a thunderstorm had passed in the early morning leaving the ground wet, but the air crisp. We both hate the high humidity and temps much above eighty. Never really thought of it, but it seems we both liked our music the same as the outdoor temperatures…in the 60s and 70s. No wonder we never could get used to the Florida weather years ago.

About an hour later, we passed the "Welcome to New York" sign. Ginny clapped, then found and played the old 70s tune "YMCA." As she often did, this day Ginny made Jesse dance on her lap to this song. Jesse never seemed too keen on doing such, but I must say it was funny to watch when Ginny would raise Jesse's paws symbolically spelling out the title to the song. Just seeing how happy my darling wife was dispelled any residual melancholy feelings I'd had about leaving. As we drove along I turned to Ginny to point out we could, as we did years ago, take bike trips along the lake. She looked at me and said, "I would love that…"

Back in the late 90s and up to the time we moved to New Jersey, Ginny and I would often take short excursions on my '97 Honda Magna motorcycle. Many times we'd take a ride along the shores of Lake Ontario out to a small town called Pultneyville. Matter of fact, the last bike trip we took in New York before moving to New Jersey in 2003 was to this destination. Other times we'd just take short local rides, perhaps to catch a light dinner of Buffalo-style chicken wings or to one of several area parks. Yet in all those rides, I would always say something to her before we got underway: "Make sure you hold on tight." She would always reply in the same way: "Don't worry, I will never let go." She'd wrap her arms around my waist as we rode along. Often times she'd squeeze tight along the ride…a nonverbal conveyance of her love. It would be great to take those long rides again; I could hardly wait.

(Refer to Pictures section, picture 22)

I will readily admit an inequity that Ginny would point out: "You may be retired, but what about me? When do I get a break from what I've been doing all these years?" While I generally would say I was a fairly attentive guy—sensitive to what she thought and felt—this division of labor was something I'd not given much thought to until she raised the issue. But it was going to be OUR retirement, not just mine. Things would be different; I would start making more of the meals. Though I'd not told her, I'd committed to myself that I would be doing a lot of the cooking and cleaning in the new place. I was going to pamper her; something I didn't do nearly as much as I should—an understatement for sure. I could just see her face when the time came and I said I would cook dinner or that I'd clean the bathrooms, etc. That was my secret plan and I knew she'd be tickled pink.

We made our usual stop along 81N at a rest stop New York State had begun and completed during our many trips North since August 2002. It marked the two-thirds point on these now familiar 300-mile trips. Over the last year or so we'd made these trips without stopping for lunch. Ever since they'd closed the Arby's at Great Bend, the last exit going north out of Pennsylvania, we opted to catch a bite to eat or just coffee nearer to our Rochester destination.

Great Bend and the old Arby's site brought to mind our old routine. Of course, the one who missed that the most was Jesse. I'd go get us lunch consisting of three of the large hot roast beef sandwiches, one large drink (iced tea), and large fries. Ginny and I would pull off some of the beef as we ate, gingerly feeding it to Jesse. We'd kid about the way she'd just vacuum it up, no chewing involved. Being a member of the hound family, Jesse had a voracious appetite. Wolfing down her food was nothing new, as that was just the way she ate. Yet when it came to Arby's, her focus on "the next bite" was so intense. Far be it that either of us took more than one bite before returning to feed the Jess.

Looking back, I figure I'd made this trip North—alone or with Ginny—somewhere between fifty and sixty times over the last eleven years. As we played our favorite old tunes I looked over at Ginny. Though Jesse was on her lap, she was busy making what appeared to be yet another list. Rather than disrupt her train of thought, I just smiled and kept driving along for what was the most tedious portion of the ride. This stretch of 81N from Binghamton to Syracuse was so boring. Often times I'd be musing over plans we had in the coming days. Today though was an exception. My mind drifted back to a time in my life that I'd largely ignored, had walled up deep inside. In so many ways we were "living the dream." Here we were, retired before the age of sixty, buying a home free and clear, financially secure though by no means rich, and I was married to my best friend; the love of my life. Yet deep inside me I bore the stain of an ill-fated time some thirteen years prior that was and always would be my greatest regret.

In July 2000 I left my first job after twenty-three years. While I did so wholly on my own volition, the reasons were varied and nuanced. I was struggling with what people often term as a "mid-life crisis." But that term seemed to lack the dire nature of what was happening within me. In many ways I felt I'd failed. I had issues of self-identification, personal satisfaction, and uncertainty about many things. In what seemed to have occurred overnight, I was now middle-aged. I'd lost that sense of idealism and adventure that was so much a part of me in those earlier years. Though I can't cite a specific point when or where it happened, I'd become rather cynical and all too judgmental. A "break" from everyday work was something I was sure I needed. Taking time off, as I called it, would enable me to get my act together...or so I thought. Taking off that summer of 2000 would afford me a chance to do some things and address some issues. This included the idea of kicking back without being all too concerned about deadlines, due dates, or immediate time constraints.

Initially my life seemed to improve; I got plenty of sleep, and had a chance to really use my motorcycle. The truth was, "seeds of discontent" had not popped up overnight, but had slowly seemed to work their way into my mindset. Looking back, things began to unravel in the late 90s.

Ginny was quite supportive of this "break" from work; she felt it would be beneficial both to our marriage and me. Her supportive attitude was something I'd long taken for granted. She was always there for me; I can't say the reverse is true. Like when her dad passed away back in 1988. I was clueless as to what she was going through. Worse, I hadn't taken sufficient time to really understand how the loss of her dad affected her and therefore I was ill-equipped to help her better cope. When the ten-year point of his death came I lacked empathy for how something like that could still have such an impact on her all those years later.

Over the next six months things went downhill quickly. I began to feel trapped in a life that didn't measure up to what I felt I wanted. I questioned decisions I'd made or failed to make. This was followed by a series of bad decisions beginning late that summer. One of these involved another woman. In late summer I did something that to this day brings back a terrible sense of shame. I'd broken a solemn vow of fidelity; soon after Ginny learned of my unfaithfulness, it devastated her.

By late autumn of 2000 I'd become an emotional mess. I was miserable and couldn't seem to set myself straight. In early December I felt I needed some space so I moved out, renting a room in town. I thought a break from each other would be good for both of us. But I didn't even ask her, I just made the decision unilaterally. Our 23rd anniversary on the 17th of December came and went, as did the holidays. Initially I did not reach out for help but instead largely kept to myself. In a very real way I was totally alone; self-imposed isolation. I was literally running away from my problems. Rather than face them and work through them with my wife, my solution was to temporarily suspend our relationship. If that isn't the ultimate example of selfishness and stupidity then I don't know what is. I'd convinced myself she no longer understood me and therefore didn't really love me as much as she professed. I figured she could not accept that who I'd become was not the same person I'd been. Well I was right. I'd become cynical and self-centered. I was in the throes of a horrific mid-life crisis without a clue as to how to remedy the situation. In hindsight, I seemed hell-bent on a path of self-destruction. No matter how long I live I will never forget the hurt I caused Ginny during this period of our life together.

Communications with Ginny became more regular in early January, though they were largely perfunctory. We had responsibilities that still needed to be addressed despite the turmoil I'd brought into our lives. When I look back upon this time, there's a sense of self-contempt and loathing that pervades me. What had happened to me? Who had I become? What was I doing? To this point it my life, nothing I'd experienced had been so painful. Even in hindsight I cannot fathom the why of it all.

The time we spent apart though, seemed to help me bring some things into focus. My holing up alone gave me time to think about what I was doing, to examine my motivations and the real issues that were affecting me—affecting us. Fortunately, after a few weeks away, it became clear to me that all I had done was run away from my problems. One afternoon when I was chatting with a good soul while on-line, they pointed out I'd never be able to address the real issues all on my own, no less solve them. Even to this "stranger," it was apparent I'd become selfish and that my whole reaction to things was rather immature.

While neither my extended family nor close friends really understood the tempest within me, I confided in several of them. They most often listened without passing judgment. I knew that Ginny was speaking to some of *them as well, trying to understand what was happening. Several of them had given me some rather sound advice by asking a simple question, "How do you expect to work things through when you're living apart?" This was exactly the same question Ginny had raised; yet at the time I wouldn't even listen. In late January she and I got together to discuss things. I told her how sorry I was for all that I'd done and asked her forgiveness. She told me to come home so we could try to work on things. I moved back home the next day.*

Over the coming weeks, several months actually, we struggled. At times our relationship was tumultuous. Ginny had always been a trusting soul; my words and actions had caused this to temporarily change. She'd become guarded, perhaps fearing openness would be met with another betrayal. Yet through it all she remained steadfast in her belief that together we could work things out. She said to me, "I believe in you, I believe in us, but I can't do it alone, you must feel this way too or we can't fix things." It became clear to me that the one person who understood me and truly knew me and accepted me was not the problem but the solution. What she had told me, what she had suggested, and what she had implored me to do, was what I should have been doing from the start. It was exactly the sort of candid council that I needed, but I hadn't been listening. I knew she was right but didn't want to admit how badly I'd screwed up. I know what I needed to do but it wasn't going to be easy; certainly not for a person who once prided himself on being objective and rational.

One day in May while I was out on some errands I heard a song on the radio. It was by a new young singer, LeAnn Rimes. Her song was titled "I Need You." As I listened closely to the lyrics there was only one person that came to my mind when I heard that song; my loving wife Ginny. That afternoon we talked for a very long time. I apologized again and literally begged her forgiveness. I promised her she'd not regret giving me another chance. I remember she told me she'd long since forgiven me for my infidelity, but said just please don't ask me to forget what happened. All our problems didn't just melt away due to this one talk. But from that day we'd begun a dialogue of openness, respect, and most importantly, love, that enabled us to move forward. I came to see that a big part of my problem was my failure to communicate my thoughts and feelings. Few if any of us are clairvoyant. No matter the issue, openness and truthfulness will always produce the best result.

Over the years since that terrible time I will readily admit that I remained so very ashamed at my behavior. Once in a blue moon Ginny would say to me, "Whatever got into you that you thought you could solve your problems the way you were headed?" I most often would simply apologize again…and tell her that I truly don't know why I did what I did. Yet I never could understand myself how anyone could have been as screwed up as I'd been. She had forgiven me, but I hadn't forgiven me; not sure I ever would.

I never again strayed from our vows or looked outside my marriage for comfort or for answers. Some might contend that my giving Ginny all sorts of jewelry was perhaps overcompensation for the guilt I felt, but they'd be wrong. I just always wanted her to have nice things. She seldom asked for anything, no less jewelry. She'd tell me, "I don't need things, I just need you." Truth be told I think I've always needed her even more than she did me. She is my world; she is everything to me.

I've referred indirectly to this time in my life to some who I've met since and others I've known for a very long time too. I simply tell them it represents the time Ginny saved my life. To this very day, Lord knows, I was, am, and will always believe that I've been blessed with the love of the most wonderful woman, my dear wife, my Punkin. No doubt about it, she is my better half.

We took 481N around the east side of Syracuse. This was a slight de-viation in the route I'd taken back when I began these trips, but doing so enabled us to bypass the traffic and construction typical to the more direct route along 81N on to the NYS Thruway, 90W. As we swung around the city, anticipation seemed to increase. These many trips over the years would now be a thing of the past. Once on the thruway we had one last rest stop; the one where we always bought a coffee. At times when you drive familiar routes such as this, the mind wanders.

It struck me as rather special that she and I had most often shared a drink rather than just getting our own. Even when we were first dating and we'd go down to Bill Gray's or Vic & Irv's, we shared our drink. We never felt it odd, though for the life of me I can't think of any of our friends who did the same. I smiled when I thought about it. When we'd go for a bite those Saturday nights out, Ginny always ordered her one burger plain while I always had "everything with extra hot sauce" on my two. I always ate quickly; perhaps a vestige of having three brothers. Maybe that's where Jesse got that trait? Once I wolfed down my first burg-er, Ginny would ask for the now-empty paper plate. She'd then dip her plain burger into the residual onions and hot sauce that remained. I'd ask her why she didn't just order her burger with the same fixings. She'd look at me quizzically and comment, "What's the matter, don't you like sharing?" Fact is we shared a lot of things food-wise. Whenever we'd dine at a nice restaurant Ginny and I rarely had the same main course. I often would order prime rib, she preferred some sort of seafood or small steak. Yet invariably during the course of the meal, she'd cut a piece of lobster or shrimp or whatever her meal was and feed it to me. Her desire to share even her food was but yet another example of her love.

We got to my parents' by mid-afternoon that Wednesday, August 28th. It happened to be my mom's birthday. My mom seemed even happier than usual to see us. Knowing we were back to stay in Rochester, well, you know how moms can be. As far as their acceptance of Ginny, from the start of our relationship they treated her like one of their family. Perhaps in part because they knew how happy she'd made me but also because Ginny was about the nicest gal you could meet. Ginny was not the least bit pretentious and she had always showed utmost respect to both my parents. Who Ginny was as a person was evidenced not by what she said, but what she did. She'd often say, "It's actions, not words, that count."

I never quite understood why, but that three-hundred-mile trip always took its toll on me. After arriving at my parents', my first order of business after bringing in our luggage and taking Jesse for a potty run was to zone out watching a little television. This sort of bothered Ginny as she felt me doing so was a bit impolite..."You should come into the kitchen and talk with your mom and dad." She was right of course, as she most always was about everything. But this day she tolerated my antics and didn't say a word. After just a short bit I could hear her laughing. She has a neat laugh. I noticed that long ago; one of the countless things about her I so loved. Of course like many things, I just sort of took it for granted. I should have told her more often just how great it was to be with her. After a short respite this day I got off my duff and joined the others in the kitchen. Jesse was underfoot, roaming around the kitchen just in case anyone should drop a piece of food. We talked for a bit and I noticed something: Ginny was smiling ear-to-ear, she was so very happy to be home in Rochester. We would be around all our family and friends; that meant the world to her. Seeing her happy meant everything to me.

My mind wandered as I sat there half-listening to the banter. I was re-calling another role Ginny played. She did not drive a car. The problems she had with her leg pains and back when she was a teen prompted her to decide not to get her driver's license. She was always afraid if she had spasms while driving she might hurt someone. On all our car trips through the years she was the "copilot." Years before GPS, this meant she was the designated map expert. I sort or cringe when I think about the times we'd be in some unfamiliar place and the traffic was heavy. She'd be as cool as a cucumber, telling me to take this exit or that. Me, all too often I'd be impatient and not listening so it wasn't unusual for me to miss the turn or exit. But Ginny was largely unflappable. She'd just tell me to pull over and get my bearings. Those trips are somewhat analogous to life in general. Sometimes things happen you don't expect. While Ginny would always take the time to think the matter through, I'd all too often react. Guess it's just another example that proves how lucky I was to have a "copilot" in my life.

My parents have a fairly big home given it housed a total of nine members of my family back in the late 1960s. My parent's anniversary was the 30th, so Ginny and I had planned to take them to one of their and our favorite restaurants, Hedges. However it was clear to my parents that both Ginny and I were too tired this day, so we'd postpone the outing until sometime after we got settled in. No hurry this time, as we'd not be leaving town. Going to Hedges during our trips up in August was sort of a tradition. The timing coincided with their anniversary and my mom's birthday. Hedges is located on the southern shore of Lake Ontario. It offers one of the most scenic evening views of the sunset. (The picture on the cover of this book was taken there). Over the years we had many great dinners and with them, fond memories we cherish to this day.

(Refer to Pictures section, picture 27)

Home at Last

Finally, our closing day arrived, September 6th. There'd been times we thought we'd never get to this point. A myriad of issues seemed to conspire against us. They'd all been resolved and our entire household would be delivered the following Monday, September 9th. Even though we weren't the camping sort, we decided that night to sleep in our new home. Though neither of us have a fondness for air mattresses, it didn't matter that weekend. We had lots to do and most of all we just wanted to be in our new home.

Monday was a very busy day, as expected. The crew who unloaded the huge van did a good job overall, though a few items sustained some damage, most notably a desk that we'd just purchased the year before. Ginny and I had packed all the boxes ourselves. The result was nothing in them was damaged. All in all, I'd count this as a successful move. By end of that day Carol and Bill came over—our first visitors to the new home. There were boxes everywhere, but furniture had been placed in all the right rooms and we'd be sleeping in our own bed that night.

I recall Ginny making the bed for that evening. She commented how much she'd missed sleeping in our own bed. Rather, she said "my bed." It doesn't seem all that long ago that she shuddered at the idea of sleeping on a hard mattress. Ginny often would point out to both Jesse and I that this is "Mom's bed." She just happens to share it with us. The top of the mattress is three feet off the floor, so the addition of "bed steps" was made soon after we purchased it to help Ginny get up and in. I just sort of jump up a bit myself to get on the bed. Most nights she and I read before going to sleep. But not this night; we were so tired we hit the pillows and were asleep within five minutes. It was the most restful sleep we'd had in quite some time.

She and I had done a good job orchestrating the start-up of utilities, even having all the carpets cleaned that weekend before the moving van came. In subsequent weeks Ginny, with some help from me, did what she'd always done before. She transformed our new house into a warm and inviting home. Home is a funny word really. Most people use it to denote where they live, be it a house, condo, or apartment. Yet one can live in any of these and never have it become their home—for, as the writer once noted, "Home is where the heart is." To me, home is wherever Ginny is; that reality has passed the test of time and will never change.

(Refer to Pictures section, picture 29)

Our first big get-together after moving up here was a celebration of my brother Rick's 60th birthday. Only eleven months separate him and me. Rick (Ricky) was the one who blazed the trail in our family; sometimes to my parents' chagrin. When we were kids we did everything together, yet in our teens we seemed to find our own niche and develop our own friendships. Though we shared some of the same friends, he and I more or less took different paths in our lives. His 60th party was held at the Reunion Inn, my idea. That place was and still remains special to both of Ginny and I; lots of fond memories are tied to that place.

In October we got a real sense of what it means to have dozens of trees on your property. Even with the purchase of a new lawn tractor, with a large bagging attachment, we spent hours collecting and raking leaves that first fall. I also bought a gas-powered backpack leaf blower too; it was invaluable. Though perhaps even more troublesome, the oversized gutters on the house proved to be great leaf catchers. I bet I was up on a ladder cleaning them out at least three times that first season. I'd need to find a better solution, for in time that effort would wear on me.

In October we hosted our first big party in years. The "housewarming" party included many old friends and some family members. They, more than any other factor, were the reason for our return to Rochester. In life you may live in many places but you only have so many who qualify as dear friends and family. Soon after the party Ginny got a nasty cold. The cold really knocked her out unlike any I can recall. For almost three weeks she coughed, was listless, slept poorly, and had no energy or appetite. On one occasion I had second thoughts about going to an appointment I'd made, as I didn't want to leave her alone. I also didn't like the idea of her having to take Jesse out when she was feeling so poorly. But Ginny insisted I go to my activities, that she'd be fine, so I went. That night I told her we were going to make chicken soup. Ginny, like her mom, made great chicken soup. Over the years she'd most often make it when the weather turned nasty or when she or I had been feeling poorly. I did the majority of the soup making that evening. She loved it, and so did I. I also served with it slices from a big round loaf of her favorite Champagne bread. That batch of soup was enough for at least two dinners and several lunches. Ginny savored it and I was pleased to see her appetite had returned.

In early November, Ginny was feeling better and was anxious to get things organized in our huge basement. She'd noted that she needed to find some things that had yet to be unpacked…like the old "milk box" space heater and our bathroom scale. To this point, we still had many boxes as well as dozens of Rubbermaid 18-gallon containers all over the place. We had eight to ten four- or five-shelf units that all needed organizing too. The Rubbermaid units contained most all the seasonal decorations that we'd use throughout the year…Easter, Halloween, Thanksgiving, and of course Christmas. Yet honestly, it was our Christmas decorations that comprised most of it. I'd often comment that the only difference between our home and a Christmas store was our displays had no price tags. There was no hiding it…Christmas was and would always be "our" holiday. On nearly every one of our vacation or day trips over the years we would find and purchase some sort of Christmas ornament or decoration. It was a nice tradition she'd started. The memories from all those trips would return each year as Christmas decorations were set up.

In our marriage, I was the planner, but Ginny was the organizer. She always knew where everything was in our homes. Often, being impatient as I was, I'd go looking for something, only to give up and pronounce it lost. I can't count the number of times she tell me, "It isn't lost until I say it is." And wonder of wonders, she invariably find whatever it was I couldn't. I sheepishly admit this applied to everything we owned, including many of my own things. In most instances, Ginny preferred to organize stuff herself. My help, she contended, was often not all that helpful to her. So I left her to organize the basement stuff that first November.

Later that same month when I went down to "inspect the progress," it seemed to me that she should have completed more than she had. Being critical by my nature yet now married all these years, I broached the matter delicately. But Ginny saw right through my not-so-obvious queries. I guess like most husbands, I possess both selective hearing and sight skills. She told me she seemed to tire so easily, that she had no stamina, but was doing the best she could. Then she stated that she'd found the bathroom scale and guess what…she'd lost another few pounds since July. Rather than say something like, "We're getting older," I opted for the more delicate response of saying she needed to give herself a break. We'd been going "like sixty" since early summer, she'd just gotten over a bad cold, and there was no urgency in getting all the boxes put away. "What else is it you really need right now?" I asked her. "I need the Thanksgiving decorations…they're all together in two Rubbermaid bins." She'd tagged the outside of the bins to note their contents but not unexpectedly, many of the tags had come off during the move. The next day I found the two bins…all by myself, sort of. With the Thanksgiving holiday less than a week away, we got them all out and placed throughout the rooms that weekend. Ginny put up all the window stencils. For some reason she always liked to put up those white stick-on window stencils; I think we had them since soon after we'd married. She was a big fan of traditions.

Reminds me of precious quirk she has. When Ginny gets totally focused on a project, a book, or whatever, she has this thing where her tongue pokes out slightly to one side of her mouth. From the very first time I witnessed it, I found it to be so endearing.

This year she'd thought it might be nice to have a big Thanksgiving meal in our new home, perhaps inviting a number of folks from my family. It turned out though, that plans had already been set, with my sister Cindy and her husband Brian hosting my parents. Though Ginny was a little disappointed, she understood that the plans had been in the works for some time. I'd not said anything to anyone other than to our son Jason and his fiancée Samantha. So 2013 would be as it had been in recent years, just the four of us. Oh, and Jesse too of course. I told Ginny next year we'd do the whole thing.

Thanksgiving is a "big" holiday to most families, but I can recall the first Thanksgiving Ginny and I shared back in 1974. In her family Ginny was the second youngest while in mine, I was the second oldest. Among other things it meant that her older sisters had families of their own. That made for one big family get-together. Her dad was the "cook" when it came to both the turkey and the gravy. Ginny made the best gravy; she learned how from her dad. That first holiday together there were no fewer than fifteen of us at her home. Ginny and her sister Carol had even made menus which listed all the foods we'd have that day, including several hors d'oeuvres, and at least a half-dozen kinds of pie. There were two tables, though we sat at the main one, side-by-side. My mom always made a great Thanksgiving meal too, but this one I found amazing. It was then I first tasted the appetizer liver and bacon; it's been a favorite of both her and me ever since. That was also the very first time I tasted Ginny's lemon meringue pie. It became my favorite pie from then on. For a guy fairly small in stature, I can really pack it in when it comes to food. That 1974 Thanksgiving was a true feast to be remembered. Yes that day as it would be for many years to come; Thanksgiving dinner was our favorite holiday meal.

The day after Thanksgiving, Ginny broke one of her front teeth while gnawing on one of the turkey wings. As luck would have it, we'd yet to find a new dentist in the area. The break or chip hadn't exposed the root nerve but had made it very difficult for her to eat hard foods. I moved with unusual vigor and got her an appointment early the following week. Going to the dentist was something Ginny absolutely hated to do. No shot to the dental profession, but she never liked going there, no matter how congenial or proficient the dentist.

Early on in our marriage I learned that Ginny had an almost obsessive fear of going to the dentist. It wasn't that her dentist was bad, she simply hated to have anyone put sharp objects in her mouth and she hated the oral pain as one was just supposed to lie there and not move. As a result, other than regular cleanings, Ginny insisted on having nitrous oxide as a sedative in addition to Novocain. She had grown comfortable with the dentist we'd had in New Jersey; now she had that added anxiety to deal with a new dentist. She had had several crowns and an implant just in the last couple of years while we were in New Jersey. I can recall she literally cried before those procedures. I'd always make our appointments together, never wanted her to go it alone, given her trepidations. I would always be there for her. If the situation were reversed, you can bet she'd do the same for me.

In early December 2013 when we went to have her broken tooth fixed, it took her by surprise when the dentist told her she needed two more crowns or implants initiated during that first visit. He'd asked her if those two other teeth had been bothering her, and she said they had been. She'd never said one word to me about it. She told the dentist to talk to me, that I would decide for her based on the merits and urgency.

I think the dentist thought this strange, but he didn't know her or her phobia on dental work. I think Ginny also knew that the cost was likely to be high so she wanted me involved. From my perspective, the cost was a nonfactor. All I wanted was for her to be able to eat comfortably.

We were there for a good two to three hours that morning and would have to return again in about two weeks when the new implants were ready. Until the "permanent" two new teeth were complete, she was told to only eat soft foods and avoid very cold or very hot liquids. She was a basket case by the time we left that day, clearly over-wrought. When we got home I learned that she knew something was wrong in her mouth before she'd broken that front tooth, but hadn't wanted to spend all the money to fix it. I felt terrible that she'd been having problems, yet hadn't said anything. I emphasized to her that money was not an issue. We would do what we had to; and I told her never ever consider the cost. I began to wonder whether her recent sickness was the full reason for her lost appetite. She then assured me her mouth had only recently begun to bother her. The dental work was completed on schedule about two weeks later. Afterwards it seemed she got her old appetite back, and I was thrilled. There's nothing worse than seeing someone you love suffering in pain.

Christmastime, 2013

Christmas seemed to come quickly in 2013. Our plan was to have my whole family over for a big Christmas day celebration including dinner. As my parents are now in their 80s, having dinner at their place doesn't work anymore; it just puts too much on my mom even when others bring the food and fixings.

Ginny was always fond of holiday traditions. Before moving to New Jersey we often had big Easter brunches at our place. Ginny loves to cook and is a great cook. We'd had a lot of memorable big family meals, but especially at Easter.

Years ago at Easter, I introduced Ginny to my family's tradition of "egg nutzing." Now I don't rightfully know if "egg nutzing" is in fact an old German tradition. "Nutzing" is a game where two people take a hardboiled egg, colored of course, and compete to see whose egg can endure a strike from the other person's egg. Ginny learned the game quickly enough. She learned too that "cheating" was a nuanced facet of the game…like hitting the other person's egg hard and so quickly that the opponent dropped their egg. My brothers and I perfected the "cheating" dimension…even stooping to use an egg made of marble to win. Judging was done by the noncombatants. They'd rule whether the tactics were legitimate or beyond the pale. The use of the marble egg was ruled "unfair" the year it was employed, but that didn't stop my brothers from repeating such the following year as we boys played not so much to win, as to cause our brother to lose.

After a few phone calls it appeared that our plan to have everyone over on Christmas day wasn't going to fly. Unlike when Ginny was growing up and her whole family would spend the day at a relative's house; my family had established their own traditions of opening gifts at home then later going over to other family member's homes. Nonetheless, Ginny and I would host a buffet-style meal and had guests come when they may during that day. It worked out fairly well, though wasn't quite what she had initially envisioned. I think deep down Ginny wanted to be the hostess of a large family gathering including an elaborate sit-down holiday meal. Over the last ten years there'd been no opportunity to do so. Perhaps she ascribed greater significance to the "whole-day family affair"; a recapturing of the memories of holiday traditions her parents had instilled in her so long ago.

This Christmas would be different. This year I was home, so the matter of decorating the house wasn't going to be singularly her effort, but ours. I had some ideas that I felt we could do that would take advantage of the cathedral ceiling we had in the main part of the house. Our new home had a "great" room and the adjoining kitchen.

Soon after, as she began to bake some Christmas cookies I shared a decorating idea. "Suppose we use the open L-shaped space above the kitchen as a focal point for a large Christmas-themed display." I explained that we could wrap up large boxes as huge gifts, take items like our four-foot tall nutcracker soldier, large decorative tins, stuffed animals, and Santas, along with other smaller Christmas-wrapped empty boxes to showcase a traditional Christmas. She loved the idea but felt it would put a lot on me, as she didn't "do" ladders. I assured her I knew that...and that she could be my eyes to ensure the display was properly faced for ground-floor viewing.

I hadn't expected the effort to take quite as long or be as tiring as it came to be. I had to be very careful working eight feet up above the kitchen. The area was accessible but not built to take much weight. It turns out that it was also quite warm up there; something I'd not considered (heat rises, Jim). Ginny knows well that when I get overheated I get cranky...not an excuse, just sort of how I am. Nonetheless, in a period of a couple of days we set up a grand holiday display. It looked like something a store would put in its main window. Ginny absolutely loved it and told me several times just that. She later commented that she had sort of the same idea but knew she couldn't do it herself. Afterwards, we hung the four-foot diameter Christmas wreath that we used to display outdoors at our New Jersey home. This year it was placed on the great room wall adorned with new three-inch-wide wired ribbon. Red velvet rimmed in gold. Replacing the old ribbon with the same flare as before was not an easy task, but Ginny excels at crafts. I think it came out even better than it had looked before.

Over the next two to three days we brought up from the basement many other Christmas decorations, including the eight-foot artificial tree. I don't know quite how she pulls it off, but it seems each year she outdoes herself. The house was aglow in Christmas-themed displays. Later she put on a CD containing "music box" tunes. For whatever reason, that music seems to best capture the sights and sounds of the season. When looking at our home from outside, the decorations were understated. She'd placed single electric candlesticks in each of the windows. The effect is so very inviting and peaceful. Others may like extensive outdoor displays, but I prefer the approach my wife employed.

December 17th marked our 36th wedding anniversary. We mused about the prior year when I'd taken her to New York City to see the musical *Wicked*. Our friend Tom had strongly recommended it. He was right; it was excellent. We'd also gone to New York City for our 30th. That time I'd taken her to Radio City Music Hall for the Christmas Spectacular, a grand holiday show. Ginny had always wanted to see that show. In the tri-state area they begin advertising for it each year before Halloween. It's a big deal. We had such a wonderful day, even going to the famous FAO Schwarz store, the same store featured in the old Tom Hanks movie, *BIG*. New York City takes on such a glow during the Christmas season. But it was the holiday city lights reflecting in her eyes and her beautiful smile which meant the most to me.

(Refer to Pictures section, picture 30)

In 2013 we opted for a quiet night at home on our 36th, as it fell on a Tuesday. Yet as she's done so many times in the past, she made us a very special anniversary meal. This year it was chicken with herb sauce; a favorite of ours. For dessert she'd made my favorite; lemon meringue pie.

As has been the case on so many of our anniversaries, we spent some quiet time "snuggling" to end the day. Ginny always says, "Snuggling is something we punkins do best." I couldn't agree more.

Over the next few days we completed our Christmas shopping; largely on a single trip to Eastview mall. As we walked from store to store, holding hands along the way, it struck me. So many people seem to rush through their lives never really stopping long enough just to observe. Much of my life I've been that way too. I knew I would have no problem adjusting to the slower pace we two had planned in our retirement.

This year Ginny and I agreed to keep it rather austere as far as gifts to each other. The truth is there was nothing either of us really needed aside from new denim jeans. Given she'd lost some weight her current jeans didn't fit her well. But otherwise, we didn't need anything. I asked her if she wanted anything special to which she replied, "You've given me everything I would want in moving back here and just being with you." It's moments like that that remind me just how lucky I am to have such a wonderful and loving wife.

Christmas Eve found us at Church, which is a tradition we've held to since before we were married. When we first were dating we'd always go to the midnight mass but unlike back then, now midnight finds us fast asleep, even on the weekends. I don't know how we were able to "close the bar" as often as we used to. It seemed most every Friday and Saturday we'd be found at this or that tavern along with many of our friends. Back then we could burn the candle at both ends with no ill effects. These days however, time is catching up with us.

I'm reminded of the midnight mass back in 1978, just days after our first anniversary. My two younger brothers were home from college, so they along with my three sisters and parents all went to mass with Ginny and me. My parents decided to go to our old church, Saint Margaret Mary's. That was the parish my family had belonged to before they moved to the east side of town in 1965.

Four of us, my brothers Ron and Michael, along with Ginny and me arrived early so as to save seats. My parents and sisters would follow. Knowing them, they'd get there not five minutes before mass was to begin. It used to drive me crazy, being late to whatever the event may be.

The air was cold with flurries predicted. As we walked towards the church I pointed out to Ginny the grammar school that my brothers and I had attended. Told her "there's the spot where my mom parked the '56 Chevy on my first day of school...I refused to go in...it took both my mom and Mother Dolorosa (the principal) to release my death grip on the car... when Mother Dolorosa got me inside, she took me into her office and put the fear of God in me for having given her and my mom all that trouble. Ginny smiled at the image and said, "Let's hope our kids don't have the same reaction."

Midnight mass was to be a "high mass," which meant it would be long but they'd also have their choir singing that night too. I'm not much of a singer but Ginny has a beautiful voice—she'd been in her high school choir. Still, everyone I know likes to sing Christmas songs, so I was look-ing forward to it.

As I look back now I recall there were several things that made the night memorable. After the rest of my family arrived and the mass was to begin, the advent wreath was lit. It was a huge wreath, which was suspended from the high ceiling on wires. The wreath must have been about six feet in diameter and consisted of pine boughs woven together along with the four advent candles. One of the altar boys misjudged the candle's height as he was lighting it. He'd inadvertently touched the lit punk to the tree *boughs. Flames jumped up from that section of the wreath. Thankfully, quick action by the priest extinguished the flames.*

As we exited church at a bit after 1:00 AM, huge snowflakes were falling in the still night air. You could almost hear the snow as it fell to the ground. It must have been snowing for some time, for there was a good four inches of freshly fallen wet snow covering everything. The silence was soon broken as all the people made for their cars. The snow was heavy, which made for great snowballs. My brother Ron— or was it Michael— tossed the first one, hitting me in the back as Ginny and I made our way to our little red VW bug. What ensued was perhaps not your typical after-mass fare, but it was fun. Ginny laughed when I got hit in the head only to change her tune when I tossed a snowball her way. I don't think any midnight mass we attended before or after had the same appeal as the one that night.

Afterwards, we headed straight to my parents for a little Christmas cheer. When we got home, we spied the lights on across the street where my best friend Paul and his family lived. Despite the hour we figured the lights were an open invite, so my brothers, Ginny and I all headed over. Sure enough, Paul's whole family was up, having just returned home from midnight mass at our current parish, Saint Cecilia's. It was a wonderful night, almost magical.

In 2013 Christmas day came with barely any snow on the ground. I didn't mind that, since with so many members of my family expected, it made for a safer trip to our place. Ginny had baked a large ham and a turkey breast, which I'd sliced up for sandwiches. There were salads, munchies, cookies, as well as side dishes. As usual she'd outdone herself; though I really did help that year. We exchanged gifts with my parents as well as Jason. Given the size of the families, we'd stopped giving to individual sisters and brothers. As I've grown older the gift side of

Christmas has largely lost its appeal. Just being with your family, your loved ones, that's what means the most to me; and to Ginny. Material possessions lose their luster but kinship and love never do.

While many folks like to go shopping for deals those days right after Christmas, even I don't relish the idea any more. I used to pick up strings of lights and other price-reduced decorations on the 26th, but not anymore. Ginny and I spent time on the 26th opening the gifts we'd given each other, munching on leftovers and eating Christmas cookies. She'd made me Russian teacakes, which are my favorite. She's always been partial to plain old-fashioned iced cookies.

On the 27th or 28th Ginny's sister Carol, along with her husband Bill and daughter Kaity came over to our place for a belated Christmas celebration. In the years we lived in New Jersey, we'd stop over to see them all on Christmas day for few hours. It struck me that this was the first year in so many that we hadn't traveled during this holiday season…it was a nice feeling. While it's great to visit folks, being home for the holidays is what we liked most. No concerns about the weather, no specific time schedule dictating where we had to be, that's what I really like.

Ginny and Carol had not seen each other since our housewarming party. Upon seeing Ginny, a look of concern was evident on Carol's face; and Bill's too. They could see she'd lost more weight. Ginny reminded them she'd been sick for those weeks in October, then had the whole cracked tooth problem and implants, so she'd not been eating all that well. She assured them she was feeling much better, and had been eating a lot of Christmas cookies. The visit was neither too long nor eventful but they could see how happy Ginny was to see them and be back here in Rochester with family and friends. Of all her sisters, Ginny was closest to Carol in age but also in that "sisterly way." They were each other's confidants over the years, particularly when it came to issues about raising kids.

2014, *the new year*

As had been the case in recent years, we had no plans to go out on New Year's Eve. That's a sharp contrast to what we'd do when we were young. Yet I would contend that this change was consistent with most folks in their fifties. I know that most of our friends no longer went out on New Year's Eve, though some might catch an early dinner out. They sure weren't pulling "all nighters" either. Even the idea of going out, contending with the crowds and drunks on the road is one that quickly dispels any such thought.

So this year when the clock struck midnight Ginny and I were already fast asleep. We'd thought we might stay up to watch the celebration in Times Square on TV, but by the time 11:00 PM rolled around, we were both fighting to just stay awake. Still it felt so good to be in our warm and cozy home.

The start of 2014 saw me spending quite a bit of time working various sample tax returns as part of my preparation for certification to support filing individual returns. I'd decided in the autumn to join the local Tax Aid group, which completes and files returns at no cost for the elderly and lower income individuals. I'd been doing my own taxes since I first filed back in 1970s. In later years, I also completed them for a few family members and friends. The training I was undergoing, mostly online, would enable me to file for folks with all sorts of tax issues, including small businesses under some circumstances.

Ginny was glad to see me using my time in a productive manner and was pleased that such efforts would help others who generally don't

have a lot of income or the money to pay a preparer. While the requirements varied by region, locally we had to pass "advanced" certification
to become part of the team. I'd begin doing real returns in just under a
month, so working the various examples was quite useful but meant I
was often hogging the computer those days.

I don't remember which day it was exactly, but in early January Ginny
told me she was having trouble swallowing her food sometimes. Immediately we both thought of the issue she'd been through a few years
back, which had resulted in corrective surgery. That medical issue
involved the top of her esophagus; the condition had been diagnosed
as Zenker Diverticulum. Ginny was certain it was the same thing yet
again. Back in 2005 a surgeon performed a resection that seemed to
correct the problem, yet the problem can recur. She described the sen-
sation, of food getting caught at the top of her throat that made her
feel like she would choke or just couldn't swallow. That was the same
description she'd used eight years before.

I looked at her that morning and asked if she'd lost any more weight.
She said she hadn't used the scale in a few days but would check as she
often does, after her shower. When she did, she told me her weight
was down four pounds since late November, before her dental work.
It didn't surprise either of us, given the "soft food diet" she had until
her mid-December implants. Besides, I saw that her appetite had returned afterwards. For various reasons, since last summer she'd not
been getting sufficient calories. It didn't matter the reason, whether
due to stress from the move, her bad cold, or the dental surgery. I
felt we needed to put some attention on understanding what was
happening. Particularly now that she'd just indicated she was having
difficulty swallowing. We needed to get her to the doctor and to get
more calories into her daily diet.

Soon after we spoke that day I made a trip to the grocery store to pick up something I hadn't in years...Ensure. We used to help her mom shop and most times her list included this high-calorie adult nutrition supplement. I knew enough to buy Ginny the chocolate flavored one, but she still resisted drinking "that stuff." Though we didn't know why she had lost over twenty pounds since May, I knew the Ensure would help. I also felt we could increase calories another way; more desserts. We seldom had dessert but that would change. I said to her, "Not only are you going to have more desserts, but I will make them for you." She just smiled and said, "You don't do much baking, sounds like more work for me." But I would prove her wrong.

Making the doctor appointment was a bit problematic; just like the issue with the dentist we'd yet to choose a new PCP under our new (local) healthcare plan. The very next day I'd get things rolling. Turned out we were able to find a doctor who was taking new patients. Matter of fact, he'd been my PCP at one time back before we'd moved to New Jersey. When I went to make an appointment I was told we'd need to get our records sent to them. Now, we'd done just that with our dentist so it wouldn't be a big deal; or so I thought. When I called our New Jersey doctors—both worked out of the same medical facility—I was told they had to have a written request to transfer the records...had to be via US mail; emailed requests were not accepted. Fine, I thought, but then you can send them digitally to our doctors here; they agreed. I made the same request of her New Jersey-based OBGYN, but that office told me they weren't set up to move the files electronically—they have to send hard copies at a cost of four dollars per page. I gave both old offices the new doctor's contact information. It took almost two weeks before the process was completed. The day they told me they had received them I made her initial PCP appointment. The soonest they could see her was February 11th. The doctor was booked solid unless the matter was an emergency, which of course there was no indication it was.

Aside from the recent difficulty swallowing, Ginny wasn't very concerned. She pointed out that her current weight was identical with what it was when we were married. She told me this with some degree of pride, to be honest. Lord knows she'd never been really overweight as long as I've known her. However, I felt she'd lost too much weight too quickly. Over the next couple of weeks her weight stabilized, in large part due to the Ensure and the dessert plan I'd put in place. I was insisting that she drink two little bottles of Ensure daily in addition to her regular meals. The only food that really seemed to give her problems was bread; exactly the same situation as back in 2005 before her surgery. True to my word, desserts were served nearly every evening.

Beginning in mid-January, I began to hone my cooking and baking skills with her help. Initially, she sort of did most of the work but that soon changed. By February 1st I had made homemade Tollhouse chocolate chip cookies, chocolate fudge (her mom's recipe), oatmeal cookies, and her favorite, chocolate-covered vanilla cream puffs. The only recipe I had much trouble with was the cream puffs. I learned there's a "feel" you have to develop when making them. As the egg mixture is heated using a double boiler, it is stirred to a point where its consistency changes...it gets thicker. This I learned by cooking the first batch too long. The cream puffs won't rise unless you get it just right. But I did learn how to make them and she ate them. They were very good, if I do say so myself.

Over the next two to three weeks Ginny felt much better. Her weight had stabilized, and then actually picked up slightly; no doubt all those desserts were having some effect. We tended to keep a lot of "dry goods" in stock at home as well as canned and other pantry goods. Yet we'd not done a great amount of restocking since we'd moved back. I recall one trip we had to make in early February. She was low on several items including Hershey's chocolate syrup, Coffee Mate, soap, shampoo, and conditioner to name a few. I would tease her at times about some of her preferences. For instance, she always and only used Ivory bar soap. Though it used to be a popular household product, I knew few others who used it anymore. Years back the company would advertise it as being very gentle and "99 and 44/100 pure." She was a brand loyal person for sure. Syrup, peanut butter, soap, deodorant, coffee creamer; the list was long. I'd tease her about trying new products, but she'd say, "If I like the one I use, why should I change?" That day when she picked up the chocolate syrup I commented that I thought we already had some at home. Her reply seemed funny to me: "We do but I don't want to run out, besides, I have coupons."

When we were first married, nearly everything we bought had to have an accompanying coupon and be on our shopping list. Ginny would explain that by keeping to the list and using coupons we could hold down the amount spent. Years back when the local grocery store chains were in heated competition, some stores would double or even triple the face value of coupons. Ginny would love to see how much we saved. In part I believe she felt it was one way she could "contribute" to the budget, as she did not work outside the home. As the years passed, this coupon fetish never changed. No matter the store, she always seemed to have a coupon. Though we really didn't need the savings to "get by," she always felt that being thrifty was the way to go. She'd often say to me: "Why spend more than you have to, why pay full price?" I admired her frugality. She wasn't one of those folks who spent a lot of money on frivolous things, especially when it came to herself. On more than one occasion when I'd stop at the store on the way home from work, I often picked up more items than were on the list she'd given me. When she saw what I'd done she would say "I had a coupon for that." In our home I'm the impulse buyer while she's just the opposite. Over the years I learned to take my scolding for having overbought rather than argue my rationale. The fact is she was right most all the time, but I seldom admitted it.

As February began, so did my volunteer work with the tax preparation group. I think Ginny was glad to "get me out of her hair" but also, she felt I needed to be doing something useful as well. I was now "working" on both Mondays and Wednesdays doing taxes from about 9:00 AM to around 2:00 or 3:00 PM. I found it nice to meet other folks—both new coworkers, but also the clients. I've long been gregarious, often striking up conversations with complete strangers. So the tax work gave me an outlet for more social interaction.

The next day (Monday) I was going to be working, so I thought we should have something that resulted in leftovers…a staple in our home. I asked Ginny what she felt like for dinner. "How about chicken and souped up Minute rice?" she responded. In our household for some reason we tended to opt for a fairly routine meal plan. Weekends were the time for "big meals" like beef or pork roasts, Tuesdays were most always Italian food, and Saturdays nearly always hamburgers or steaks. I'm not sure why we tended to set up such a routine, but it worked well for us. The only time it didn't was when we lived in Florida. It was so hot most all the time that both she and I would often just not want a big meal. That's funny coming from me, as I seldom ate breakfast or lunch; a habit I developed in college which has more or less stayed with me over the years.

As dinner was served that Sunday I noticed Ginny wasn't eating a lot yet I knew how much she liked this particular meal. When I asked her why, she said she was having problems swallowing the chicken. I was glad her doctor's appointment was the next day. We needed to find out why; though both of us were fairly convinced it was that old problem rearing its head again.

The doctor's office was quite busy when we arrived. It was then I noticed that there were four doctors working out of that one location. When the doctor's assistant/nurse came to get Ginny, right away she struck me as exactly the type of person you'd want to have in that role. She was soft-spoken, friendly, and yet very professional. It being February, Ginny made a point of removing her boots and coat before being weighed in. Then she was taken to an examining room to have her blood pressure taken. The doctor's assistant then had a brief chat to gather background on the reason for her visit. "Wendy" handled all of this, and then told us both that the doctor would be in momentarily. Upon seeing him, I recalled that he was the same doctor I had in the past.

Back in early 2003 I'd somehow strained my back at work after improperly lifting a large binder. It caused a twinge in my back at the time but by early the next morning I couldn't even walk. I drove the 325 miles nonstop to our old home. This was the same doctor that had seen me. Back then he'd taken me to task for driving all that way without resting but there was no way I was going to be stuck for the weekend in New Jersey with a bad back all alone.

The doctor asked Ginny a lot of questions. She provided some background information and explained about the medical condition she'd had a few years back, then about her bad cold in October, and finally about the soft food diet she had for the two to three weeks late in 2013. The doctor felt it may take some time to isolate the cause and reach a diagnosis, but told us we'd start the medical assessment using an upper GI specialist. We'd have to contact the specialist's office to schedule an endoscopy. That procedure would be done in just two days.

The morning of February 13th Ginny was nervous about the endoscopy procedure. It's one where they have to sedate the patient then "scope" out the esophagus all the way down to the stomach. Most people don't like medical procedures of any kind, and my wife is no exception. Yet

she had an aversion to doctors and hospitals that dated back to her
teen years when she'd had severe leg pains.

*I was going to be leaving for college in just a few days, January 12th.
I'd met Ginny just four months before on Sept 4th, 1974. Yet here I was
going to see her in the hospital. It had been a planned stay, which she'd
explained to me a couple of weeks ago. Ginny had suffered from severe
leg pains and cramps for the last couple of years. She'd seen all sorts of
doctors and specialists during that time but none had come to a solid diagnosis. In the past they'd performed all sorts of procedures, even taking
a biopsy of her thigh muscle on her right leg. She vividly remembered it,
as it was so painful. For some time she'd been on several pain medications
and an anti-inflammatory, but none seemed to solve the problem.*

*I would go to see her everyday beginning that day of her hospital ad-
mission on January 6th. To cheer her up, each time I went I brought
her a little "gift." Let's see, there was the "I love you" statue, some Ciara
perfume, a little "love bug" in a small wooden cage, and some other items
I can't recall. But today, January 11th, was the day she'd be discharged
from Genesee Hospital. Rather than go up to see her there, I'd visit her as
soon as she got home. I had a special gift, or at least I'd hoped she'd feel
that way about it.*

*I'd gone to a jewelry store (Jerry's) the prior week to purchase a 14K gold
medallion and chain. I had it engraved. On one side it had her name
(Ginny) and on the reverse it said, "To My Punkin, Love Jimmy." I was
concerned she'd think the sentiment was over the top, given ours was still
a budding romance. I'd never felt this way about any other woman. So it
was with some trepidation that I made my way down to her house after
she'd called to tell me she was home.*

As soon as I'd arrived, her mom told me she was downstairs in her bed-

room. *When I walked down I saw that she had the gifts I brought her displayed, each in their own special spot throughout her bedroom. We both were well aware that the very next day I'd be heading off to college. That was unfortunate since we'd had so little one-on-one time that past week. I began to have second thoughts about giving her the piece of jewelry. Perhaps I should hold off for now. I didn't want to "rush things" and screw up what had already become a great relationship. As I stood in her room, she turned to me and kiddingly inquired, "So what did you bring me today?"*

At that point I almost froze, or at least was sort of tongue-tied—a condition uncharacteristic of me. What the heck, I thought…so I pulled the box out of my pocket and handed it to her saying, "I brought you something special." She looked at me in an odd sort of way. I wasn't sure that was a good or bad sign. But when she opened it up and saw her name she was thrilled. Only then did I point out it was engraved on the back too. She turned it over, read it. Her eyes welled up with tears. Now look what you did, I thought to myself. Yet she reached over as I sat on the edge of her bed, gave me a big hug then told me, "I love you too." I will never forget that. I don't even remember what happened the rest of the day, all I know is my heart soared and so it seems had hers. She wore that medallion all the time; even shows in our wedding pictures. It was, by her own admission, her all-time favorite piece of jewelry.

The endoscopy procedure didn't take too long, though it seemed so to me as I waited for her to come into the post procedure recovery area. I'd brought a book to read to try to kill time and get my mind off things but today, I just kept thinking about her. The doctor came out to see me…told me all went well and that I could go into the recovery area. I was so pleased to see Ginny. She was still quite groggy at that point. After a bit the doctor came over to review the ten pictures they'd taken. He commented that all looked good, that he saw no problem at the top of her esophagus, no repeat of the Zenker Diverticulum, though he could see she'd had the past surgery. He did note that he thought her throat was a bit constricted so he "stretched" it a bit while he was there. That I knew was a procedure that Ginny's mom had had done a number of times. I thought perhaps this issue of difficulty swallowing was hereditary. About thirty minutes later they told us she could leave but would have to use a wheelchair; such was their policy for any sedated patient. I went to get the car, got her in, and went straight home. They suggested she could eat later, but the effect of the anesthesia might make her nauseous if she were to eat too soon after.

The very next day was Valentine's Day. Ginny said she felt the best she had in some time. She even had a ham sandwich, a former lunch mainstay that she'd stopped some weeks ago because swallowing the bread was difficult. She was very pleased, and I was absolutely ecstatic.

That weekend we made beef stew, one of her favorites. I served it with the Champagne bread she so enjoys. She had two helpings! Our stew is unlike many others, it's a bit spicy, loaded with meat, and not too many veggies. Ginny loves veggies so I had to include green pepper, celery, carrots, and small potatoes. Me, I've never been a fan of any cooked veggies.

If anyone was to stop in to visit us in February it wouldn't take them long to see one of my quirks. We don't take down our Christmas decorations until late February, well past the time most others do. This isn't because we're indolent, but reflects the fact that Christmas is our favorite time of year. I can recall one year when the tree didn't come down until early March. I asked her to hold off taking it down; she gave me that look, the raised left eyebrow. Her mom had that same "look" at times…an inherited trait perhaps. That year she relented for just one more weekend. Truth be told, Ginny so loved this time of year too, but felt the holiday decorations should be down by the end of January. It's a huge effort to put it all up, yet it's a joyful task. It's just as big an effort to put it all away. I say tougher, since here in the Northeast we have such dreary winter weather. The good news for Ginny this year was that I was there to help take everything down too. Yet the tree and all the trimmings would be the last to go. In 2014 we'd set no records for extending the season, as she insisted it all be put away before Valentine's Day.

A follow up visit to her PCP took place on February 25th where he re-affirmed the good results from the endoscopy. While her appetite had returned, her weight loss was still an issue. The doctor felt we needed to continue with internals so she was scheduled for a colonoscopy on the 27th. Ginny grudgingly agreed…this would be her first one; I'd already had two of them.

The effects of the pre-procedure diuretics really knocked her down. While I understood the doctor's desire to eliminate "digestive tract issues" as a cause, I felt the idea wasn't good. How this procedure was going to be of any benefit when part of the prep involved withholding food really mystified me. In the end we deferred to his recommendation. In hindsight I'd wished we hadn't. The procedure went fine with no unusual findings, but she did not rebound well in terms of either appetite or energy level. Over the following few days her problem swallowing resurfaced, worse than even before her endoscopy. She seemed to have symptoms of having caught the flu, though she didn't have a temperature. She told me nothing sounded good to eat, though I insisted she had to.

The two pounds she'd gained since Valentine's Day had not only disappeared but she'd lost another three in just the last three weeks. Her follow-up appointment with her PCP had been set for March 24th. It was clear to me on Sunday March 9th that we needed to get in a see the doctor; we couldn't wait. That morning I'd made her scrambled eggs that she ended up choking on, and she couldn't finish even a small bottle of Ensure. As I helped her take her shower that day, it struck me how emaciated she looked. I'd seen her sick with the flu, but never like this. The euphoria I'd felt only three weeks ago had now been replaced by a deepening concern that the medical folks weren't on the right track. That scared me but I'd never let Ginny know. I had to stay positive and affirming.

The morning of her appointment on March 11th things were not going well. She'd not had a good night's sleep, having twice needing to get to the bathroom. Both times I'd helped her, as she was now so weak. As we waited our turn to see the doctor I was really very concerned. Her weigh-in confirmed the weight loss we'd noted. All told, it meant she'd lost over 20% of her weight since early summer of 2013. In the eyes of the doctor's assistant I could see compassion tinged with concern. The doctor on the other hand, did not seem as concerned, though suggested she go for an outpatient procedure at the nearby hospital. The "swallow test" was scheduled for that Friday, March 14th. Before we left, the doctor commented that if this procedure did not uncover an issue, we might need to investigate matters from a psychological dimension. When I heard this I knew how Ginny would react. It was just like the doubts conveyed to her those many years ago when she had the severe leg pains. The doctors couldn't isolate the cause back then, so they too suggested they could be psychologically-based. Sure enough, on the way home from her appointment this day she began to cry, insisting this was not in her head, that she really couldn't swallow.

I never thought about it until now, but it strikes me that doctors want to find root causes that are physical. Failing to do so, some have a tendency to point towards behavioral causes; aka psychological issues. Ergo, if they

can't find a definitive physical reason, the problem therefore must be of
the patient's doing; sort of a cop-out in my opinion.

Beware the Ides of March

Although neither Ginny nor I are superstitious, I had a bad feeling early the morning of her swallow test. We both had tended to be early birds of late, though Ginny was never one to relish those early hours, particularly soon after we were married. I guess over the years my early rising tendencies coupled with her love of good coffee helped eliminate the grumpiness that came with the sun's rising. Today Ginny wanted to take a long shower before her test. The test involves swallowing barium-infused liquid that is then monitored—similar to a real-time x-ray video. I think she had a premonition that things would not go as hoped. She seemed so weak as I helped her into and out of the shower. As I toweled her off, she became apologetic. I would hear none of it. "I'm here to help you, so just be quiet," I said with a smile.

We had no issue finding the lab area where the tests were performed, though it was quite a walk from the main hospital entrance. We arrived before 10:00 AM as scheduled, and with no one else ahead, we went right in. We were briefed by the technician, Mary Ellen. She was a very nice woman who then explained how the test would proceed. Ginny stated that she wasn't sure she could even swallow the liquid as she had a difficult time consuming even one bottle of Ensure earlier. The tech said, "Don't be concerned, just do your best." But before the test began, the tech asked her a question that floored me: "Have you had a small stroke recently, because the left side of your face seems a little droopy?" Ginny, then I, assured her that nothing of the sort had occurred, at least as far as we were aware. Then the clincher…her left pupil was also more dilated than her right. At this point we'd been there less than ten minutes…and my concern, and Ginny's, was now obvious. Something was definitely wrong.

Ginny began with the first of three liquids, each of varying viscosities. It took no more than thirty seconds from starting before the problem was evidenced on the monitor. The liquid did not go down; it simply pooled about six inches down her throat. Something was restricting or blocking the fluid, preventing it from going down. Moreover, the tech noted that her esophagus was "inactive." The tech explained that the walls of the esophagus propel food to the stomach not by gravity but by rhythmic waves of muscular contractions called peristalsis. Ginny's esophagus showed no movement at all. The test was stopped.

Just based upon what the tech and attending lab doctor had seen, we were told Ginny would have to be admitted to the hospital for more thorough testing. I remember the tech said that such had only happened twice before in her seventeen years of work in that lab.

As some preliminary paperwork was begun, I sat beside Ginny as we waited for a person to come to get us. She began to cry, saying that she knew the problem was not in her head; it was true she really could not swallow. Within minutes, we were carted off to the ED (Emergency Department) where we waited for the next three hours or so. Somewhere around 2:00 PM, the plan was to run a couple of CT scans (computed topography) on both her upper chest area and her head. The latter was suggested by the tech in consultation with Ginny's PCP who'd been contacted by phone. Right before they came for her, Ginny asked that I go home to attend to Jesse's "needs." I grudgingly agreed, as I knew I had to take care of the dog. I countered by saying I'd be gone less than an hour.

As I drove home, a million things were going through my mind.... none of them good. I know Jesse greeted me, as she always did, as if I'd been gone for days but I don't remember much of anything else. All I knew was that I had to get back to the hospital. I zipped back, no doubt exceeding the posted speed limit. This time I had to park the car on the uppermost level; it seemed to take forever. After making my way down to the ED, I was told Ginny had been transferred to a hospital bed; she was on the fourth floor.

As I walked into her room, I spied her roommate, an older and rather boisterous woman. As I rounded the curtain separator, there was Ginny lying in bed. I could tell she was happy to see me based on the big smile she wore. How she could smile amazed me, but she was most often like that...that woman has an absolutely beautiful smile and can-do spirit. I gave her a big hug, and then asked how the CT scan went. She sort of shrugged her shoulders and said she'd heard nothing on the results so far. She was told a doctor would be in "shortly" to share some initial findings. Shortly is a word often used in hospitals similar to how the word "momentarily" is used by the airlines when estimating a flight delay. A couple of hours later we did get the visit.

The doctor had excellent bedside manners and took his time explaining to us what they knew and didn't know so far. There were two main findings. The first was that Ginny had some sort of "lesion" on the right side of her brain. Further, there appeared to be one or more lesions on the right side of her esophagus. I pressed him for specifics..."Do you mean tumors?" To that the doctor said it was too early to know for sure, further testing was going to be necessary. One test was a lung biopsy that would need to be scheduled, likely for Monday the 17th. Another test was for an MRI that would occur later that day; it would be targeted on her brain. At that, the doctor left, leaving Ginny and I to think about all he'd said. Ginny began to cry, then said to me, "What have I done to the Punkins, this is all my fault." I held her in my arms and said, "No it isn't, it's no one's fault."

If there were any fault, it was mine. I should have known better. Ginny's dad had died from lung cancer. He smoked cigarettes much of his life then switched over to small cigars by the time I'd met her. Whatever her predisposition was in terms of need to or desire to smoke; I should have understood there may have been a hereditary likelihood that she too could contract cancer. Though she was a "moderate smoker" and it was her choice to smoke, I should have insisted she at least get annual chest X-rays to serve as an early warning to any possible problem. But I didn't think of it; it never occurred to me, so now we'd pay the price for my thoughtlessness. When we'd been dating I told her I would always protect her and keep her safe. I'd failed her; that much was already clear to me.

There are times in life that truly test our ability to stay positive. My gut reaction was that of blind rejection of what we'd been told; of denial. Yet I knew I had to stay positive, for that's exactly what Ginny would do if the roles were reversed. It's in that frame of reference I told her, "Let's just take this one step at a time." At this point what they knew was limited. About an hour after the doctor had left they came to take her down for the MRI. I went down with her and waited in an adjoining area. It didn't occur to me until afterwards that I should have told them to give her a sedative to help relieve her anxiety. It wasn't long before we were headed back up to her room. Here too they said a doctor would be by later to share the results.

If asked what the pinnacle of the medical profession would be, I'd likely have told you that the doctor would be a brain surgeon. The doctor who came to share the findings was a neurosurgeon who had the appearance of some guy out of *GQ* magazine. My guess is that he was in his early to mid-40s, over six feet tall, and rather handsome. He looked just like I would have expected, though I'm sure that it's unfair of me to generalize like that. After brief introductions he told us that Ginny did in fact have a brain tumor, nearly the size of a tennis ball. He then assured us that it appeared contained and operable; he could remove it. The only thing he cautioned us on was that we needed to make sure that the tumor, and not something else, was at the core of the problem. To figure this out they needed to do some analysis of the type of tumor to determine the proper next step. He closed by saying that if all checked out, he could perform the surgery as soon as the following week. To be honest, I felt this was good news and didn't hesitate to share that with Ginny as soon as he'd left.

They had hooked Ginny up on IVs earlier in the day…just saline—no food yet. I knew she'd had very little to eat that day, so I asked the area nurse when she would be getting some food. She told me that Ginny was scheduled to be tube-fed, but under no circumstances was she allowed anything orally; not even water. The nurse explained that given the apparent blockage, anything she drank or ate could be choked up, inadvertently causing her to aspirate it into her lungs. Aspiration could result in pneumonia or asphyxia. What that meant to me was that all the food and drink I was pushing her to consume could have brought about aspiration. I was upset with myself for pushing her so to eat and drink. Look, I'm not a doctor, but if a patient of mine tells me they can't swallow and there's a chance that there's an obstruction causing it, further investigation was in order.

It was now after six o'clock, so Ginny insisted I head home to take care of Jesse and eat my own dinner. She told me "I'm a big girl, so I'll be fine until you're back in the morning." What she really meant was, "I know you have to go, but don't worry about me, just make sure you're back tomorrow morning." I knew this from having been married to this wonderful woman for over thirty-six years.

The Ides of March took place on Saturday in 2014. As promised, I was back in to see my darling around 8:30 AM. I'd been up since before 5:00 AM, but I needed to make sure Jesse "took care of business" before I left her again for several hours. I was smart enough the second day to make sure to get an all-day parking ticket before I left in the early afternoon. That hadn't occurred to me the day before. I can't tell you the weather that day, but I will always remember seeing Ginny as I walked in. She had feeding tubes running up her nose and IVs her arm. As I spied her, she could only manage a plaintive smile; a far cry from just yesterday. Again I gave her a big, though careful hug, as I went over to her side. I don't know what I expected, but I didn't expect all those tubes. They made it hard for her to talk but she said they'd come in last evening to insert them. Told me how badly she gagged when they shoved them down. She said it took them three tries. I felt horrible, as I would've stayed with her had I known what she'd have to endure.

This day I brought a book to read. It was a good idea, since I'd not known her talking would be minimal. No matter—I needed to be with her, that's just how we've always been. Being with her was essential to both her and to me. I did the same routine as the day before, leaving in the early afternoon to return about an hour or so later. Today when I returned, Ginny said that the neurosurgeon we'd spoken to the day before was going to be stopping by again, though she didn't know why. I sort of figured the doctor was simply making his rounds of patients or potential patients but I was wrong.

When the surgeon came into the room, his disposition was a bit more sedate than it had been the day before. He told us that more work needed to be done, but that he suspected we'd have to hold off on the brain surgery. He explained that he'd taken a closer look at her MRI, CT scans, and the swallow test video. Though the planned right lung biopsy would take place on Monday, he was fairly certain of a somewhat modified diagnosis. He went on to explain that about 80% of brain tumors source from other parts of the body; they are the result of metastasis of other cancer within the body. In short, in all likelihood, the brain tumor, no matter the size, was not the number one problem. He noted that the obstruction of her esophagus was the larger concern. Though he told us the biopsy would confirm it one way or the other, he didn't want us to get our hopes up. Though he didn't say it, I got the sense he knew exactly how bad the situation was, but didn't want to be the messenger of bad news. Still, I had a lot of respect for the man, as he really didn't have to come to tell us what he did. He could have left it up to others.

I said nothing about it that day or since, yet I can recall an argument we two had the prior summer. Ginny and I both smoke...her a bit more than I. If you asked her, she'd tell you she smoked about three-quarters of a pack per day but the truth is it was more like a full pack. The prep for the move was quite stressful at times, which I'm sure was part of the reason for her smoking more. One day I said something to her, told her she was smoking too much. To that she responded rather defensively, "I had one father and don't need another." Normally I'd have let that go, but that summer day I said to her, "It's not the cost that concerns me; I plan on growing old with you so I want you around for a long long time." I got no reply.

In hindsight, I had no idea how long Ginny had been sick with cancer...that hated word. So many things were going through my head that Saturday, but deep down I knew that my job—my role—was to keep her positive...to let her know that nothing was certain at this point. Even the surgeon wasn't yet certain. We needed to take this one day and one test at a time. For the rest of that afternoon and early evening we didn't talk a lot, she couldn't really and I, well I didn't want to either give false hope or prattle on with conjecture.

The Letter

On that Sunday the 16th, I awoke even earlier, 4:00 AM. I hadn't had bad dreams but to me it felt like things were spinning out of control in our lives. Something like this doesn't happen to us…it happens to other people, not us! My guess is no one ever thinks such terrible stuff is going to happen to them. I made coffee then sat down at the computer to write Ginny a letter. I don't think I'm an exception, but it seems to me we take most things in our life for granted. I needed to put my feelings down on paper and write to her just as I used to write those many letters way back in my college days. This is what I wrote:

March 16, 2014

Dearest Ginny—Mine,

I got up early today, as is usual. This house is really not a home without you here. If willing things to be different were all it took, you'd be here with me and well once again.

I cannot tell you how sorry I am that I was as forceful over the last few weeks…pushing you to drink more of the Ensure and Boost. All the while you kept telling me that you couldn't drink any more or eat any more food. I just knew you continued to lose weight, which meant we were losing ground. I should have been more understanding…should have listened more to your words of being unable to consume any more food or drink. But now we know why.

"Mine"—funny word really, when you think of it. To most people it denotes a possessive statement; perhaps almost demeaning…that is unless the word applies to what we call one another. "Mine" to me is a term referring to a part of myself. Fact is, you will always be mine…

and the same goes in reverse…as we two really are but one.

We have quite a challenge ahead of us in the coming weeks and months, yet I will tell you I will always be there for you. We can do this…we can beat this. The strength that you may lack is within me therefore we will have the strength to endure any and all of the obstacles that lay ahead. Every step of the way, I will be there with you. It's going to be hard at times, but we will not only endure, but succeed.

You know me like no one else; almost from the day we met. You know that come this September we will celebrate having met forty years ago. That was the night I met the woman that would become "mine." You know that once I get my mind set on a goal there's no changing it. I know that you too understand that the challenges ahead are going to be difficult but like me, you've got a stubborn streak. Once the course is set, you'll do all you can to make it a reality. And you will never be alone in this, I will be there, for it isn't a matter of what you must do or I must do….but what WE must do.

It is hard to express to you how very much in love with you I am. You are, as I've stated to many folks over the years, my better half. You've made me a better man simply by my association with you. I am so very lucky to have been the one for you. We are as inseparable as the proverbial "two peas in a pod." That will never change. We are going to beat this…not you, we. Whenever and whatever is required, we will do it.

At times perhaps I look back…wish I'd been more understanding… more sensitive or empathetic. I possess quite a few faults and a few good traits as well. But I am who I am and no one knows this better than you. I will focus on making sure you know that no matter what challenges lie ahead, we two will overcome them…together, just as we have done so in the past.

I love you Ginny…I will be there whenever you need me. Nothing else matters when compared to you, for you are my life…you are my Punkin…you are mine. This isn't a declaration as of today…it is as it has been and always will be. I love you so my dearest…we're going to beat this, together!

Your Hubby, Jimmy.

I printed it off, stuck it in an envelope, and then went to take my shower. As I drove to see her I felt I just had to make her understand. This was not her problem—it was our problem. She is the most important person in my life; she is my life. If she fully understood that, she would fight with all her will. I felt the odds were against us, but then this has been the case before, yet we battled through. We could do this.

Walking in, our eyes met. Unlike the day before, I was prepared to see all the tubes that surrounded her angelic face. Right away I said to her, "I have something for you" as I handed her the letter. She had a quizzical look as she began to read. I should have expected her reaction, for she began to cry. I interjected, saying it wasn't supposed to make her sad. She replied, "I'm not sad, this is the most beautiful letter I've ever received." I explained that although things looked bad, we couldn't let them get us down.

Again I'd brought a book to read, perhaps a subconscious expression of my need to escape. She seemed to be able to talk more readily today. She began by telling me of her restless night. Her roommate had insisted on leaving her room light on all night. When the attending nurse had turned it off, the woman wailed. So naturally the attending nurse turned it back on, which is how it stayed all night. It struck me that the woman didn't belong in a hospital but rather a nursing home. Her chatting to herself, loudly crying out for assistance whenever she felt inclined; these were typical of her behavior the entire time she roomed with Ginny. I know I should have been more compassionate but my only concern was for my wife, not this stranger. Ginny needed her rest. This may sound callous to most folks, but it's the way I felt. When I learned the reason the woman was there was that she had fallen in her home, it only cemented the notion that she should not be there. She was discharged a couple of days later into a nursing home.

I was fairly impressed with the nursing aids and the attendant nursing staff for the wing Ginny was on. Most seemed both competent and caring, though a couple of them ought to look for work that doesn't involve people. To me they lacked any degree of empathy. This assessment may seem harsh yet I feel it was accurate. So far the doctors seemed quite good overall, though to that point no one had had a heart-to-heart talk with us. You know, informing us of the dire reality. I'm sure this is a task no one wants to do, but without it, the patient and their family can only guess. This new reality was foreign to us.

The day before, I'd made some calls to family and a few friends letting them know that Ginny was in the hospital and that they had ascertained she had a brain tumor as well as some sort of restriction affecting her ability to swallow. Ginny had asked me to let them know how she was doing but also to tell them that she was not up to visitors. The one exception was her sister Carol. My mom seemed a bit perplexed by this, as she really wanted to come see her. Some people don't like visitors because they are "at their worst"; sort of a vanity issue. But Ginny's motivation was driven by her desire not to be an object of pity; not to be the focus of attention. Ginny hated being the center of attention; she has always been this way.

We were told that her lung biopsy had been scheduled for the next day in the late morning. The thought of it had Ginny on edge. While we both wanted to know the full scope of the problem, part of us really didn't. That may sound contradictory, yet I think our reaction was fairly typical. So far in this short stay, the news seemed to get worse each day. We'd have to wait to see if Monday was going to break that pattern.

To this point, Ginny was largely restricted to bed, due to all the tubes, including both gastrointestinal and urological catheters. She hated being bed-ridden; she wanted to get up and get out in the worst way. We were told that this would change. She was scheduled to get a stomach tube inserted, which would enable the removal of the feeding tubes that encumbered her. That fact concerned her but I told her she was looking at it the wrong way…the feeding tube was progress. It would mean she'd be able to get out of bed and walk around. I knew without it she would be kept in the hospital, unable to go home. When we asked when that procedure would be done we got an indefinite reply, but likely later in that week.

We'd done the same routine as the previous days, me heading out to take care of our dog then returning. While it was sort of a pain in the butt, it also served to give us both a short break; not from each other, but from the monotony of just waiting for the doctors to make the next move. Just sitting around waiting gave me a sense of helplessness. Before I left that Sunday evening, Ginny had asked if I was eating properly. I told her I had zero appetite. I can't really explain it, but even though I knew I was hungry, I had no desire to eat—none. She made me promise to stop and pick up some ready-made meal at the store on the way home. I reluctantly agreed. I hadn't told Ginny that the day before all I ate was two bowls of cereal, a stick of string cheese, and a small packet of Lorna Doone cookies; the latter two items were shared with Jesse.

Test Results

Jesse knew even before I'd ask her to "get into your kennel" when it was time for me to leave. I hadn't told Ginny, but each time I'd come home, twice a day, Jesse would greet me with kisses before running to the door to give Ginny the same welcome. "Mommy isn't with me," I'd tell her, "but she loves you very much." It broke my heart to see Jesse's reaction, as she just did not understand why "Mom" hadn't come home with me as she always had before.

That Monday I got to the hospital at 8:30 AM to find Ginny "resting." Though I was quiet, she awoke as I sat down in the one real chair in her room. She smiled at me and asked how I was doing. How I was doing? Here she was in the hospital asking me how I was doing. This was classic Ginny. No matter what was affecting her, she'd ask the other person how they were doing. You don't see that selflessness in most people, including me. That day I simply told her I was fine, but more importantly I asked her how her night had been. That early morning it was just trivial banter exchanged. We both knew a lot was riding on the results of that day's testing that including a chest CAT scan and lung biopsy. They came to prep her, and then took her away around mid-afternoon. This time they told me I could not come, as there was no waiting room for inpatient relatives. So I stayed in her room reading, but she was all that was on my mind. I admit it; I was scared.

They brought her back on a gurney, not the wheelchair she'd left in. The nurse told me she'd be groggy for a bit given the sedative. When I asked how it went the nurse said someone would come see us the next morning after they'd had time to assess the results. But I wanted to know now, before she awoke! I simply nodded in reply.

I sat there, just looking at Ginny. They'd positioned her so she was lying on her right side. I so wanted to just rip off all the tubes, take her in my arms and take her home. Perhaps ten or fifteen minutes later she stirred. She started to talk but her voice was quite raspy. No doubt they'd removed the feeding tubes to perform the biopsy then had to reinsert them. I only hoped she didn't have to go through the same dreaded sense of choking she did that first time. Her first words to me were, "Hi, mine."

She rested fairly well the rest of the day. I know both of us were quite anxious to hear the results of the tests but some things ought not to be rushed. I stayed until early evening after the night nurse had first been in to see her and check out how she was doing. The next day would be pivotal; I knew it and so did Ginny.

The day began like the others before it, with me parking up on the roof-top of their large garage. Early morning passed with her lying there, really worse for the wear it seemed, due to the biopsy. She seemed to have to clear her throat or cough more than before. My query as to results told us that it wouldn't be until mid-morning that someone would come to see her and discuss them.

It was about 10:30 AM when a pulmonary specialist came to see us. Right away I noted his quiet demeanor. He told us they'd taken the sample tissue—two of them actually—both from her right lung area. The results indicated she had "a small-cell cancer—stage four" and that the last CAT scan appeared to confirm the presence of several tumors. Then I asked a stupid question: "How many stages are there?" To that he responded, "Just four, I'm afraid." At that moment I wanted to scream out and tell him they were wrong—that they'd made a mistake. He was very sullen but also expressed empathy. I'm sure we weren't the first couple to which he had delivered such awful news. He told us we'd be meeting a doctor from the Oncology department later that day. He told us the name of the physician but it went in one ear and out the other. I couldn't fathom how this could have happened to us. As he left, the silence was deafening. I broke it by saying, "We can beat this." Ginny was softly crying. I didn't know what else to do or say, so I repeated it. She responded, "I know, the Punkins can do anything."

We often hear folks say that bad things can and do happen to good people. Yet deep down, none of us ever imagine that we would be the ones it happens to. It seems to me the question of "why me?" is not the right question but rather "Why not me?" I had always prided myself on having a plan…well, this wasn't part of any plan I'd ever envisioned. Through this all, I never cried in front of Ginny. She, not I, was the victim here; she was the one who would suffer the ramifications. I had to somehow instill in her a stubborn and unending will to live. That was MY job, not to feel or even think of the impact it might have on me. So damn it, that's what I was going to do. Our story was not written to end like this, of that I was sure.

The Fight of Our Lives

The afternoon of March 18th we went to meet with a doctor, an oncologist in the hospital's cancer center. I had dispensed with the raw emotions that had overcome me from our morning meeting. I was never a person who'd give up—who'd succumb—and neither was Ginny. We would fight this thing no matter what it took. The meeting began right on time but didn't go quite the way we'd expected.

The oncologist began by briefly going over the results of the tests to date. Ginny had a brain tumor that had metastasized from her lung area. The brain tumor was now impacting her motor functions on her left side. This is why right before the swallow test Ginny had had difficulty writing; she's left-handed. The doctor paused, and then stated: "If you do nothing, she has three months to live, if you opt for radiation

treatments that could improve it to four to six months, a year at best."
I remember the feeling as tears just started rolling down my face. As
I looked over to Ginny seated on my right, the effect on her was the
same. Upon seeing our reaction the doctor said, "I'm sorry if I've said
something that upset you." Really?

I wanted to strangle that doctor! How could anyone just sit there and
recite a canned talk of life expectancy. The very life of my darling
Ginny was what she was talking about. No doubt this was one smart
doctor, trained well and likely a graduate near or at the top of her class.
But her whole manner struck me as lacking any sense of compassion.
Doctors have a tough job, especially those who must deal with death.
Yet without compassion what good is all the medical knowledge? To
this day I will tell you, a doctor who lacks compassion should go into
research, not into practice where they interface with patients. We can
all understand candor, and although we wanted an honest assessment,
what we got felt sterile and uncaring.

Once we got past our initial reactions, I became all business myself. I
told the oncologist that we wanted to begin radiation treatments immediately. She told us that Ginny's treatment would be in two stages.
The first would be focused upon her brain tumor. For that she recommended full-brain radiation therapy. This consisted of a series of ten
treatments that would begin the very next day and be repeated each
day, except for the weekends. The second stage of treatment would
then be on her lung cancer, which would begin two weeks after the
first treatments ended. This was the plan…our only plan.

One thing I must mention. Ginny has had long brunette hair since
I've known her. She loved to have her hair brushed. Over the years I'd
been her coiffure much of our marriage; just the basics, such as trimming and coloring. The oncologist told Ginny that her hair would

have to be cut short, for they would be fabricating a "helmet" that would cover her entire head…there was no room for long hair within that helmet. While I said nothing, I knew this side issue would throw her for a loop.

As I walked aside Ginny in her wheelchair making our way back to her room she saw how mad I was, I just couldn't hide it. I'd largely concealed it during our meeting with the oncologist, but Ginny knew me like no other. She knew I was furious at what I considered an all-too-casual manner and indifferent attitude emanating from that particular oncologist. She also knew I'd stay quiet about it until we had some time together, just the two of us.

After the attendant dropped her off in her room and the nurse got her back into bed, Ginny and I had a chance to talk. I saw she needed to talk and I needed to listen. She went right to the topic of her hair. Ginny was not a vain woman but she did love her hair worn long. I told her that she should not worry, because hair grows back. Besides, I told her, she would look stunning with a pixie haircut. She replied, "I thought you liked my hair long?""I do, but it's only hair. We have to do whatever it is that tips the odds in our favor."

I knew full well that it was possible that all her hair would fall out from the effects of radiation. So I added, "I don't care if you are bald as long as I have you, nothing else matters." She gave me a sad smile, but I think she was in fact relieved at my affirmations. I never bothered to bitch about the oncologist. Venting of my opinion wasn't going to change anything, and would distract from focusing my attention on Ginny rather than my gripes.

We were shell-shocked. Even though I sensed exactly what the doctors had told us was the case—hearing it, having it confirmed—was absolutely devastating. It was if our world had been blown apart. This just could not be happening…but it was.

I stayed with her the rest of that afternoon even after she suggested there was no reason I needed to stay as late as I'd been staying the last few days. We didn't talk a lot; she couldn't and I could only reiterate that nothing is certain; that plenty of people had beaten cancer before. It was a bit later than usual that I did leave that Tuesday. I was in no hurry to go or do anything. During that afternoon Ginny's sister Carol and her husband Bill came to visit. So did Kim, who is a long- time RN who works at that hospital. Kim and her husband Lyle are two of our oldest and dearest friends; we go back to the dating years.

That evening at home I remember making some phone calls to family and a few friends. I remember crying and no matter how many kisses Jesse gave, I could not stop. I didn't care what anyone thought or said. I seem to remember saying a prayer that night when I went to bed. Truth is I hadn't prayed much in recent years. I had no idea if God would even listen to me. All I know is, that night I made all sorts of promises if only He would help us.

By Wednesday morning word had gotten out to the nursing assistants in regards to the need for Ginny's hair to be cut. One of them explained that she used to cut hair so would be glad to do so. Ginny was hesitant. She knew it had to be done but I think she felt it was just one more thing being taken from her. While I'd never been accused of being overly sensitive, I had to help her overcome this seemingly trivial fear. She looked at me so sadly again, saying "But I thought you loved my hair long?" I replied, "I do but I love you more…we need to do this for us," I said, "Besides, you're going to look so cute." With that she relented.

As the attendant cut her hair, the look on Ginny's face was so pitiful. I encouraged her by telling her how adorable she would look in short hair. Clumps of hair hit the floor, each about a foot long. I could tell the gal had done this before as she shaped the cut; it was no hack job. As she was finishing up she bent to pick up the hair before tossing it out. I intervened. "No, I will take care of it." I picked up most of it, placing it into a small plastic bag so I could take it home.

Tears began rolling down her cheeks as they brought her a mirror so she could see her new hairstyle. Despite all the tubes, I sat aside her wrapping my arms around her, and then whispered in her ear, "I love you, mine."

Another doctor came to see her to tell her that the next day they would be performing some minor surgery to insert a feeding tube directly into her stomach. He pointed out that she'd no longer have to deal with the discomfort of the catheters that ran from her nose to her stomach. The procedure was scheduled for early morning. He noted that they needed to do this before Ginny underwent her first "full-brain" radiation treatment. The first treatment would be the next day, likely mid-day. After the doctor had left I told Ginny she needed to rest, but that I'd be right there. She suggested that maybe I should get an early start back home but I told her that I'd like to stay with her for a while longer. She lay on her side, opposite the way she normally slept in our bed. When I pointed this out she said she knew that, but if she laid the other way she couldn't see me. She soon fell asleep.

An hour or so later a nursing aid came in to check on Ginny. Though she was quiet, Ginny awoke. I don't think she got a decent sleep those first few days. We talked only briefly before I told her I'd be heading out but would see her early the next day. I so hated leaving her there but it was where she needed to be, at least at the time.

When I arrived on Thursday morning I was somewhat surprised to see that the stomach tube procedure had already been completed. Gone were those nasty tubes up her nose, replaced by equally unsightly tubes leading directly into a "valve" on her stomach. Around it a large dressing covered most her abdomen. I could see the wound had been oozing. She was a bit groggy but told me they just brought her back a short time ago. Said that they told her they would change the dressing later. I could see the feed tube was "on," but at a very low setting. I asked the nurse why so low as she'd been getting more nutrients when the feed was through her nose. It was then we were told that they reset to a new baseline when the tubes go in. They would then increase the flow once everything checked out. I didn't say it, but it struck me that since coming there five days ago, Ginny must be losing even more weight. I'm no doctor, but I felt that if she kept losing weight she'd have no strength left to fight. I got the sense the hospital was doing everything by the book, independent of the specifics in Ginny's case. She needed nutrition to regain some strength and stamina yet I was sure she was slipping further, getting weaker. I'm sure they were doing everything in their normal regimented manner, but I'm not a person who believes "the book" is always the best method to use. Such was abundantly clear to me in her case.

About mid-morning Ginny asked me to raise the bedside restraint so she could use it as a handle to pull herself into a sitting position. She had to do this in order to hunch over to cough and clear her throat. I didn't know at the time, but my raising the sides of the bed would become an issue.

Shortly before Wednesday noon they came to take her to her first radiation treatment. They told me I couldn't go, not the first day. While the treatment would take less than half an hour, that day they had to fabricate the helmet that she would wear. It would cover her entire head, including her face. I knew the idea of her whole head being covered made Ginny nervous, fearful in fact. Before she was taken I told her not to worry…just to think of why she was doing this, so she could go home. We'd been told that as soon as the stomach tube was placed and the radiation program underway, they would likely let her complete the process as an outpatient. But they would not release her until they could see that her body was accepting the new feed path and was properly processing the food. The latter was some issue, as she had not had a bowel movement since the past weekend. Matter of fact, she'd been anything but "regular" since the colonoscopy procedure she'd had way back on February 27th. Having her subjected to that earlier outpatient procedure had not been a good idea. That I needed hindsight to know this doesn't excuse the fact her doctor should have known better given her condition. News flash: if a patient is losing weight, any procedure that worsens that condition isn't a good move unless the procedure is imperative.

I returned to the hospital shortly after 1:00 PM that day. She had just returned from her treatment. As I entered she was hunched over, coughing mildly. One side of the bed was down so I went over to raise it as before. After I did, Ginny told me that the nurse who came in right after she'd returned told her she couldn't have both sides of the bed raised. The reason was due to an issue of "restraint." Apparently someone at some point in the past had made a stink about a patient being restrained in his or her bed. It's not easy to release the bed sides if you're in the bed, ergo, having the sides up is considered to be an inappropriate action of restraint. So hospital policy is that at least one side must be down unless the patient is being moved to another area while in their bed. This struck me as a stupid blanket policy. In Ginny's case, she used the sides to help pull herself up in order to cough. She didn't have the leverage or strength to do so without them. If you knew Ginny you would know this—she always follows the rules—but not me.

Rules: doesn't matter what sort of rule we're talking about…don't run beside a pool, don't exceed the speed limit, or don't do X or Y. Over the years I'd tease her about this. I on the other hand, while not flaunting rules, often viewed them as a guide. Like speed limits…doing a touch faster than the posted speed was not going to cause you to get a ticket. Ginny and I had a number of "discussions" centered on my refusal to take all rules literally. So while some might say that rules were made to be broken, Ginny's take was that rules were made for a reason, so obey them. Then there are people like me, who believe rules are to be considered as guides, nothing more.

A bit later that afternoon a nurse came in and noticed that both sides of the bed were up, so she lowered one. As she did this, I spoke up. This particular nurse clearly understood why I'd raised the side; she did not see it as a big issue but did say that other nurses might come do as she'd done. If that happened she noted, just explain to them you need them both up. I thought her approach was quite reasonable. She went so far as to tell Ginny that if anyone said anything, just tell them your husband raised it and why.

That day ended as each had since her arrival, but that day brought some hope with the start of aggressive radiation treatments and with her new stomach tube giving promise to a near-term discharge. Also, her roommate was being discharged to a home. Perhaps, I thought, Ginny might get at least some needed sleep tonight.

Each day since the previous Saturday, I'd brought a book in to read and pass the time. For the life of me I couldn't tell you what book it was, but having it helped me. Thursday morning as I entered her room, she was wide-awake and seemed well-rested. She had in fact slept fairly well the night before. That is until one of the nurses came in to take her temperature and check vitals sometime before midnight. It took

Ginny quite some time to fall back asleep, but she had. I really don't understand why folks wake sleeping patients to gather data on them. Who isn't better when they get a good sleep? That being the case, why would you wake a person to take readings when getting rest should be a top priority?

Noteworthy of that Thursday was that they finally increased the feed rate. Also, it became clear that Ginny needed a sedative to help her cope with her feeling of claustrophobia when she was undergoing the radiation treatments. They had given her one the first day when they'd been fashioning the helmet, but it hadn't been recorded in her charts so she didn't get one this day. When I returned from home after lunch, Ginny was in tears as I entered. She told me how horrible it felt to be "trapped" inside the helmet and hear only the sounds of the machine as it emits radiation to retard or destroy the tumor. She said she told the nurse who took her down but because nothing was on her chart, they couldn't give her any sedative. Unlike the day before, there was no attending physician at her treatment, just the technician. She opted to go ahead with the treatment as she didn't want to risk not having one that day. It took me a short while to allay her fears; I assured her she'd get meds every time thereafter. I was upset…despite Ginny's assurance that she'd had meds the day before, the nurse said she couldn't give her one because it was not on her charts. Inferring both that the chart was "gospel," which meant it had to be followed, and that Ginny was confused and so hadn't really been given a sedative that first day. I'm sure too that the extent of the nurse's investigation was to look at her chart rather than call down to Radiology. Turns out that's precisely what it was, for I confirmed it.

Thoughts of an early discharge on Friday were dispelled early that Thursday afternoon, day seven. Ginny had no "B.M.," so they could not even begin to process the paperwork. She was disappointed. I was too but had already come to terms with that reality the day before, as I knew they wouldn't let her go just yet. Though I did not say it, I also knew that as a general rule, hospitals don't discharge patients on the weekends so if it wasn't Friday, Monday was our new target. That said, the soonest she could leave would now be the 24th. On a brighter note, her feed rate had been increased yet again; a good sign, I told her. Today was also the day I'd meet a representative for a third-party home nursing care group. We hadn't decided if we'd use such a service, but I at least wanted to understand some specifics, like how often they came and for how long each time.

Friday was perhaps most remembered as the day I was trained how to feed Ginny via her stomach tube. It wasn't that complicated, but each step is important, so I paid close attention. Initially I watched closely as the nurse gave her the feeding. The liquid was akin to the Ensure I'd been foisting on her orally since January, but was not quite the same. It had supposed greater nutritional value than the oral counterpart. It was however, made by the same firm—Nestle—the giant Swiss multinational. One difference I later became aware of was that it cost ten times as much. Not that this was the least bit an issue, but I wondered how different it really was or if the fact it was "by prescription" made it possible to charge a lot more for it; my bet was probably more the latter than the former.

By the close of Friday I'd learned not only how to feed Ginny but also how to change the dressing on her stomach. Changing the dressing was a lot harder for me to do, as I tend to get a little squeamish when it comes to blood, wounds, etc. I'd never make it as a doctor but I sure as hell was going to be the best "aide" Ginny could ever have. As I relay this, I also will note I'd met the home nursing rep that afternoon. He was quite helpful in explaining things. For starters, the nurse could come every day if that's what we wanted. They had various plans with various co-pays involved. Again the issue of cost was irrelevant to me, though I'm sure that it is an issue for many folks not as blessed as we. The rep explained that the visiting nurse would be there anywhere from a half-hour to a bit over an hour depending upon the duties and needs. This wasn't full-time or even what you might call part-time duration; just thirty to sixty minutes per day. In any case, that meant I would be the primary care provider for my wife. I'm told most guys abhor such duties. Yet oddly, I was looking forward to doing them. My wife had taken care of me our entire married life. So my taking care of her was natural. I didn't care what others would do under my circumstances, but I did know that nobody but me could care for her to the degree and depth I would. There is nothing I wouldn't do for Ginny. If any medical issue arose, her PCP was but ten minutes away by car.

The weekend brought new faces to the staff in that hospital wing. Like most other jobs, most of the staff only worked Monday through Friday; that is unless we're talking about a doctor being on call. I took care of an entire feeding on Saturday and Sunday, also changed her dressing too. I caught myself more than once closing my eyes as I removed the old dressing, but I'd get used to it. While she didn't say much about it, I could tell that Ginny was proud that I was going to do this for her. To her this 'duty' was a labor of love; she said so in so many words the following week. It made Ginny feel special, which I found strange for she already was special, and had been since the day we met. I didn't say anything but when I left that Sunday evening I was concerned. She had yet to show them her digestive system was properly functioning. Such was requisite for her to leave.

Sunday night I packed a small bag with clean clothes for Ginny. I knew we didn't have a green light for discharge, but I was committed to be ready. I put the bag into the car before I went to bed. I did not want to have something distract me in the morning and forget to take it.

Monday, day eleven, began like most recent days…not too cold, just seasonal for the area. Yet in my mind that was the day I was going to bring her home. I was adamant about this, even though I'd not pushed it hard while with Ginny. As I went up to see her, I found her upset… she'd been crying. Apparently a nurse had come in and chastised Ginny for having both sides of her bed up after she'd been told that was against hospital policy. The nurse told her she'd checked with some head honcho who told her that it was a legal matter not up for discussion. To say I was upset upon hearing this would be an understatement. I was livid; spitting blood mad I'd say. How dare someone scold a patient about some stupid rule like this, especially given she needed the sides to be up. Ever since her biopsy the previous Monday, Ginny felt congestion and needed to expel the fluid or mucus that was hampering her breathing. In hindsight I'm sorry we granted them permission to do the biopsy, as it only seemed to exacerbate her weakened lungs.

I went over to find the particular nurse who'd had this issue but I couldn't find her. Instead I found the head nurse for that wing. I told her several things, including the fact I did not want whomever that attending nurse was to interface with Ginny again. Further, if anyone had a problem in regard to the sides of the bed being up, they needed to see me, not Ginny. I did not raise my voice but I can assure you the message was crystal clear.

A piece of good news…Ginny was pleased to tell me that she had finally had the "movement" that had gated her release. I know it sounds banal, perhaps even a bit crude, but I'd never been so happy to hear about such a thing.

Upon checking into the status of her discharge, I was told that they were still missing some medical authorizations to proceed with the release. I asked how I might help, but was told the process could not be rushed. The nurse then told me we shouldn't get our hopes up, as she felt it was unlikely to happen this day. I set her straight, telling her that Ginny was leaving today even if it meant I had to carry her out in my arms. So it was best they figure a way to accelerate their normal procedure. At this the nurse asked me if I could contact her PCP, for his was one of the needed authorizations. I was on the phone to his office within minutes. I told Ginny that Jesse would be fine, I was not going to leave her mid-day today; the next trip home would include her.

Early afternoon came…I got a third follow-up from the home nursing rep. I reiterated what I'd told him on Saturday; I would not need their services but would like to order the special food supplement and devices (plastic syringes, etc.). He seemed a bit put out. He told me most every patient who is fed via stomach tubes uses their service. It's both safer and more efficient. I then simply repeated my decision—I would be fulfilling all her daily care needs—feeding, medicines, and dressing changes. He began to tell me that most patients prefer an outside service as it is less of a burden on the family and creates a social bond between the nurse and patient that cannot be had otherwise. I thanked him again but declined.

I was told one discharge step that needed to occur dealt with us meeting with the hospital-assigned social worker and their nutritionist. I was told normally it takes a day or so to see them sometimes. But I insisted we'd been there since the 14th, they, not I, should have taken the initiative to see us. The nurse seemed surprised the social worker hadn't seen us before. Within an hour both these people came to see us. The nutritionist answered my questions about devices and nutrition; they would send a script to our pharmacy. The social worker's only concern was whether I'd signed up for visiting nurse services. She acted like a walking advertisement for that third-party group. Mind you, the social worker never said a thing about Ginny's mental or emotional state of mind or offered up any suggestions on other services that we might find useful upon discharge. Though I did comment on our continued interfacing with the oncology group as an outpatient for radiation treatment, nothing was asked or stated by the social worker that struck me as the least bit useful. I'm not sure what the hospital's definition of social worker is, or what the role's scope of duties involves, but it sure didn't fit any I would have expected.

As the clock approached 4:00 PM, we got word. They had all they needed to initiate discharge. By 4:15 PM I was out front with the car to pick Ginny up to take her home. Her hospital stay had taken a lot out of her the past eleven days. Yet her smile was evident as I helped her into the front seat of the car. She was finally going home.

Going Home

There were no children waiting for Mom to return. Our only son Jason had long been living on his own. Still, there was a small soul who had longed to see her "mom." That would be Jesse.

Soon after we'd found Jesse back in September 2003, it became apparent that although she'd been bought for Ginny, Jesse had an affinity for me. Ginny would tell you that such is no wonder given all the food and treats I tend to give the dog. She's probably right, as she most always is, but let me tell you; Jesse and Ginny have one very special relationship too. Some people have gone so far as to coin a name, "fur kid," to denote the extra special relationship that so many pet owners have with their pets. Jesse is very much our fur kid. I can recall back in 2006 when she somehow hurt her back, as Dachshunds are prone to do. We worked with her vet to try to alleviate the pain and correct the problem. In the end Jesse had to have back surgery. The truth is I never even blinked when told it would cost several thousand dollars. She was just like our child, as silly as that may sound. Through it all, Ginny was there to care for her while I went off to work. Sure, there was a special bond between Jesse and I, but there was also a very special bond with Ginny. Over the years Ginny used the term, "ducks in a row" to describe Jesse's need for things to be just so. If either Ginny or I were out of sight when we three were on a trip, Jesse would cry. She needed to see both of us. We were her ducks and so we had to be seen. Even if we'd just hit a rest stop along a highway, when either of us disappeared, she would cry—sometimes quite loudly, to our chagrin. No doubt some passerby would think to themselves, what's wrong with that dog? But a dog lover was always quick to conclude, must be that mommy or daddy is in the restroom.

Today I was late getting home to feed and "de-water" Jesse. During the last eleven days every time I came home I'd get a greeting like I'd been gone forever. As stated earlier, Jesse would then run to the door that connects to our garage and wait for Ginny to enter. Today Jesse was in for a big surprise.

I brought Ginny into the house, asking her to not say a word. I helped her to the living room floor, as I just knew someone was in for one great greeting. In releasing her from her kennel, her safe place, Jesse gave me kisses but then took off for the door, only to find Ginny sitting on the carpet. Jesse jumped and squealed then began to cry. If you've ever seen any of the YouTube videos of soldiers returning from over-seas to be met by their pet dogs, you may understand what I mean. The cry was not of sadness but sheer joy; and the look on Ginny's face was both precious and priceless. We both knew this was going to be a tough fight to beat this thing, but right then, all was right in our world.

It was now up to me; I was the 24/7 care provider. Considering this is the same guy who years ago showed a real disdain for changing dirty diapers, one might wonder if I had what it would take. Yet everything had changed from my perspective. There are many old adages that could be used to describe the current situation, such as "when the going gets tough, the tough get going." But none of them really can convey my motivation other than the single word we call love. I love my wife more than mere words can convey. This effort wasn't an obligation or responsibility; it was simply the fact I would do anything and everything to meet her needs. My view was simple; my sole reason for being was to care for her...period.

Since the day after she got her feeding tube I'd taken her on short walks in the hospital wing. These were necessary for her to try to regain some sense of mobility, though she could not be left on her own. She did not have any strength or stamina and her weight had fallen another five pounds during her stay; no surprise there. That first evening I set up a small area adjacent to our bed that had all the paraphernalia we'd need except for her "food." Her first "meal" at home went well, as I remembered every step inclusive of the pre- and post-cleansing of the line. She had to receive all her meds the same way of course, with me either crushing and dissolving them or carefully measuring them in the small syringe. I think Ginny was pleased with how proficient I'd become and perhaps a bit less concerned about my ability to take on this new role.

When it came time for bed, Jesse figured she'd get in first, which was the old norm. That first night though, we set forth a new routine. I'd help Ginny to the bathroom to take care of whatever and then support her slow walk to our bed. Even with the bed steps she hadn't the strength to get into bed on her own. I'd let her position herself then I'd lift her up and into bed. She was so thrilled to be in "her bed" again. She would get her best night's sleep in days that night. It was so great to have her home.

We both have long been avid readers. Most often we read in bed for a while; it has a nice mind-quieting effect before sleep. But since early March, Ginny hadn't done much, if any, reading of her many romance novels. She'd say she was too tired or had a headache. In hindsight it seems to me that the brain tumor had likely been the reason. Ginny was not a competitive person but she'd tease me about how slowly I read. I'd tell her that was an unfair comparison for she was a voracious reader compared to anyone I've ever met. It was playful teasing…your font is bigger, your pages hold less, etc. Given how much she loved to read I wondered if she'd regain her prior enthusiasm for it.

Though we both grew up in large families; she with four sisters, me with three brothers and three younger sisters, the act (or art) of teasing was a mainstay for me, but not her. Early in our relationship it became clear that Ginny did not like to be teased. She felt that such often lead to other, less benign, behaviors such as criticisms. Like most things I think she was right in this regard. What one person may think is amusing doesn't always translate that way to another. I'd like to think I learned to adapt given her feedback, but the truth is she was more flexible and accepting than I throughout our relationship.

When it comes to humor my wife had one "character flaw" that would surface from time to time. She would laugh uncontrollably after witnessing someone fall down. My first observation of this came early in our dating, yet it stayed with her for all our years. The night I proposed to her comes to mind but perhaps the most vivid example occurred while we lived in New Jersey. I was bailing water out of our paddleboat docked along the lakeside retaining wall. It was a hot summer day and heavy rains had filled the boat, causing it to ride low in the water. I'd just finished trimming and mowing the lawn so I was quite tired. But I knew more rain was expected that evening so I felt I better empty the boat. Ginny was out on the back porch reading at the time or working her Sudoko puzzles. With the boat nearly emptied out I inadvertently dropped the small bailing container in the lake. Reaching out to retrieve it; I reached too far and went head-first into the lake.

The water was quite warm on that July day, so it wasn't an unpleasant dunk. The water was about three to four feet deep in that spot so I simply stood up; no harm done except perhaps to my pride. I looked up, hearing intense laughter. Ginny was making her way down to me. The words "are you alright?" came out, but were richly contrasted by her reaction. She could barely speak or catch her breath. Now mind you she could not stop laughing, deep down uncontrollable laughter. You've heard the phrase, "laughed till you cried"; well, she had tears. I couldn't quite pull myself up as the boat's position, the slippery rocks, and my own ineptitude conspired to cause me to slip yet again back into the water. Now it grew silent, not out of concern, but Ginny's laughing had clicked up to the next level where not even an utterance is possible. In my embarrassment I did not see the humor. Apparently this showed in my face, which only made her laugh even harder. She actually went up to the house and called my brother Rick, to share with him my predicament. She quickly returned, carrying the cordless phone and a towel and said to me, "If you have a moment your brother would like to talk to you." This too apparently met her definition of what's funny as she handed me the phone and continued her unbridled laughter.

I remember asking her on some similar occasion what it was that caused her to laugh so uncontrollably when she saw someone fall down. She smiled at me and said, "You mean like the time you fell in the lake?" and proceeded to laugh as if it had just happened. I don't know about that woman; clearly there's something wrong with her. But you know I wouldn't change her one tiny bit.

Now in fairness it only seems right that I share one of my character flaws. I like to scare/spook people. I've been doing it since I was a kid. Initially just family, but as the years passed no one was exempt. The first time I did so to Ginny we were at her house. Her bedroom was in the basement. She'd gone down to get some things from the laundry room for her mom. Overhearing them talk, I snuck down and slipped into her room, which was opposite the laundry area. I stood behind the closed door waiting for her to finish folding the clothes. When I heard her coming I jumped out just as she started up the stairs. She let out a scream and I couldn't stop laughing. When her mom heard the commotion, she came to the cellar stairs only to look down and see all her clean laundry all over the floor. "What are you two doing down there and why is the clean laundry all over the place?" Ginny, having recovered from fright, declared that "It was Jimmy's fault". I admitted it. Ginny then punched me in the arm (I deserved it) and told me she'd get even. She did just hours later. Throughout our marriage I'd pull such stunts from time to time and Ginny would always retaliate in kind. While it may sound childish to many, I relish the many fun memories of those "spooks."

That first night back home Ginny awoke in the wee hours. I'd sensed her stirring and awoke as well. She apologized for waking me but had to go to the bathroom, and knew she couldn't yet do this on her own. I helped her down and into the bathroom. On return I lifted her back up into bed after she'd placed one foot upon the bottom bed step. She plaintively stated aloud, "I'm pathetic; I can't even go to the bathroom without help." I sort of chastised her while at the same time assuring her. "Ginny, give yourself a break, you've just returned from eleven days at the hospital and are in a weakened condition. You need to learn to depend on me; I'm here for you." She just smiled and thanked me for my help.

I awoke first in the morning just after 5:00 AM. Ginny was still sleeping so I dug Jesse out from under the covers. Jesse wasn't ready to get up, as conveyed by her growl. I knew Ginny hadn't slept soundly in days, and that she needed the sleep. I turned on the coffee maker without a second thought. While innocent enough, that was really quite thoughtless of me. I realized that only after she'd awakened a bit later to the smell of fresh-brewed coffee.

When we were first married neither of us were coffee drinkers. I'm not sure exactly when that changed, but it sure did. Our morning coffee ritual was honed over many years. Both of us developed an absolute love of that daily routine. In recent years I often used a vanilla-flavored creamer, but Ginny never altered, preferring only her Coffee-mate dry creamer; never any sweetener.

On every trip we ever took together it was always my first job of the day to get us both a cup of coffee. If that meant driving to a coffee barn or going down to the hotel lobby, so be it. Our day could not begin without our cups of coffee. In later years we most often had it twice a day, early morning and then early afternoon. Weekends were special in that only then did we share the afternoon coffee time. Most times we'd buy only the Eight O'clock ground coffee but Ginny would not use it during the week for her afternoon break; she saved "the good stuff" for only when she had it with me. During the week she'd say, "Any old ground coffee was fine." In a microcosm, this trivial mannerism said so much about her. She was perhaps the most selfless person I've ever met; a rather rare attribute.

I heard Ginny stirring in bed so I left our computer room to help her down. She said to me, "is that coffee I smell?" Only then did it hit me, she couldn't have coffee, she couldn't have anything she could taste. I felt so stupid, I should have known better. I apologized, but she'd hear none of it, as she told me she didn't want me to change my routine or go without simply because she couldn't have it too. She then told me that the two things she missed the most were her morning coffee and having an ice-cold can of ginger ale. She'd only begun to drink ginger ale over the last couple of months so I was surprised by her fondness for it. It struck me how much she'd lost by not being able to eat or drink. While there was a way to get her nutrition, it provided no sense of pleasure; that was gone. We are all sensory beings. The loss of any of our five senses diminishes our ability to relate to our world. I'd never given much thought to it, until then.

The new daily order of business was as follows: feeding, meds, and changing her wound dressing. On this, her first full day home, changing the wound dressing was particularly nasty. The incision had oozed quite a bit during the night so the entire works had to be removed, the area cleansed, and then dressing replaced. I admit it wasn't my idea of a fun thing to do. At one point Ginny told me she could do that part, but I refused her help. This was my job; hers was to start to regain her strength so she could get better. Nothing more and nothing less was acceptable. Some of you might think it rather crude to speak of things like changing a dressing. But even something as basic and necessary as that has with it the opportunity to serve as an act of love. Compassionate souls know this to be true, but it was my first realization of it. That says volumes about my own lack of insight and understanding when it comes to such matters. My "teacher" was giving me yet another lesson in life. What, if anything, I would learn would depend on whether I was listening with my heart.

That day, our son Jason and his fiancée Samantha stopped by to do their laundry. This would afford me a chance to pick up some things at the grocery store, including more meds. We tended to keep quite a store of food at home with most of the perishable meat kept frozen so it wasn't going to be difficult for me to take care of my own meals. Eating had become simply a chore for me; I had no real appetite anymore. That day we'd also be taking delivery on a full month's supply of Ginny's "food"; that high calorie nutritional supplement that I'd feed to her at least three times daily. I would feel better once I had plenty of everything she would need here at home. I was bound and determined to give her at least 1,500 calories a day; 1,200 was the minimum I'd accept. I knew she just had to gain weight after seeing the home scale reading of only 105 pounds the night before.

Ginny would turn fifty-eight years old on the 28th of the month, but to this point I had no gift to give. I asked her what she'd like for her birthday...she simply said, "To get better so I could grow old with you." She saw right away that her saying that aloud bothered me...she could see that my eyes began to tear. Then she declared, "What I really want you to find me is a 'husband' pillow." I had no idea what she was talking about. Turns out that this is the term used to describe a pillow with arms. Many folks use them on couches or on the floor to give them added back support. Ginny's back was bothering her a bit as she often had to hunch over to clear her throat. She figured the husband would make it easier on her. I found exactly what she was talking about at a nearby Bed, Bath & Beyond when I was off running errands later that morning. She'd love it. Still, it seemed like such a utilitarian present. She couldn't eat anything, I really couldn't buy her clothes, and if I came home with a piece of jewelry she'd kill me.

Ginny had lots of very special jewelry I'd purchased for her over the years. Aside from "dangle" costume jewelry earrings, she never initiated any of the jewelry purchases; it was always me. I recall on one vacation trip back in 2005 I'd bought her several nice pieces of jewelry but "hit the limit." I literally had to plead with her to let me buy the last one. It turned out to be one of her favorites; one she wore quite often when we'd go out for the evening. Sometimes she'd kid me by telling me I needed to take her out to more fancy places so she could wear all the jewelry I so often insisted on buying. It's kind of funny when I think about it. She didn't like me spending a lot on her, for anything. She'd say she didn't "need" it. I'd always counter by saying "Okay, but do you want it?" Most times she'd answer no, adding, "I only want to be with you." I think that's why she liked going out to TGIF's on Friday nights when we lived in New Jersey. It wasn't expensive, gave us an opportunity to socialize, and she and I got out of the house. Wait…one more thing…it meant she didn't have to cook every night. She liked that aspect too.

Upon returning from my errands the first order of business was Ginny's second "feeding" of the day. Though Jason expressed interest in seeing how it was done, I didn't want him or anyone to witness it. It's hard to explain, but to me this was a very personal thing—an intimate act—but I suspect few folks would understand what I'm trying to say. Maybe it was just me, but I felt that Ginny too had the same sort of sense about it. I religiously checked the meds schedule to make sure she wasn't due for any. All told, she was on at least four meds initially. Except for the Codeine pain-killer, I couldn't tell you their names, but I knew what each was for, as I'd taken notes on the matter. I'd already gotten quite good at using the pill crusher in order to mix it into her food.

Ginny spent some time on the couch in the living room the next day. It was the first time in nearly two weeks that she was out of a bed for any length of time and now with no tubes dangling around her. She liked the freedom, I could tell. Watching television was about her only activity though, as reading and even doing her crosswords or Sudoko seemed onerous. She told me she'd get a headache soon after beginning those other activities. We were both hopeful that as she continued the radiation treatments, that aspect would improve. She had already noticed a slight improvement in her left hand's dexterity.

My wife had the patience of a saint. On the other hand, I'd often say when they were handing out attributes I stood in the passion line twice but skipped the line for patience entirely. Ginny would agree. In this regard we were very different. I was aptly impressed with her ability to figure out any puzzle. She was amazing when it came to jigsaw puzzles, as she could do a 2,000+-piece puzzle like a wiz. She'd amassed many boxes of these during our years. I bought her a puzzle board back in the 1980s that she used all the time. It got to the point it became worn out; ratty you might say. So just a few years ago I bought her this super duper puzzle board that had removable portions and even zipped up for carrying. She used it a few times but then told me it was sort of heavy to move around, unlike her old cardboard unit. She didn't fess up to this though, until I'd noticed her using the old one again. I think she didn't want to hurt my feelings, for she knew how thrilled I was to find it and give it to her as a birthday present that year.

I had called some of our friends, suggesting that they might want to come see Ginny now that she was home from the hospital. Over the next few days several made plans to do so. I was perhaps overly protective, not wanting too many folks to come at once, as it would surely tire her out. But I knew Ginny wanted to see them now, unlike when she was an in-patient. I'd also spoken to my two younger brothers, Ron and Michael, but told them the weather forecast for the upcoming weekend was "iffy" so I wasn't recommending they attempt to come see her. Maybe the following weekend would be better. While they both understood, Michael and his wife Connie seemed intent on coming up on her birthday weekend along with their daughter Molly. Their two boys, Christopher and Peter, were both away at school or otherwise committed.

My brother Michael and his family were our most frequent out-of-town visitors when we had lived in New Jersey. They would come up for a long weekend in the summers. Visits always had to include frequent use of our paddleboat, swimming at the lake community's little beach/club, and of course, walks into town with the requisite special ice cream cone purchase at Denville Dairy. Initially, all five of them would come, which meant we best make a lot of fresh fruit salad. That was Christopher's favorite. Peter would eat almost anything, though Molly was a bit of a "picky eater." Ginny always enjoyed their visits, as did I. Through them we were able to see their kids grow up. Michael and his family were also the last guests to visit us before we'd moved back to the Rochester area. They'd visited us on the July 4th weekend in 2013.

I remember the last visit particularly because I got a bit melancholy reflecting on some things. I thought about all the other little day trips I'd told Ginny we'd make sometime, like the huge model railroad display in Flemington, New Jersey at a place called Northlandz. We'd passed it several times as we drove down to see my other brother Ron and his family. I'd always have a reason why "now" wasn't a good time to visit it. Same goes for the various Revolutionary war sites, located right in Morris County where we lived. Ginny's interest in our domestic wars was born from her visits as a child with her parents to the Gettysburg Civil War museum. She would tell me how frequently they'd gone as a family, most of them weren't thrilled with those trips, but Ginny had been. Over the years she had read many books on the civil war. Many of her romance novels were from that time period as well. In hindsight, her interest had been spurred by her dad, a person whom she so loved. Even though he'd had only girls, when it came to the civil war and auto mechanics, Ginny was always right there, anxious to learn and share his fondness of these things. I think it gave the two of them a special bond.

It struck me that I was on the opposite end of the spectrum of hedonism, almost an ascetic at times. That wasn't the type of person I'd been years ago, but I had to admit, it was who I'd become. I could always come up with a reason for not making one of those planned day trips. "Who's going to look after Jesse?" I always could come up with an excuse why now was not a good time to do this or that. In light of all that had happened or may happen, it struck me that I'd denied Ginny some great experiences and *good times for no good reason. A good life requires balance, yet it seems I'd let ours get out of whack. It wasn't her that had caused this, it was me. How was I ever going to make up for that and would I ever have the chance?*

That second evening home from the hospital I went to the fridge to see if there were some leftovers I could eat as dinner; I spied a small bottle of water pushed towards the back of one of the upper shelves. I hadn't noticed it before. It was given to Ginny at the doctor's office after that initial test, the endoscopy. I remember that she had downed another of the same bottles in the recovery area. She'd said how it had so quenched her thirst. I'd found her another one that day but she had only taken a sip from it, so I brought it home for later. That was February 13th, some six weeks ago. So much had changed in just those six weeks. I continued to search through the fridge to find something but it appeared I'd already eaten all the leftovers. I went to grab a Pepsi; the only cola she and I liked, when I saw next to it two cans of ginger ale. Those were hers. I wasn't going to drink them. They would be there for her when she got better.

It was this day, her second full day home that I learned that the smell of food cooking made her sick to her stomach. I'd cooked up some Kielbasa sausage using a touch of olive oil to fry it in a skillet. Before long she called down from our bedroom asking that I close our door so the smell didn't come in. It hadn't occurred to me that the smell might have been either enticing or revolting to her. Sometimes I guess I just don't think. I ended up eating alone watching some news program. I hated eating alone.

When Thursday the 27th rolled around, though her birthday was the next day, I found I couldn't wait any longer to give her the husband pillow. She absolutely loved it and put it to use right away. It wasn't her favorite color (blue), but rather a medium tan. I figured it would go with any surrounding…like that mattered. When I mentioned I should've bought a different color she told me she loved the one I'd got. Now of course this meant I'd have nothing to give her the next day, her real birthday.

Later that day I took her to her radiation treatment at the hospital. I smartened up after that first time we went as an outpatient. Now we exclusively used their valet parking option. The first day I'd dropped her off out front, placed her in a wheelchair then parked in their big garage. It took me ten minutes to get back to her, and just as long on the way out. They had told us there was parking in the back for cancer patients like her that came for treatment but the lot was full. It wasn't just cancer patient cars that filled it up either, for I saw several folks walk out of the main hospital to retrieve their car from that small lot. It worked on a pass key basis—if you knew the 4-digit code, you just drove in. Seems folks had figured they could save money, as it was free compared to using the hospital's four-storied garage. It's rather obvious what had happened; it doesn't take a genius to remember the code, no less share it with friends. These treatments generally took us less than thirty minutes so we spent more time in route than at the hospital. But this was just fine by Ginny. She liked getting out of bed and out of the house. Today she'd completed the seventh of ten treatments on her brain tumor.

Ginny's sister Carol had been to see her both in the hospital and since coming back home. Carol commented that her sister-in-law, Pam, wanted to come see Ginny, as she was practiced in an unusual type of healing therapy known as Reiki. Ginny thought it sounded intriguing and liked Pam a lot, so they'd arranged for Pam to come on Thursday. Pam's only precondition for the visit was that she not be paid; she wanted to do this as a friend. It was a nice visit. Ginny lay on the couch in the living room as Pam did her thing; I left them alone. I frankly didn't know or care to know anything about Reiki therapeutic healing. All I wanted was for Ginny to have a little time to talk with Pam, as they'd always hit it off. The hands-on healing that is purported certainly wouldn't hurt Ginny and psychologically would help, at least in terms of the calming effect.

It was either the 27th or 28th when we went in for the treatment that the nurse in radiology took a close look at Ginny's dressing. Even though I'd changed it earlier that day, the nurse changed it again. She commented that it looked good and that she could see I was cleaning around the valve too. She asked Ginny how she was doing. Ginny's reply I'm sure the nurse had heard a million times…Ginny was so easily tired and would get nausea several times a day. These both were side effects from radiation. The only concern I voiced was that the liquid Ginny would cough up at times had some pink in it. The pink tinge we thought was due to the fact that her liquid pain med was colored red. I was concerned she had or easily could get pneumonia. The nurse agreed the concern was well-founded, as Ginny may have aspirated some of the food or liquid she was being fed before she'd been admitted to the hospital. But the cough hadn't gotten worse. It wasn't like a cough from a cold, but as if phlegm had built up in her throat which she had to get out. Overall, she got as clean a bill of health a person with cancer can get.

On her birthday one thing she asked me for, I knew I could provide…a shower. Ginny knew she'd be receiving visitors over the next day or two so she wanted to take a shower; not a sponge bath with a separate hair washing. The nurse had explained to us how this could be done without getting her wound too wet. The problem as I saw it was she hadn't the strength to stand up that long, as we learned the prior week. Unlike our big shower in New Jersey, the one here was too small for two to take a shower at one time. No matter, I knew what we could do.

One of our outdoor plastic chairs snugly fit into the shower but with enough room to enable Ginny to sit while holding a plastic covered "pillow" over her abdomen. I squeezed in beside the chair to act as her set of hands to wash her and her hair. More than once I inadvertently knocked open the shower door, sending spray into the bathroom, but our set-up this day had worked. She got "all pretty and clean"; an old phrase I hadn't heard her say in years. As I dried her hair, some of it just fell out…not clumps, but enough that she noticed. I saw she began to tear up so I started to joke around about this being a very special service that I only offered to my most prized clientele. You see, Ginny would tell others at times that she would have to see her hairdresser ("James"). As I finished up drying and brushing her hair I kissed her on her head, then on her lips as she sat upon the small stool I'd set up in the bathroom. As she gazed up at me she had such a forlorn look. I said "I love you, mine"…and she smiled.

After her shower as I got her situated in the bed, she brought up a matter that I'd rather she hadn't. I'd joked a bit earlier about me being good since I hadn't bought her a piece of jewelry for her birthday. Upon hearing that, she said, "I've been thinking—I want us to go through all my jewelry to set aside a piece for family members and my closest friends. Something they can remember me by." This caught me totally off guard. Here it was her birthday and she was talking about giving away her jewelry—about dying. I didn't initially acknowledge what she'd said until she said "Did you hear me?" I told her I'd heard her but asked her why she would bring up such a thing. "I want to go through all my jewelry with you and pick out pieces for each person." She then cited some examples, indicating both the specific piece and the person. She began to list each person whom she wanted me to gift a remembrance. I got a piece of paper and wrote them all down. Though I'd marked down the examples she'd noted, I told her I didn't want to do it today—not on her birthday. She looked at me from the bed, agreed there was no rush to do this, but made it clear what she wanted done.

"You know my tastes in jewelry may not be the same as others, but you've given me so many beautiful pieces I just know I have something for every person on my list." She then noted two more examples tied to her sister Carol and her niece Kaity. The topic was closed, for this day at least. I hated the implications and I can't be more vehement about it…hate, despise, loath, detest…you get the point. I would never bring this up again, but I knew she would.

The remainder of the day just sort of passed without any ordeal or event. I so wished the weather would warm up a bit, as I wanted to get her a wheelchair so I could take her on walks until her strength returned—initially around our cul-de-sac but eventually around the near-by park.

Michael, Connie, and Molly did come that weekend of her birthday. Though they did not comment to me, I could see the alarm in their eyes. Ginny had changed a lot since they'd seen her last July. Yet just like the other visits from friends and family, this too was good for Ginny. They stayed at my parents' place, though there was plenty of room in our new home. They all understood that Ginny simply wasn't up for any extended visitors. That birthday weekend also brought a visit from some other long-time friends, Paul (best man at our wedding) and Ron, both dear old friends. As with others, I could see deep concern in their eyes upon seeing Ginny's frail condition. I didn't talk much during any of these visits. I wanted to give Ginny all the time with friends and family she could take without tiring her out. Deep down I was scared—frightened at what lay ahead. I had kept a stiff upper lip to this point, had been Ginny's "rock," as it were, but I didn't know how much longer I could do this without the façade cracking open to reveal my fears. As odd and illogical as it may sound, I remained very much in denial. I couldn't bear even the thought of losing her…it was absolutely unthinkable.

The day after her birthday one of those memorable moments in life happened. I'd just finished giving her a late afternoon feeding. I'd gone back into our bathroom to get something. When I came back out a moment later, I looked up at Ginny as she sat in the bed; she was crying. I asked her what was wrong…was she in pain? She said to me, "I don't know how to tell you this, but I don't think I'm going to be able to give you the 60th birthday party I'd promised." Initially I didn't know what to say, so I just walked over to her and took her in my arms. After about a minute I said, "Don't worry about such things; just know you will always be with me…always."

I was a tough-minded caregiver. I insisted Ginny consume at least four infusions of food a day, five was being pushed too. Yet it seemed no matter how much nutrition I pumped in, she wasn't gaining any weight and she seemed to actually be getting weaker.

On Monday the 31st on our way home from her treatment Ginny reached over and turned down the volume of a tune I was playing on XM radio. She said to me, "I need to ask you something." "Hey, I was listening to that song" was my reply. She then switched the radio off. "I need you to promise me that if things don't work out as we hope you will continue on." This was not something I wanted to hear so my reply was simply, "There's no need to talk like that; you're going to get better." But she persisted. "You need to promise me you will continue." I began to lose it. I didn't want to talk about this because we were going to beat this. She looked at me and said nothing. "Okay" I said, "I promise…but you're going to get better."

The rest of the way home the radio was off and there was only silence in the car. She had said what she needed to say to me. I just could not "go there." Even the thought of losing her so terrified me. We had so much more to do together. All the trips I'd said we'd make when I retired. All the meals I told her I would cook for her since she too was entitled to "retire." I didn't look at her that rest of the way home; I didn't want her to see that I was crying.

We got back home around noon. I needed to give her another round of meds and feeding because that day we'd try to reach the 1,800-calorie intake. The earlier topic was not mentioned again, but it was on my mind—hers too, no doubt. Though the nurse in the Oncology group had told me it wasn't unusual to get some "leaking" around the valve on her stomach, I was still concerned. The day before, Ginny and I noticed that same pink liquid around the valve. It had leaked into the dressing right after I'd given her a feeding and her pain meds. The liquid Codeine was red in color, perhaps to convey that it was cherry flavored (not that she could taste it). But suppose it wasn't that, suppose it was blood? All I could figure is that perhaps her digestive system couldn't take the amount of liquid I was giving her so some leaked out. I was very careful whenever I fed her, making sure never to infuse the food too quickly as I didn't want to upset anything. Still, we'd seen this leakage again and her spittle at times was also tinged with pink.

I don't recall if anyone had come to see her that afternoon. I do recall she told me she wanted to lie down and rest in bed. I'd hoped she could come out into the living room instead. She rested comfortably the next two to three hours, though she never did get to sleep. I didn't end up going in to lie beside her; I felt I'd disturb her rest. Instead I relegated myself to the living room with Jesse, opting to read the current fiction book I'd borrowed from the library. I went in to see her again when it was time for her to eat. She told me she just wanted to rest but I sort of pushed her to take a feeding. Like I'd noted before, I knew she needed the calories if she was to regain any strength. She relented fairly quickly, though I think she did so purely to satisfy me. After her feeding, she asked if I'd come in to just lie aside her—just to be with her. I said I would be in right after I took care of few things. The truth is I never did end up going in to lay with her that day. I really wanted to, but something came up…a phone call or something ended up distracting me. There are times when opportunity will knock softly. If we fail to answer the call it will come back to us in the form of regret. You'd think by now I would have understood this harsh reality.

Tuesday April 1st marked the final radiation treatment for her brain tumor. Afterwards we met with the radiation oncologist to talk about "next steps." Ginny had regained almost full use of her left hand by that point, so I knew the treatments had had some positive effects. At the same time we both knew that the next series of treatments, for the tumors in her chest, would no doubt continue her feeling of nausea and weakness she'd had those last two weeks. But we had no choice; it was something we knew we just had to do.

It didn't really register at the time, but when the oncologist said we'd wait a couple of weeks to allow her to regain a little strength, I pushed back. I told her that time was not in our favor so we only wanted to wait one week before beginning the next series…that would be April 8th. The doctor agreed, but I got the sense she was doing so just to placate me. In retrospect, I felt she knew some things she wasn't sharing with us. While she had never misled us, she also wasn't as forthcoming as I felt she should have been. This is not a matter of fact or something I could prove, simply a feeling. I'm sure doctors wrestle with the balance between medical efficacy and empathy all the time. We are all human. If we allow ourselves to get too close to any given situation we run the risk of not only losing our objectivity but of becoming emotional wrecks. There isn't an easy answer for doctors and other medical professionals. All I know is that from my perspective finding the right balance to professionalism and empathy is critical. Some patients might say they don't want to know the truth, but I'm not one of those. Hearing things we don't want to hear is the only way we have any hope of limiting the scars of regret.

Before we left the cancer center that day they asked us if we wanted to take the "helmet" that Ginny had to wear during each treatment. Ginny said she wanted it, which surprised me. Upon seeing it, I understood why she had hated the treatments. The darn thing covered her entire head, leaving her literally in the dark. As we drove home I asked her why she wanted the dumb helmet. She told me because she had been so frightened to do this, but she had done it. "I did it for us, for the Punkins" is what she said as I drove home. She added, "I never could have done it without you and all the help and support you'd given me. I never felt alone. In the dark during the treatments I would think of you to remind myself that I could do it—we could do it. Just like you'd written to me in that letter you gave me in the hospital." Ginny made me feel very special, for I had long known I had a wonderful wife. She loved me so much she had done this for me, subjecting herself to the nightmare of those treatments.

I wasn't going to miss those almost daily trips to the hospital. They seemed to drain Ginny. Soon after we got home that day, she fell asleep. I think the stress was released from her in part because at least this first step was now done. She ended up taking two more feedings later on that day. I'd wanted to get in a full five, but it wasn't in the cards that day. Early that night as I slept, something very special took place but I wouldn't know about it until the next night.

April 2nd began in a fine fashion. That morning Ginny had taken her first two feedings with no issue whatsoever. She had a touch of pain late morning but it coincided with her normal 5 ml Codeine dose so it quickly faded. Her script cited a dosage that could be given every six hours. A time or two I'd cheat that a bit, but not by much. All seemed to be going well. We had no appointment to keep that day, no need to get her dressed and head over for treatment. But then things changed.

At about 1:30 PM she called me into the bedroom. She said she had a terrible stabbing pain that went from her right side shoulder blade to her chest. I looked at the clock…she'd had her pain meds just a couple of hours ago, wasn't due for more until about 5:00 PM. I could see she was in severe pain…I gently rubbed her back but it persisted. I started to get mad and began to vent. "This is bullshit, how am I supposed to take care of you when my hands feel tied…what am I supposed to do, give you more meds?"

I placed a call to the cancer center to speak to a doctor or nurse. The person who answered told me the only thing she could recommend is for me to bring Ginny in to the ED (emergency room). The thought of doing so struck me as utterly futile and one that would have her just sitting around for who knows how long before someone came to see her. My response to the nurse was simply, "I would sooner take a set of pliers and pull out every one of my teeth than bring her back to wait in emergency." I think my reply sort of shocked the nurse, as it grew quiet on the line. Then she said, "Alternatively, you could take her to her PCP." I told her that is what I would do and then thanked her…but I did not apologize for my vehement reaction to her initial suggestion. The next minute I was on the phone with her PCP's office…the doctor would see her right away.

We got to the nearby office straight away; it was 2:25 PM. She needed the walker to get around, yet did not have the strength to get up from the waiting room chair. It was then I saw one of the fellows I'd been working with from the tax preparation group. I acknowledged him but didn't get into any conversation. The look on his face was either pity or empathy—I couldn't tell. I'd been absent from the work since March 12th. They all knew Ginny had been hospitalized yet only now had anyone other than family, friends, or doctors seen her.

I helped Ginny to her feet and we made our way into the examining room area. The look of deep concern was evident on Wendy's face. It had only been a couple of months since she'd first seen either of us. The weigh-in was evidence that we were losing the battle; she was down to 100 pounds.

When her PCP came in, he too had the look of concern. Yet right away he told us he'd prescribe a stronger pain-killer; Hydrocodone. It was clear this had moved into the palliative care stage. At the time, I didn't know what that word meant. The office called in the script. I picked it up on the way home and administered it to her right away. The stabbing pain relented.

I felt so powerless. All I could do was watch this damn disease literally consume her in front of my very eyes. Nothing we did seemed to even slow the progression as the cancer decimated her. Yet Ginny and I weren't giving up. You can't get a hit if you don't swing, so swing is what we did.

That afternoon there was no repeat of a pain episode. The new pain meds were used twice more that day. The label noted, "Take as needed." As she convalesced the rest of the day, she only managed one more tube feeding as opposed to the two we'd planned.

We went to bed early that night, before 9:00 PM. As had been our recent routine, I read as she laid aside me with Jesse between the two of us. Ginny's right hand rested on Jesse's little rump, I placed my hand atop hers, turned and said, "I love you, mine." Ginny smiled and said to me, "Last night you fell asleep reading your book. Before I woke you to turn off the lamp, I noticed your hand was on Jesse so I placed my hand on yours and said those very same words you just did. I know you love me and I love you too."

It was in the wee hours I awoke as she touched my arm. She had to go to use the bathroom. It had reached the point I had to support her every step, no longer just there in case. Our reality was becoming ever more obvious.

On April 3rd Ginny had asked to use the phone. She seemed more rested than usual, which seemed like a good sign, but I said nothing of the sort. By noon she'd already had two feedings with another planned for 3:00 PM. Just as we'd done every day, sometimes twice, I changed the dressing surrounding the stomach tube. It was in good shape, which was heartening.

After one of her phone calls Ginny called me into the bedroom. I noticed her eyes were brighter than they'd been in days. She stated, "You're going out tomorrow for dinner and a couple of beers with Gary." Right away I told her no. I wasn't going out to leave her here alone. "But I won't be alone, Jan is coming to stay with me and chat." Still I told her no. "Too bad, it's all arranged; they will be here at five o'clock this Friday." I still protested, but to no avail. Even in her current state, I've learned over the years not to get into an argument I can't win. Ginny was absolutely adamant. "Yesterday I saw how mad you got when I was in pain—you need a break." I replied, "I wasn't mad at you, I was mad at the fact I couldn't help you, I couldn't make it go away." She replied,

"I know you weren't upset at me, but you need to take a break…it will help you in the days ahead. So please just do this for me."

Ginny noted that I hadn't left her side but twice since she got home from the hospital, and then only briefly even though Jason and Sam had been there both times. "You need to get out so that you regain some sense of perspective. There is only so much you can do…like it or not, you must accept that." Like I said, I've learned not to argue with her, especially when she's right; which as in the past is most of the time.

Mid-afternoon after her second feeding, I was cleaning up the various syringes and containers we use. As I put them back on the side table next to the bed Ginny said to me "I was wondering…have you thought about what you will do if things don't work out as we planned, where do you plan to live? Here?" Truth be told, I hadn't given any thought to it and was completely avoiding what it implied. Was I in denial? You bet I was. Not only had I not considered what might happen, I refused to consider it. As noted, our story included growing old together and doing all sorts of things we'd been planning. I couldn't comprehend even the thought of such.

I turned to Ginny, having considered what she'd asked and replied "I don't know, but this place is too big for just one person, I'd probably not remain here." I will never forget her reaction and reply. She said, "Oh, but I love this house." To which I replied, "Then I'll live here, I will never sell it." At that she gave me one of her beautiful smiles.

A bit later that afternoon I called my mom to ask her if she could stop over the next morning so that I could run some errands. My mom said she would, might bring my dad too. My dad's health had been on the decline for some time, but he wasn't bed-ridden or anything like that.

April 4th arrived in bright splendor compared to the recent weather. Though it was spring on the calendar, we'd yet to have any really nice days. But on that day, the sun was shining and the temperature was due to go into the upper 40s. It was a perfect setting for one of the errands, which was to go borrow a wheelchair. Then I could take Ginny on walks; something she too was looking forward to. I so wanted to take her outside for some fresh air.

My parents got to our place around 10:00 AM, pretty much right on time. I told them I needed to be gone a couple of hours, no more. I gave Ginny a kiss, told her I'd be back, and told Jesse to be a good girl.

I wasn't familiar with the place that loaned out wheelchairs and similar support equipment, but got a good idea of where it was from my brother-in-law, Bill. I hadn't told Ginny where I was going, for I wanted to surprise her. I needed a few things off the grocery list too, but my main goal was to get the wheelchair.

I found the place with no problem. It was staffed by a single volunteer that morning. The woman and I spoke for a bit. She gave me a brief history of how they came to serve the role of sourcing home health-care-related equipment. They had all sorts of stuff, but all I wanted was a "good" wheelchair. I didn't want some beat-up piece of junk. She found one exactly like what I was looking for. I was thrilled and couldn't wait to tell Ginny about it and show her.

As I drove towards my other planned stops, I decided instead to go home. I wanted to show Ginny the chair and I really didn't like the idea of not being there if she needed me. It was just after eleven o'clock that I returned, which sort of surprised my mom. After getting the chair out of the trunk, I went in to receive my usual warm greeting from Jesse. I saw my dad in the living room sitting on the couch watching a little television, so was my mom. Before going to see my wife I asked my mom how Ginny was doing. My mom seemed a bit distracted and replied, "Oh, she's fine...your father however, has had problems trying to find something worth watching." I then walked down to our bedroom to check on Ginny.

I went in to find Ginny sitting up in bed with an odd expression on her face. I asked how her visit with my parents went, to which she told me that my mom had been in only once to check on her—they hadn't really talked. I found that odd because my mom had been a little put out with me when I'd told her that I didn't want anyone visiting Ginny while she was in the hospital. Hearing what Ginny had just told me I walked back to the living room to suggest that my mom visit with Ginny while I could help my dad find something he wanted to watch. Over the next twenty minutes or so they visited and I stayed with my dad. He seemed antsy to get going home. I don't think he'd eaten any breakfast yet. He tends to keep unusual hours, often staying up most of the night watching television, only to fall asleep sometime before dawn when most of us are just getting up. I'll just say that like Ginny, my mom was endowed with a great deal of patience, which was a good thing given my dad's proclivities and quirks. They left shortly afterwards.

I fed Ginny right after they left; including giving her some pain meds as she mentioned her chest was bothering her a bit. As I fed her I told her what I'd brought home. She smiled, noting that she'd need it, as she just didn't have the strength to walk very far even with the walker. Ginny seemed tired so I suggested she rest for a bit. I had some stuff I wanted to do around the house but would be there in a flash if she needed me. She fell asleep almost right away. It made me smile to see her so peaceful. In recent days she'd often sleep sort of half-sitting up, as the congestion in her chest made it uncomfortable for her to lay flat.

A couple hours later, I heard her stirring. I walked in greeting her, "Hey there sleepy head, it's about time for some more food…got to make up for yesterday's short rations." She just smiled then told me she'd rather wait a bit. It wasn't until about three o'clock that we got her third feeding complete. I looked at her—my goodness, she was so frail. Even just going to the bathroom was a real effort, no matter how much I helped her. So far the severe pains that had so affected her two days before had not returned. I was thankful for that, as I hated to see her in pain. I left to clean up the feeding paraphernalia, and then went into the computer room to check the news and play a couple of games.

It was just after 3:30 PM when I heard her call my name, "Jimmy"; just the one word. Something was wrong, so I jumped up and ran to the bedroom only a few feet away. She was bent over on the bed coughing. Unlike past times I could see she was having a hard time. I put my arms around her back as she struggled to expel the mucus. As I watched pink fluid started to come out. It seemed she'd broken whatever blockage there was; but it didn't stop. The fluid turned from pink to red and it kept coming. She was struggling to catch her breath. She looked up as I sat aside her, my arms still around her, holding her. Her eyes were filled with terror—a look I'd never seen before. I told her, "It's alright, I'm right here…you'll be okay…take your time." Blood began to pour from her mouth. Her eyes met mine; she could not talk, she could not breathe. Reality struck—I was losing her. Her head dropped forward then rolled to the side. I called out "Ginny, Ginny!" I remember crying out to God for help, but I knew she'd left me. I grabbed the phone and called 911.

Within minutes a small army of help sounded their way to our house… fire trucks, rescue squad, police cars, and at least two ambulances. The 911 operator had asked me to try to give her mouth-to-mouth; I'd been trained years ago. To do so, I had to lay her on the floor of our room, which I did. But when I tipped her head back, blood pooled in her mouth. I knew before the first person came through the front door that she had passed away. She had died in my arms.

For the longest time they worked on her, trying to resuscitate her, to bring her back; but to no avail. One of the seasoned paramedics spoke to me afterwards to tell me that even if she had been in the hospital, no one could have saved her. It appeared that a blood vessel had broken, likely in her right lung. There was no open pathway for her to take in air. The action caused her to aspirate blood into her lungs instead of air. There was nothing that I could have done to prevent it...nothing anyone could have done.

Ginny's sister Carol came with her husband Bill. Bill was a senior officer with the local volunteer fire department. Bill had received word over his emergency pager, heard the house address, and just knew. He'd called Carol, so they both got there shortly after the arrival of all the emergency personnel. I cannot put into words what was going through my mind, body, and soul. I sort of went into shock; best that I can describe it. All I know is that the most important person in my entire world had passed and with her, the life we had together. My world had ended...I lost the love of my life, my darling wife Ginny.

I will close this portion of my writing to say that at 5:00 PM Gary and Jan came to our house. I only then recalled that he was going to take me out to eat while she would spend some time with her dear friend Ginny. I'd completely forgotten all about it. I did call some folks that Friday but I don't know who, aside from our son Jason and my mom. I just don't remember.

Part III

Unlike the two previous parts, this part takes place in the present. It has now been over eighteen months since Ginny passed. To me it seems like a very long time, yet it is not. How this part ends is unknown, however how it began and the direction it is taking is critical to the outcome and in order to understand the path I've chosen.

The tragic loss of a beloved spouse will elicit the full range of emotions. Some of these persist while others tend to fade. I will try to give you this understanding the only way I can, which is from my biased perspective. How I did cope and to the extent I am coping with the realization of my new life is of course debatable.

The grieving process, while common to anyone who has suffered a great personal loss, is also uniquely driven by the nature of the relationship that existed. No two people are the same and as I will mention below, the grieving process itself is not linear. Despite what you may have heard or read there is no definitive end that you might place upon the calendar. At least for me each step along the way is not really ever completed; it is revisited multiple times before a sense of closure begins to take root.

Parting Gift

Those first few hours, even days, remain a blur. What I recall so vividly is that I was able to endure primarily due to the help and support from my family. My sister-in-law Carol and her husband Bill were my lifeline during those initial days and weeks. There are no words that can ever convey the depth of my appreciation for their having stepped forward at that critical time.

I know I had to make some immediate decisions tied to matters of funeral arrangements. Though Ginny and I had not been active church members for a number of years, we both maintained a belief in God and of the promise of an everlasting life. There would be no church services; however memorial services would be held, along with a separate celebration of her life.

I remember the funeral director asking whom I had chosen to give the eulogy. When I informed him that I would be saying a few words along with a couple of others, he noted it was not customary for a husband to give the eulogy. He indicated that a spouse is prone to breakdown given the emotional stresses that speaking to a group entails, so he recommended I reconsider my role. Yet I insisted the eulogy was something I would do. I know no one but I was capable of doing what needed to be done. It wasn't either pride or arrogance speaking, just the reality of the lives we two had shared. There would be no "showing," as her remains would be cremated, though her urn would be there. In addition, I wanted to have specific music, favorite songs of hers and mine, as well as a continuous loop of pictures of her over the years.

There was nothing more important to me than making her memorial services a success; something she would like. In a very real sense it gave me the opportunity to give her a final gift. I identified the specific songs that would be used as background music while Carol found each, which we then put onto a CD. The pictures were largely sourced from the vast archive that Ginny and I had gathered over our nearly forty years together. They were supplemented by a few pictures obtained from other family members and friends. All told, there were 163 pictures; each capturing precious moments in her life, and our life together.

Her memorial was set to take place one week after her passing. The eulogy was a daunting task in that I wanted to convey a brief story of this wonderful woman who was the most important and influential person in my life. I spent hours upon hours on this effort. After two or three days working on it, I made a change. I removed most of the anecdotal references in favor of trying to provide insight into the nature and character of my darling wife. I knew how difficult it would be for me to maintain composure. To overcome the risk of breaking down, I had to find the resolve to at least temporarily set aside my grief. By late in the day on Wednesday, April 5th, the eulogy was complete. I began reading it over and over, initially to myself then aloud. It was the only way I felt I could muster the control to get through it. I'd end up reading it no fewer than fifty times.

The following is the end result of the week's efforts excluding the pictures. I'd actually chosen more songs but was restricted to these twenty-three given memory limitation on the CD.

The Eulogy
"To My Punkin, Love Jimmy"

These are the words engraved upon the very first piece of jewelry I gave to Ginny. She wore that gold medallion for years…always said it was her most precious piece. If you look closely, you will see it in a number of the pictures here today. Earlier this week I was in a panic, as I did not know where the necklace was. I did find it; I had to know it was still here with me.

I want to thank each of you for coming here today to pay your respects to my beloved wife, your sister, friend, mom, aunt. I hope to see most of you at the "Irish wake" tomorrow. Ginny specifically asked that I hold a celebration of her life and not grieve too long.

So many of you have kept her in your prayers; she felt that, and told me just how special it made her feel. Please continue to pray for her, though I am convinced that she is already in heaven.

I want to take just a bit of your time this evening to share some closing thoughts on the woman who has been such a large part of our lives. I ask that you indulge me. Eulogies are seldom surprising or informative, but I expect you may learn some things from my talk that none of you knew before.

This week as I was preparing this, I had plans to share with you two anecdotes, stories of our life involving both how we met and how I proposed. But ask me about these tomorrow, for this evening I need to take this time to set the record straight on some aspects of our life.

Ginny never wanted to be the center of attention, matter of fact she hated it. I've known this since the day we met. Just weeks before our wedding in December 1977 she was so nervous about being the focal point on her "big day" that she asked if maybe we could elope instead. I told her not to worry and that I would be with her every step of the way. Well today, she is singularly the center of attention. However unlike then, these recent days have been filled with sadness rather than the promise of our future.

Ginny was rather introverted unless you took the time to get to know her. If you did, she would open up her heart and her mind in an effort to help her better relate to you. She was a great listener. To some of my guy friends, she became like "one of the boys" in the things we'd do together. It didn't bother her to be the only girl at times, as long as she was with me. I recall a trip to Toronto that was just such a time. Paul, Michael, Ginny, and I had a great time…for me she was THE reason that after all these years, the trip was so memorable.

In the 70s when we met, society was changing. Women were taking on career aspirations in ever-increasing numbers. However, she held no such interest. She told me then she had always "just" wanted to be a devoted wife, mother, and homemaker. Some folks looked down on her for that, but then that was both their mistake and their loss.

Going back to how we met, she always seemed to feel that if she and I were to marry, that she—not I—would be getting the better part of the bargain. Let me make it clear about her misconception. As a couple we were well-matched, balanced as it were…hand in glove. Attributes and abilities that I possessed helped me become a fairly successful businessman, BUT success in our marriage and our life was rooted in HER abilities and attributes. Ginny's unwavering love, depth of understanding, kindness, insight, and determination was what mattered. As it may not have been obvious to many of you, **she**, not I, played the pivotal role. She has been <u>my rock</u>, my very foundation for nearly forty years.

Those that knew her well knew that she possessed the very essence of humility, dedication, caring, and acceptance. Unlike me, she was not quick to judge others. Yet a person like her could easily be hurt as she often wore her heart on her sleeve. I always knew when I messed up in our relationship. When I did, her initial reaction was often to become quiet, but sometimes when I really nutzup, then her Irish temper would surface. Over time I understood that her temper acted as a mask, a shield to protect her injured feelings. Unfortunately she married a slow learner.

Ginny inherited a trait from her mom I must tell you about. I call it "the look." Anyone who knew her well will know what I'm talking about. "The look" can best be described as follows…she'd tilt her head to the right, her left eyebrow would rise up in a point, and then her face would take on an almost "I dare you to continue" look. It's hard to describe, but many of you have seen it. Oh how I miss seeing that look.

Over the years, Ginny's counsel had been sought out by many of you. She was especially good at "affairs of the heart." Ginny was always one to put others ahead of her own needs. Unlike a lot of folks she hated spending money on herself. I smile when I think of one long running joke we shared. I would tell her at times that she needed to see her hairdresser for a trim or perhaps styling of her beautiful long hair. You see, for most our life, I was her personal hairdresser. She would say, "I need to make an appointment with 'James.'" Over the years I've relished being her go-to guy for trimming, coloring, conditioning, and brushing. She so loved to have her hair brushed, just ask our son Jason, for she loved it when it was brushed for fifteen minutes or more.

Ginny & I were married over thirty-six years…like most married couples we had our share of tough times, but the good times far out-numbered those. I truly admired her many virtues. I just wish I'd told her that aloud more often. It seemed at times that she had unlimited patience…another quality I sorely lack. She complemented me and my many frailties…and she said I did the same for her, though she really had darn few weaknesses. In our married life she did not get the credit she so richly deserved. From the outside, to many it appeared she had an easy life. I mean really, how tough is it being "just a homemaker." Well, what most did not see is that it was Ginny that made us a suc-cessful couple. Sure I was extroverted, quick-witted, "book smart," and most often loud as well as verbose…these traits often made me the center of attention. Yet my success, our success as a couple, was almost singularly due to Ginny. She made us who we were…she was by far my better half. Without her, I am so lost it is nearly indescribable.

I want to leave each of you with a message of hope, but mine is also a cautionary tale. Don't ever think you or your plans make a whit worth of difference in the big picture of life…because they don't. Like the fifty-year-old Beatles song said, "All you need is love." Everything else pales in comparison. Each and every day we should tell those we care about how much they mean to us; setting aside the petty differences that so often come into our personal lives. Today before your head hits the pillow tell that special someone you love them—hug them, and keep them in your heart. Act as if today is your last day to be together. I promise if you do this, you will never regret it.

Both Ginny and I believe in God, though we have not been active churchgoers in recent years. We believe in being the best person we can be. In sharing with others who have less, of being a source of love, compassion, and kindness to all, and that we should strive to make this world a better place by our presence. Perhaps most importantly, we believe in the power of love, the single unifying force that binds our world. This past weekend I spoke to a long-time family friend/ priest. I told him that I absolutely NEED to believe that Ginny is now with God, with our Lord Jesus Christ. How can I not believe this, for it is my sole consolation given her passing? Ginny is now with her dear parents and other members of her family who are no longer with us in this world. I can picture her playing with Schatze as I play with her dear pet Jesse. Jesse so misses Ginny too. I have lost my soul mate, Jason has lost his mom, Carol and most of my extended family has lost a dear sister…and many of you have lost a lifetime friend. In our grief let us remember her as she was before this illness took her from us. She was always so vivacious, so full of life and love. The many pictures we've displayed today are evidence of that fact. Working on that picture project and the favorite songs selection, together with her sister Carol, has given me purpose and focus this past week. I want Ginny to be proud of this, my final gift to her. I wanted her to know once again that she could count on me.

If I stop and consider it all, I do believe she knew how much I loved her, even though our parting was cut short. I don't know how I can live my life without her…but I promised her that I would continue. We were married for 13,258 days…oh, what I wouldn't give for just one more day together so that I could say goodbye to the love of my life. There is nothing else I can do but go on this journey with her in my heart, though no longer in my arms. I will try to keep going—one day at a time—but my heart is broken, for the one person who made my life complete has been taken away. I love you, mine…then, now, and always, I will be your Punkin.

Memorial Services Song List (alpha order as recorded)

Song Title	Artist/Year
100 Years	Five for Fighting 2009
Beach Baby	First Class 1974
Both Sides Now	Judy Collins 1967
Cherish	The Association 1966
Elusive Butterfly	Bob Lind 1966
Everything I Own	David Gates & Bread 1972
For All We Know	Carpenters 1971
I Won't Last a Day Without You	Carpenters 1972
If	David Gates & Bread 1971
Landslide	Fleetwood Mac 1975
Love is in the Air	John Paul Young 1978
Mandy	Barry Manilow 1973
My Cup Runneth Over	Ed Ames 1967
Somewhere in the Night	Barry Manilow 1978
Best of My Love	Eagles 1974
Long & Winding Road	Beatles 1970
The Story of My Life	Neil Diamond 1986
The Sun Ain't Gonna Shine	Walker Brothers 1965
Your Love	Jim Brickman 1999
Weekend in New England	Barry Manilow 1979
When Will I See You Again	Three Degrees 1974
You're My World	Helen Reddy 1977
My Valentine	Jim Brickman 1997

The Aftermath

The memorial was attended by many who've known Ginny and me over the years. They included family and friends as well as some more recent acquaintances. Some were friends I hadn't seen in years. Not sure why this happens in life, but sometimes we lose track of people who once loomed so large in our lives. It was good to see them all; I just wish it had been under different circumstances. Some people made endearing statements, which I so appreciated. Other attendees, although well meaning, made perfunctory declarations that I could have done without: "She's in a better place," or "It was God's will." After the memorial, I felt pretty good; I felt Ginny would have been pleased. I went out to dinner with Carol and Bill. For that moment at least, I felt a sense of peace.

The "Irish wake" was set to occur the next day at the Reunion, the tavern where Ginny and I had met so long ago. Many of the same folks who'd attended the memorial came to the wake. The time flew by, or so it seemed. As the wake drew to a close I became anxious, as it signaled an end; one I was not prepared to handle.

Over the coming days and weeks I struggled to come to terms with what had occurred. In a very real sense I'd begun a journey of self-discovery that few of us ever consider. I found it increasingly difficult to cope with any facet of life. In part because I wasn't living, just existing. My life seemed surreal.

There is nothing more important at such a time than support from others. While some of them had suffered the loss of a parent, fortunately none of my long-term friends has suffered the loss of their spouse. I found I had to fight the desire to simply curl up and die. I wanted to be left alone, yet I knew that isolating myself was not the right thing to do. Both a brother and a sister urged me to find a support group to help me through this period. This I knew was the right move, though I learned there are very few such resources. Yet I did find some help from support groups. However, before I share those experiences I want to comment on the overall topic of "support."

Support to a grieving individual can take several forms, including financial, emotional, and spiritual. I will address only emotional support within this context. In an effort to support those grieving, sometimes people say things they should not. What a person in grief needs most from family and friends is to be heard; to know they can talk about their feelings without being told by others what they should do and/ or how they should feel. The single most beneficial support you can extend is simply to listen, even if at some point the person begins to weep. Tears are not a sign of weakness but an overt expression of how deeply a person has been affected. Expressing support by letting the griever know that you won't tell anyone they'd wept is just stupid. So what if they cry...let them. A general guide I'd suggest is simply this; if you don't know what to say; then say nothing. Trite or thoughtless statements are not helpful.

Based on my own experience and comments from others who've suffered a similar loss, I can say that our society as a whole is often clueless when it comes to how best to provide grief support. I can't tell you how often I was told by others to "call if you need anything." But a person in the throes of grief is highly unlikely to reach out, at least initially. Putting the onus of contact upon the grieving person is not the way to support them. Trust me when I tell you that a person in grief will need both "space" and "contact." In the end, no one but they can transcend grief; being patient with and tolerant of them is key. There is no master timeline that must be adhered to. Avoid telling them you understand, for you cannot unless you too have experienced such a loss. As far as telling them what they should do, that is most often a bad idea. Even if you know of another who has suffered similarly, basing your guidance on what another person found helpful is often not going to fit as circumstances vary greatly. Just be there for them.

My sleeping and eating habits changed. I lost my appetite and found myself going to bed by 9:00 PM and arising in the wee hours. I can't explain it but for me there is comfort in the stillness of those early hours. Most of the world is still asleep when I get up. I continue to read fiction books as a means of distraction; or perhaps escape. The house is all too quiet, its only occupants being me and Jesse.

Every time I would go out I put Jesse in her kennel, her safe place. For the first few months, upon my return she'd give me a warm greeting then run to the door to the garage waiting for Ginny to appear. At times when I witnessed this, I would try to tell her, "Mommy isn't coming home." Quite often this would lead me to tears. Those that say animals are "dumb" clearly don't have one as a favored pet or lack the perception that they too possess an awareness of their environment and seem to exhibit a sense of loss. Jesse did. To this day when I leave the house I tell Jesse, "Daddy loves you, and Mommy loves you too." Ginny used to say this to Jesse every time we'd go out—I so long to hear her say it again.

The grieving process is rather complex, with no two people manifesting the effects in the same manner. Even those who have suffered a similar loss may react quite differently. What I've learned is there is no one solution, no single right way to go about trying to cope and recover.

The support group I joined was comprised of only surviving spouses. In my group I was the most recent widower. When the eight-week program began, it had been less than three months since Ginny's passing.

Some attendees had suffered their loss as long as nine months prior. I found the program helpful, however there was a key element missing, at least from my perspective—the role of faith.

Those first few months included times of intense anger. Initially the anger was aimed at the hospital for not having better prepared my wife and me, for not being more forthcoming in terms of her life expectancy or of the risks; like the sudden and traumatic end she suffered. I did not hold them responsible for her passing but for our lack of understanding. In time, through letters and a meeting I initiated, I was able to put this behind me. I pursued the matter, knowing it could not change what had happened to Ginny but in the hope some policy or protocol changes could help others avoid what we went through. I knew in my heart that it is what Ginny would have wanted me to do.

Another aspect of anger that arose dealt with beliefs and my faith in God. I simply could not understand how He could take such a wonderful person as my wife. It took some time for me to come to terms with this and to make peace with Him. This brings up an aspect that I found absolutely central to my ability to cope; one that had been missing from the support group I'd participated.

If you had asked me a couple of years ago to define myself in religious terms I'd likely have told you I was an agnostic. To be clear, an agnostic is not the same as an atheist. The latter does not believe God exists, while the former sees no evidence to support the existence. In short, I neither believed nor disbelieved in God; I had no faith. This fact no doubt would have been a great disappointment to my parents, as well as my broader family. I'd been raised a Roman Catholic, and had attended parochial schooling throughout my primary and secondary education.

Earlier in our marriage, both my wife and I had been active members of a Catholic parish community. Yet in the late 1990s we became disenchanted with some aspects due to issues in our personal lives and some issues that were plaguing the Church at the time. The mistake we made was in allowing our loss of faith in the Church to become a loss of faith in God. So at the time I most needed it, I found I had no relationship with God. I'd long since stopped praying or actively believing. I know He hadn't answered my fervent pleas to spare her that horrid day. I had begged and pleaded with Him, to no avail.

The organization that sponsored the surviving spouse grief group I attended was secular. This was fundamental to their program which I can understand given they did not want to dissuade or otherwise limit participation. Their program therefore did not touch upon the role of beliefs, of faith.

One aspect of this surviving spouse group that I found quite helpful was that it enabled me to 'tell my story'. After the completion of the eight-week program, I began to attend the follow on program but I no longer wanted to tell my story nor did I want to hear other people's stories. What I needed were tools to enable me to cope. Attendees of such a group proceed through the grieving process at varying paces so while I fully appreciate the need some have to continue to convey and lament their loss; I found hearing such tales only made me feel worse. Yet independent of whatever shortcoming such groups may have, I would highly recommend participating in at least the surviving spouse portion.

At the same time I began attending the secular group therapy, I located a faith- based support group right within what was our old parish. The faith-based group was open to all who'd lost a beloved, be it a spouse, sibling, child, or parent. I only attended a couple of those sessions, as I could not relate to the group. The reasons dealt with such aspects as how recent my loss was compared to others, an age disparity (I was one of the youngest attendees), a gender disparity (I was the only male), and perhaps most important; I lacked a set of core beliefs. I found I had to be able to identify my plight with that of others. Failing that, I just couldn't get what I needed most, even from such a faith-based group. The "fault" did not reside with them but with the fact that my faith was weak. I needed to take steps to change that.

Early in my grieving process I had so many questions I felt needed an answer. I was absolutely lost. I'd fallen into a great abyss. I felt hollow, empty inside. In a very true sense a part of me also died that horrid day. I literally had no will to live—to continue this life—but I'd made her a promise to do just that. There was conflict within me. I was a person drowning in a sea of despair. At the same time it became clear that the only chance to survive was dependent upon me. No one other than me, no matter how thoughtful or well intentioned, could get me out of the place I found myself.

While it pains others to hear it, I would confess my preference was to be gone from this world. My life had become a nightmare to which I could not awake. Existing and living are two very different things. I absolutely knew I had to make some changes or risk the consequences. This began an effort of outside activities geared to others, a return to weekly church services, openness in my communications, and considerable time spent in reflection and introspection. These efforts continue to this very day.

Time has been both my enemy and my ally since Ginny's passing. I did not have to deal with returning to a "normal life" of everyday work. One reality that those who've lost a loved one must face is that family and friends are unable to grasp the extent of the impact such a loss entails. Others can "only imagine" how it feels but they cannot know. Worse, I discovered that family, friends, and our society as a whole, have expectations tied to grief that are largely based upon assumptions, which have little basis in reality. Over the following weeks and months my education in this regard would take me places I'd never have considered.

It is important to understand that grief is neither uniform nor linear. Linear processes can readily be measured to assess progress towards completion. The grieving process simply doesn't fit such a model. Although there are common elements inherent in the process, no two individuals will experience grief in the same way. There is no universal "best way" to approach it, no less endure it. Even among those who have experienced a similar loss, the grieving process can vary significantly. A means of coping—coming to terms with all the implications—is centered upon the nature of the relationship that existed between the deceased and the survivor. As such, self-discovery and awareness are vital towards enabling the process to progress. Perhaps the single best piece of advice I was given lies in the phrase "take it one day at a time."

While there have been a number of books written on the topic of the grieving process, at best they represent a guide. I've read a few of them. Some I found somewhat helpful, others not in the least. Nothing I'd read seemed to fit my exact situation or needs. There is no easy way through it. My approach is not the only one by any means, but it is the one I chose. Even with the well-meaning support of family and friends, grief is a rather solitary journey. No one can do it for you…you must find your own way. I didn't find value in the analysis or forensics of grief contained in a number of books. Further, some of the strong suggestions that I read about I simply rejected. Case in point; one "renowned author" noted that, "a grieving person should stop making any further emotional investment in the deceased." I not only felt this was somewhat heartless but also beyond my ability. I could not just unplug myself from the woman who I've known and loved for nearly forty years. I could not and I would not by choice.

Oddly enough, what helped me included a series of books; some classi-
fied as non-fiction, but most were fiction. The books depicted characters
under similar conditions who were struggling with coming to terms
just like me. For instance, the five books by Richard Paul Evans is a story
of one man's grief journey. The story begins in the book titled *The Walk*.
I strongly recommend it and the other four books in that series.

Because no two people are the same, how we're able to cope is going
to depend upon numerous factors, including our own personalities. I
found an outlet for my thoughts and feelings which best fit my need
was in writing. This included emails to family and friends; some
letters, a personal journal, and something I call "white papers." The
latter involved writing down all my thoughts on a particular topic and
concluded with a particular statement of belief. Perhaps a better term
for these would be "opinion papers," but writing down my thoughts
helped me form what has become a set of core beliefs.

Perhaps it's just my personality but I did not seek "answers" by im-
mersing myself in theological writings. I tend to be a nonconformist
by nature. I generally take issue with the idea of learning simply by
reading what others have written; at least when it comes to non-em-
pirical matters like theology. If we only learned by reading then it begs
the question: What prompted the author of the recommended reading
to distill their own thoughts into a new book?

Who we are is a product of our heredity, our environment, and our
experiences. The amount of the effect of any of these three factors can
be debated but each has an effect that shapes us into the person we are
today. Nothing in my background or my past prepared me for what was
taking place subsequent to the loss of my darling wife. I felt completely

and utterly destroyed; adrift in an endless sea of blackness. As I noted earlier, the idea of death was more appealing than this new reality. I knew I could not do this myself. This led me to conclude I needed both group support and one-on-one support via a qualified grief therapist.

In regard to a grief therapist, I sought an experienced professional who had experienced the loss of a loved one. I felt such was a prerequisite, particularly when I questioned the validity of advice I'd seen in a few books written by "experts" in the field. I needed real world advice and insight, not conjecture or theory-based guidance from a psychologist or psychiatrist. My approach was akin to talking to a chef rather than trying to find the right cookbook. In my life I've found that practical experience most often trumps academic knowledge.

I was fortunate to find just the right person as my grief therapist. If you're one of the many who feel that even the thought of seeing a therapist alarms you, all I can say is you best get over it. Rid yourself of the notion that seeking emotional help brings with it stigma. Seeing a trained professional can make a huge difference in one's ability to cope. It has for me. Yet I'd add this caution. Don't go looking for specific answers and solutions from anyone. In most cases I found that the answers lie within each of us and that there is no one best solution.

Often times in life when something completely new befalls us we may try to figure things out by seeking advice and counsel of family and friends; but this is generally not one of those cases. The old adage of talking to a priest or clergy seems founded in logic, however initially I didn't have a lot of luck. Finding a member of the clergy who was adequately experienced in handling grief was no easy task. In regard to grief support, only those clergy members who have both suffered the loss of a loved one and have some degree of training/experience are likely to be of benefit. In my particular case, I had a tough time finding the right "spiritual" guidance partially because I didn't have a solid relationship with God at the start.

I was surprised to find that given all the death a clergy person indirectly experiences, it seemed to me many lacked the tools and training to help me cope. Simply telling me that my wife was in heaven did nothing to help me deal with all the emotions I was feeling. I operated under the assumption that a "seasoned" priest would be quite familiar with the grieving process; that turned out to be incorrect. I was fortunate though in that I ended up finding two sources. One was a long-term family friend who happens to be a retired priest and the other, a young priest who had himself suffered significant personal loss in his life. Both helped me but in different ways. The young priest was able to empathize and provide solace while the older priest provided the benefit of his experience and overall guidance. The younger priest could draw on personal experience beyond the loss of his parents.

To this day I still speak to Ginny several times a day. I end the day with a goodnight to her and begin the next day with good morning. I don't know if she can hear me but that doesn't matter. I tell her of many things, including how much I love her—she hears that often. While some would argue that you must "let go," must "move on," I don't agree and I will never agree. That is a choice each of us must make. Every day I listen to the music we both so loved. I have all those pictures of her from the memorial CD, plus many older photo albums. I have my computer set to scroll randomly through hundreds of pictures. I have multiple framed pictures of her throughout the house, particularly in my bedroom. These provide me with a sense of comfort and elicit such bittersweet memories.

On a monthly basis I continue to see a grief therapist. Having suffered the loss of a spouse many years ago, she possesses firsthand knowledge that I find essential. I don't know how long I will continue these one-on-one grief therapy sessions. I guess the answer is as long as I feel I find it beneficial. There's no way to simply put a timeline on such.

I remain in contact with a few of the other members of the surviving spouse group I'd attended last year. I find this continued contact beneficial and while I can't speak for them per se; I believe they do too. Their calls, emails, and or meeting with them one to one has helped me and I'm told mine have had the same affect for them. While I did not continue with group therapy, some have and they find it beneficial. This is just another example that there is no one best way to cope. Each must find their own path.

I'm fortunate in that I have no firsthand experience in regard to the loss of a parent. However, Ginny had lost both her parents in our years together; her dad in 1988 and her mom in 2005. She would often tell me how lucky I was to have mine still with us. The truth is that death was something I was largely untouched by for most my life. While this was a blessing, it left me completely unprepared when tragedy struck. In the past I'd met or known many who have lost parents, siblings, a child, and one who'd lost his spouse. All losses have very profound effects upon us. However, the loss of a spouse from a loving long-term relationship gave rise in me the sense of what it means when one uses the phrase "a living hell."

Before I continue further, I want to touch base on a topic that has had a significant effect for me. The topic deals with dreams.

I never put much thought or credence into inferring or imputing specific meaning to dreams. I've already stated I have no particular expertise when it comes to such matters involving psychology or other scientific analysis of human behavior and thinking. At the same time, I don't and won't seek any such advice or professional counsel to try to explain why I dream or what my dreams mean. There are no doubt fairly exhaustive studies that have been done in an attempt to prove or disprove the purpose, value, and perhaps even meaning of dreams. Those things don't matter, for they mean what they mean to me, not what others think or feel they mean.

Shortly after my darling wife passed away I had the first of a number of dreams about her. None of them were nightmares and there was no common thread that tied them together. Each of the dreams holds meaning to me beyond the mere fact I'd had a dream. In a few cases the term "dream" may not be the right one, for either I was not really asleep or I did not see or even hear her speak but I felt a presence of sorts. At this point many of you might discount what I'm about to say or likely believe me foolish or delusional; but I am neither. All I can say is that these dreams, some in full color with sound have had a profound effect upon me. They have affected me in ways I could not have anticipated.

To be quite truthful, if I could program myself to have dreams of her I would do so every night, but I cannot. She is no longer of this world; that's just a fact. Yet I think many make a mistake when they speak of those who have died, who have passed, as being gone. This gets into the realm of a whole other topic, one of spirituality.

I've just used a term in the last paragraph that warrants a bit more explaining; spirituality. Spirituality to me is the idea that there is some aspect of existence that cannot be readily explained using our under-standing of "reality." To me reality is a term we use to describe this physical and sensory world we live in. It is the combination of what we learn from our five senses through the processing of that input. Generally such a reality is provable, or at least draws from empirical methods to explain or deduce an outcome. Spirituality on the other hand is not something that can be readily proved or disproved using the same empirical approach. Spirituality enables us to more readily 'see' meaning and purpose beyond ourselves and the cocoons of life we tend to create. This gets into the age-old conflict that has and always will exist; the debate of science versus faith. Notice I do not use the word religion; from my perspective religion and faith are not the same.

What spirituality, faith, and religion all have in common is that they require us to suspend aspects of logic, reason, and empiricism in order to accept a premise or thought. These require us to believe. What a person does or doesn't believe is affected by many things. Some beliefs, like the existence of ghosts, aliens, God, or any number of things, are so deeply held by some that they define the person's world to a great extent. Beliefs therefore, can and do define what we say is our reality. I will simply close this thought by saying that I think and feel that having beliefs is essential. These are not just a matter of belief or faith in a deity, but also belief or faith in each other. For me, beliefs are essential to relationships.

If you were to ask me to describe my wife using only one word, I could do it. The word that comes to mind reflects what I would say is the rarest of human qualities; grace. Those who knew her well will both under-stand and heartedly agree. While she embodied so many wonderful attributes she was truly exceptional, she is grace personified. So perhaps, just maybe, you will understand the reason for my steadfast love.

Letters to a Priest

The following pages contain excerpts from a selection of forty-two letters that I'd written since the passing of my beloved wife Ginny. My letters were written in response to letters from a long-term family friend who happens to be a priest. These have been edited to retain anonymity of persons and specific organizations. As such they include only those portions that topically fit this writing. "Father" happens to be a Roman Catholic priest. I'd met him when he was newly ordained in 1968; I was still in grammar school. We've not maintained contact in recent years, yet he availed himself to help me during what has been the most difficult time in my life. For that I am and will always be eternally grateful.

Over the first thirteen months "Father" (the priest) and I exchanged letters that contained many topics relating to religion, the Church, beliefs, and relationships. These communications took the form of letters rather than emails or telephone calls. That fact had a significant impact upon my ability to process, digest, and try to come to terms with both my grief and my relationship with God. I must say that having a belief in God has been central to my own ability to cope and proceed through the grieving process. I do not espouse that such is requisite; only that it has been and remains key to the path I've chosen. I would also like to convey to you that while my faith more or less aligns with Catholicism, I would not be so presumptuous as to say it is the only path to spirituality. Each of us must find our own way to God; in my view God is nondenominational.

Within the excerpts I believe that you will see an evolution in my thinking and a growth in my faith, which had been dormant for many years. My personal progress did not come quickly but developed slowly over time. Today my faith is quite strong; internalized beyond a point it had ever been in the past.

Dear Father,
April 13, 2014

Regarding My Personal Journey (letter # 1)

I am writing you to say I am trying to understand aspects of her passing; specifically why. I know in my heart that our Lord is a loving God. As such, her being taken from me is not a punishment upon her or upon me. Though the why is unknown…one of the mysteries I won't know until after I too have passed. I'm trying to come to terms with this, to a point of acceptance. This is not an easy task, for I am so sad and lost without her.

Maybe I'm not approaching this in a way you think I should. But for now all I can say is I'm doing the best I can. This is the most difficult time of my life. I told someone Friday that what I'm experiencing is worse than death to me. I was being literal. I'd promised her that I would continue on…I would never go back on that promise, never. The love I have for her has grown and changed in our nearly forty years together. I continued to be her "protector" until the day she died. I could not help her that day and that fact has been an added burden these last few days, as I'd told her long ago I'd always keep her safe.

It seems many admire those who possess true independence; the few who can withstand and sustain under any conditions that may befall them. I am not one of those people. My equilibrium was attained only when I was with her.

I've become a lost soul, merely wandering without the love of my life. I will be trying to make it, day-by-day. I will continue to talk to Ginny. I want to truly believe in an everlasting life—a heaven that would reunite me with my beloved. This path appears to be one I largely must walk alone.

Dear Father,
April 27, 2014

Regarding My Personal Journey (letter # 4)

On Friday night, actually 3:00 AM on April 26th, something both profound and mysterious occurred. I'd gone to bed early, which has become typical. What was unusual was that for the first time since her death I had a dream about Ginny. It was quite vivid. In my dream I could see her so clearly. I eventually became aware it was a dream.

We were outside a bakery located in a mall setting of some sorts. We were looking at buying some cookies. I saw a plate of chocolate chips (with pecans). We both love them but she prefers no nuts. As I reached to pick them up she went around the display, picked up a plate of different cookies, smiled at me and said something akin to "only if I can get these." I then noticed she looked younger—no glasses either. I'd estimate she was twenty-eight or twenty-nine years old. As she spoke, it occurred to me she could not eat anything, as she could not swallow. My reality had entered the dream. I walked up to her then buried my face between her head and neck, put my arms around her and said, "I miss you so, mine…I'm so sad without you" to which she replied, "I know, I know." Then I awoke. I had the sense of presence to write down the dream before it disappeared as so many dreams do.

One of the attendees at her memorial, a forty-something-year-old man, told me he'd learned of her death and felt he had to come pay his respects. He told me she was his very favorite babysitter when he was a small child. Early on in our relationship I was witness to her taking care of other people's children. She had a wondrous way with children; a connection that's hard to describe.

I still am so very sad. At times it comes quite unexpectedly; washes over me like a wave and the undertow is so strong.

I've been going on walks…yesterday about one-and-a-half miles. I spoke to her the entire walk as if she were beside me. Often tears come too, but no one sees, which is what I prefer.

Dear Father,
May 13, 2014

Regarding My Personal Journey (letter # 8)

In addressing some of what you'd written to me on May 10th I'd like to relay some comments. My "cross" seems clear to me for having lost, in this life, my darling wife. This has shaken the foundation of my world. I've only traveled in grief a short distance so far…shock has turned into despair. I now can see some things more clearly…that nothing in this life really matters except for our relationships. Nothing matters in this world but love. The love we extend not only to our spouse, but to all.

One can be in a crowd, yet still be alone. I've long believed this to be the case; it's not a new revelation. Initially I have withdrawn from life. The black void has at times swallowed me up, has made me feel as I do today, that I'd rather be dead than live this way.

Ginny always stood up to what was right even if the view was unpopular. I recall one case on our honeymoon where she befriended another recent bride who came from Mexico and did not understand our language. The task was for each bride to make a small pizza for her new husband. One gal there took the ingredients from Gaby, the Mexican bride. She told her "give it to me because you don't understand and will mess it up." On hearing this, my most shy bride, walked over to the woman, took back the ingredients and said to Gaby, "don't worry, you and I will do this together, I will show you and explain." To understand the kindness, the gentleness she displayed, is to know my Ginny. She hated to be the center of attention yet she would always stand up to do what was right. Gaby and Ginny made the two small pizzas for Joaquin and me. When they brought them out to us Gaby leaned over and told her husband Joaquin what Ginny had done…with tears in her eyes she gave Ginny a big hug. You can just imagine how proud I was of her. That selfless action epitomized who she was.

One failing of mine is that I should have told Ginny more often in our lives how much I loved her, why I loved her, and how proud I always was to be able to call her my wife and that she had chosen me to be her husband. I should have told her these things, but often did not.

Dear Father,
July 5, 2014

Regarding My Personal Journey as it Continues (letter # 12)

You'd written in your last letter:
 "Each baptized Christian enters into the dying and rising of Christ in the unique way God has willed that we do so…and each of us, differently; you in your experience of dear Ginny passing, myself in the pain and suffering post-surgery."

I fail to see that these are meaningfully comparable. When someone tells me they understand my pain because they've lost a parent, suffered a financial setback, or lost a job…these too are not comparable. While loss and suffering are not competitive sports, all losses are not equal either in their impact or their effect. Most people do not suffer the loss of a spouse until late in their lives. However, sudden and premature death is always devastating. While people like to try to comfort those in grief by saying they understand, they cannot understand any more than if I were to explain to you how it feels to go skydiving. Unless you've experienced it, you can only imagine. This strikes at the heart of sympathy versus empathy. Only those who have experienced such a loss can convey empathy. Understanding the difference is beyond the ability of most. Unfortunately that doesn't stop some folks from making statements that are callous, though their intent may be good. Perhaps they wish to convey that the affected person is not alone? But tying one's own loss to indicate that they too "got over" it is not relevant. Even if the losses are of like kind, relationships between any two people are unique. The specifics of the loss…how long the couple was together, quality of the marriage (depth of love), etc. are so individually driven that it's nearly impossible to compare one loss to another.

In your May 31st letter you mention my ability to accept the loss little by little…"that Ginny's death was a kind of death for you…but not just a death to my will and plans." You note that my new life is a complete gift to me, providing a new start—new opportunities. Here we have reality mixed in with hyperbole. I agree that in a very real sense her death was a death to me as well. Ginny's death feels like a gutting of myself—the tearing apart of my heart and soul. It is both emotional and psychological; the torment is horrific and all too real. These thoughts are not from only my experience, but also my observations of others in my group therapy sessions. I have described such as "hell on earth" for good reason. To have one's spouse taken away is most married couples' worst fear. The concept of acceptance is misplaced in my opinion, as it is not a matter of choice. Only a fool denies reality, and I am no fool.

Acceptance is not the object, it is a matter of understanding that is important and such does not happen overnight. Profound understanding takes time, but even then we will never understand the why of it as mortal beings. Such loss is not a matter of God's will either. He no more desired that Ginny die when she did and how she did than I. God does not look down upon this mortal world making decisions to take this life but spare that one. We each have our free will. We make decisions in our lives—some good, some bad. Decisions have consequences. In my eyes God is there to comfort us in our time of loss, not to confound our sense of reason.

In your May 9th letter you spoke about not only accepting one's cross but embracing it. No matter how long I live I will never embrace the loss of my dear wife. The very concept of doing so goes against every fiber of my being and the abiding love I have for her.

My faith was weak as I entered into this remaining journey. That was due to many reasons, some of which deal with my sense of what the Church has done or failed to do in my eyes. But that was a mistake on my part. The Church is not God. The fact that the Catholic Church has had issues including the long-standing failure to properly address the matter of "problem" priests, their stance on individuals who are LBGT, the Church's rigid stance on birth control, and the inability for clergy to connect with or make relevant Christ's teachings in today's world— these were all a part of my weakened faith. This is not an excuse for my turning my back on God, but it is what happened. None of these things were God's work. These are issues largely tied to religious institutions run by imperfect humans.

Ginny is my greatest gift from God…our meeting, our life together. I look back wishing I'd been a better husband and friend…yet guilt and regret are not emotions I am taking forward in my remaining life. They are corrosive, similar in that regard as anger and bitterness. I am an imperfect creature…I've made mistakes…I've learned from them… and am doing my best today.

Many people try at times to convey their support—some more successfully than others. Perhaps not surprisingly, I've found that women are
much more compassionate and understanding. Overall our society does
not handle grief well. Some run from sadness or perhaps they fear their
own mortality. It is hard for those who have not experienced such a loss
to relate to what I am going through, but it is not their fault. I found
that running away from grief isn't the answer any more than ignoring it.

These days I seek fewer confidants than I had initially. I shield myself
from well-intentioned but clumsy folks who though with good intentions, sometimes say things that are not helpful or supportive. My
participation in the group therapy sessions has been helpful. While I
can identify with only three or four of the other members of the group,
I have struck up relationships with a few. We talk over the phone, and
write to each other via email; this support is bi-directional. They help
me and I believe I have helped them.

My faith and trust in God has strengthened since the initial days after
her passing. I believe in God, in heaven, I know Ginny is in heaven,
and my sole objective is to live out my remaining life in a manner
where one day I will be reunited with her in heaven.

In a recent fiction book I read by Nelson DeMille entitled *The Quest,* I
found something. The book is a historically accurate depiction of certain events that took place in the late 1930s…but has a central fictional
premise that the chalice used by Jesus at the last supper survived across
the ages. The quest the book speaks to is that of the Holy Grail. On page
152 a concept is espoused then summarized on page 197 as follows: "If
you believe in Love, you must believe in God." For me this says it all.
It is not dogma or doctrine that He so urges we heed…but that we live
this life the best we can. True love is selfless…no greater virtue exists.
Simply stated, God is the epitome of love, the very essence.

Dear Father,
August 22, 2014

Regarding My Personal Journey (letter # 14)

Not a day goes by where I don't wish things were like they were a year ago. I miss Ginny so much that words are inadequate. I talk to Ginny many times a day. On my sixtieth birthday I walked three miles. For this birthday I'd asked my family and friends NOT to call me or send cards…I just wanted to be alone in my thoughts. They honored my request. The reason in part deals with the party that Ginny had planned; one she wasn't here for this time.

This was the first year since we'd been married that she hadn't baked me something special for my birthday. It was most always the same thing by my request, one of her delicious lemon meringue pies. Ginny made the best lemon meringue pie I'd ever eaten. I can remember the time back in the summer of 1975 when she and I "cashed in" our skeeball tickets in exchange for a Pyrex pie dish. That pie plate was the one she'd used all those years. The night we got it I thought it was sort of an odd "prize" to choose. But when I asked her, she said "It's for my hope chest, it'd be great for making you pies." Some years she'd make both a pie and a chocolate cake, figuring if there was only one dessert it would be gone too quickly. I can say this for certain, the pie never lasted more than a couple of days—three days max. Ginny was a great baker in my book, but it's not her cooking I miss, only her.

After prayers each night I talk to Ginny, right before reading a book. Often I whisper to her…asking her to come into my dreams so that I can see her. She'd done that on April 25th and then again on June 25th.

On Aug 12th she came into my dreams again. I'd only been asleep a short time but awoke at 10:42 PM. Unlike the two earlier times I wasn't aware it was a dream until almost the moment I awoke. In my last dream she held me and said to me, "Hold on Jimmy, believe in me, believe in us…one day we will be together again…you simply need to have faith and believe." I got to tell you, that "visit" made a huge difference in my outlook. When I awoke I looked over to some of the pictures of her that are now on her dresser, and I thanked her. I know many folks would dismiss such a dream as a trick my mind was playing on me; but I don't think so. Guess the key depends on what you believe.

Dear Father,
September 21, 2014

Regarding My Personal Journey (letter # 16)

Recently I met with both the deacon and the new priest at my parish. These meetings have been helpful. The meeting with our new priest occurred after last Sunday's 8:30 AM mass. I spoke to him for a bit over an hour. Though he's rather young and only recently ordained, I found comfort in his words and in sharing of his own trials and tragedies. I find that only in sharing our inner-most thoughts do we really get to know another. Anyway, he assured me that one day Ginny and I would be together again in heaven. That means everything to me, for it is my end objective, no matter how long this remaining journey lasts.

I just finished a book the priest I met with had suggested to me…*The Shack*. In many regards, the book is like me; rather non-traditional, especially when it comes to my religious/spiritual beliefs. The author, William Paul Young, did a good job overall in his writing, though I must confess I was a little confused at times. The book tells the story of the tragic loss of this man's daughter under heinous conditions. The au-

thor seemed to create a broad distinction between God and religion…
alluding to the fact that much harm/misery has been done in the name
of God by various religions. However, I don't buy that organized religions are by their own existence, unholy or less than God-like. Still, the
book was very good and I'd recommend it.

Since last I'd written an important date passed—September 4, 2014—
forty years from the day that Ginny and I met down at our favorite tavern, the Reunion Inn. We had had plans to go down there that night,
to reenact that first meeting. As the date approached I struggled with
what, if anything, I should do. I decided to go down myself. I ordered
a Genny beer just as I had that night. I stood exactly where I did that
night as memories came reeling back. I'd walked her home those many
years ago, so this night too I made the trek. I followed the exact route
we'd taken, cutting down near the very same church where we were
later married in 1977. As I walked I spoke to her, told her how much I
missed her and so wish we were taking this walk together once again.
Tears came as I knew they would, as I approached the house where she
and her family once lived.

I made my way back to the tavern where I'd left my car, far slower than
I had years ago. It seemed so surreal. As I walked back I could hear
the sound of laughter from the nearby amusement park. A swirl of
memories flooded in from all the times we'd been the source of that
laughter, never considering the world outside that moment. Just to
hear her laugh once more would be such a joy.

I can't find the words to explain why I had to take that walk. If wishing
were all it took she'd be with me now and I'd tell her all the things I all
too seldom did. As I got into the car to drive home, I said to her, "Ginny, I love you and miss you so, I promise one day we will be together
again…I love you, mine."

Today is day 171. Much has changed and yet nothing has changed. The loss I feel is still with me each day. Everything I may achieve in my remaining journey is inspired by Ginny. She is my reason for continuing…her goodness and her love sustain me.

Below this letter is a writing I recently completed, *A Personal Belief.* It reflects what I believe in terms of why bad things happen to so many good people. Right after her passing I felt so cheated and I was very angry with God. That sense has long passed. I'm not looking for you to agree with my "personal belief," but I wanted to share it with you anyway.

A Personal Belief

I find it rather incomprehensible that people, including theologians of many faiths, seem to attribute events, actions, or consequences to our almighty God regardless of the circumstances. Do we really believe that God intervenes in daily human life? That His will is somehow the prime driver that brings about human grief or its antithesis?

In reading a translation of Pope Francis' homily of March 30, 2013 he stated:

> "We are like the apostles in the Gospel, often we would prefer to hold on to our own security to stand in front of a tomb, to think about someone who has died, someone who ultimately lives on only as a memory like the great historical figures from the past. We are afraid of God's surprises."

While I feel that Pope Francis is precisely the sort of leader that the Catholic Church needs today, I wonder if he felt this way when it came to the recent deaths of members of his own extended family (grand-nephew along with his wife and small child). What good came from this loss? Perhaps the "good" is not determined by the event but rather the reaction to such a tragedy. Perhaps it holds the potential to unlock a greater insight into the nature of our God. Whether a good or bad outcome can spring from such losses is not predetermined but is up to those affected.

When my wife passed back in April, 2014 in a sudden and traumatic manner, nothing about her loss made sense to me. She was perhaps the most wonderful person I've ever known; compassionate, kind, gentle, and loving. Certainly she did not "deserve" to pass so prematurely and so traumatically. No more than when those children were slaughtered at their school by that deranged individual with a gun. No more than when an innocent child or young person succumbs to a terrible disease. It seems to me we are attributing results to our deity that simply are not of His making; are not of His will.

What is the purpose of "free will" if a result were predetermined? Some would say, "He or she was destined to suffer such a fate." This too strikes me as nonsense. There would be no purpose to life if in fact destiny was set from the day of our conception.

To me it is more likely that God created this universe with the idea that it would proceed forward in this realm we call time in a manner independent of His influence upon any specific result. Good and bad exist not because God desires a particular outcome…but on the merit that events unfold in this moral life, which have the potential to favorably or unfavorably affect His creations.

My belief is that God is the essence of all that is good…with or without form. He is the epitome of what we humans label the virtue of love…of all that is holy. God surely exists; otherwise there would be no purpose to His creation of higher forms of life…what we call the soul. Just as God, the soul exists without form. The soul is the essence of the creature but lacking any physical presence. I do not believe that humans are simply the end result of chemical and biological evolution of life forms here on planet Earth.

I struggle each and every day with the loss of my beloved. Still, I cling to a belief that one day when my time comes I will be reunited with my wife in heaven for all eternity. The love my wife and I shared was not simply a passing fancy…we two became one many years ago. That blessing bestowed upon us is immortal. My challenge is to find my way to her as best I can in a manner that enables me to favorably effect others while maturing spiritually. Not an easy task, yet one that each of us must tackle.

Dear Father,
October 16, 2014

Regarding My Personal Journey…The Gift of Love (letter # 19)

Yesterday I sent an email to the young priest in my parish. He had stopped by to see me before mass on Sunday to see how I was doing, let me know how much he liked the digital pictures (of Ginny) I'd sent him previously, and to encourage me to keep up the fight. While I know Ginny is in heaven, I miss her so terribly. I just want to be with her but know that it's not my time as yet.

In my life I've made many mistakes. There was a time fourteen to fifteen years ago that I had a horrid mid-life crisis…one that could have ended my marriage. Ginny never gave up on me…she always believed in me and in us. In a very real sense she saved my life. That experience changed my life. I never veered from our path together again. Our marriage was once again something I highly valued, yet I feel I should have told her more often how much I loved her, how grateful I was for her love.

Dear Father,
November 7, 2014

Regarding My Personal Journey…Thoughts and Musings (letter # 21)

Below is a recent writing I'd done that reflects my feelings in regard to heaven. I did this as a way to organize and summarize my own thoughts. Like others, I profess no insight per se, yet believe many folks tend to have a rather myopic view when it comes to ideas depicting such unknowns. I've met many people who have rigid concepts concerning heaven; no more developed than when they were small children. God did not give us minds to simply follow…He expects us to uncover, to delve into such mysteries to better understand. I am not one to simply comply or blindly follow.

The fact is, I am not a patient person. Ginny would agree with this statement. Many folks tell me to be patient with myself during this grieving process; easier said than done.

Having just past the seven-month mark since Ginny's passing, I must say I still find myself struggling. Despite the fact I truly believe Ginny is with God in heaven, I miss her so. I know you may not fully comprehend the sense of union—oneness—that I feel towards her, but please understand that my desire, my need, to be with her is so overwhelming. I seek not to possess her love but to be reunited in our love. In a very real way she completes me.

Defining Heaven

After having recently read a number of books, fiction and non-fiction, that purport to convey insight into what constitutes heaven, I find them all lacking to one degree or another. How does one define something with which no mortal has first-hand experience? How can anyone state such with authority, as they lack the requisite knowledge?

The most recent book I read attempted to provide some explanation or interpretation. It was written by William Shannon, professor emeritus in religious studies at Nazareth College and a priest of the Rochester Diocese. The book; *Here On The Way To There*, is described as a Catholic perspective on dying and what follows. Having been raised within the Catholic faith and having attended both a parochial grammar and high school, much of his explanations seemed familiar. Father Shannon admits that his writing is at best interpretive, as neither he nor anyone he knows can say with any certainty what constitutes heaven, no less where it is. Some seem to believe heaven isn't so much a place as a state of mind and being. I think it is neither and both.

In reading the 2013 book, and 2014 movie, *Heaven is for Real,* I felt I had some sense of the possible. I liked many of the ideas depicted in it, though I was not the least bit inclined to relate to such. Similarly, books such as *The Boy that Returned from Heaven, Five People You Will Meet in Heaven, The Shack,* as well as the five-book series lead off by the book *The Walk,* all make some attempt to convey to us aspects of God, of heaven, as well as the degree of connectivity of those who have died. Perhaps the best book I've read is *Proof of Heaven*—if you have not read, please do, for in it I found a sense of truth...at least from my perspective. Still it strikes me that none of these gave me a clear sense of the continuance of relationships. Do we retain our memories along with our immortal soul? Do those we love remember and hear us? Do they miss us?

Having lost my darling wife both suddenly and traumatically this past April, I find I have a strong motivation to both understand and accept the notion of our soul's immortality and our eventual going "home" to heaven. I have used the term "home" myself when referring to heaven in my nightly prayers. Father Shannon describes that homecoming (ref. page 120-124), so it seems my use of the word home is fitting. Yet what I do not see in Shannon's book—or really any of those I've read—is an explanation of how our mortal relationships transcend our own mortality. How does love continue, for I feel it must?

I have simply defined my heaven as being again with my wife in the presence of God and the faithfully departed. Aside from believing she is now with God in heaven, I do believe she and I will one day again be together forever. I love my wife unconditionally, and I believe as completely as any mortal could love another. I say this not to assert that the love my wife and I have is better than another's but to convey the fact that I deeply believe she and I were joined in the sacrament of matrimony, not by chance or by destiny, but were given the opportunity to exercise our free will and overtly chose/found love. While we were two separate mortals, our love possessed a singular dimension… one love, not two people that love each other.

Some friends and relatives have told me I need to "let go" of her…to move on with my life. I accept that such an approach may be how they would react to the death of their spouse, but that doesn't mean it is how I will respond. My path may not be their path. It doesn't make me right and them wrong; just different. Some have warned me…telling me to be careful that my love for my wife not exceed the love I have for the Lord. I find such comments to be less than helpful and do not feel that all loves are comparative. My love for God can and does exist…would I equate it to the love of my wife…I would not. The two are different; one is not better than the other.

I've been told that it takes time to get through the grieving process. This I accept and understand. The process is neither linear nor the same for any two individuals. The mourning I experience as a result of grieving has been both frequent and difficult. I struggle each day. Yet my belief in God and in the idea that my wife is now in heaven are integral to my being and my ability to cope with this loss. I have coined a new definition to a scientific term…my "singularity." To me it means that my single purpose in my remaining mortal journey is to positively affect others so that one day when our Lord calls me home, I will be immediately reunited with my wife Ginny. While there is a whole secular view, which has both purpose and merit, such is insufficient for me. I do not accept that she is gone, just no longer here in mortal form. She continues to exist and does to this day affect me. I continue this mortal life but she is with me…a part of me to this day. The better part I might add.

Many aspects of heaven, while unknown to us, are likely similar from one person to another. However, I do not believe heaven is homogeneous. What I incrementally need, want, or desire in my heaven may be slightly or very different from someone else. For example: They may envision fishing in a cool mountain spring but fishing never was an activity that I particularly enjoyed. I believe we in fact are granted a heaven that completes us…that serves to provide us a means to be with deceased family and friends while at the same time affording our ability to be one with God. I believe we can—though are not required—to take on a mortal form in heaven. That form has no bearing to the age we were when we died but is the age we're most comfortable in.

There are individuals who for one reason or another never were able to have children in this life. I've heard stated that there can be no children in heaven, as there is no longer any need for procreation. Yet I find this reasoning flawed. Heaven need not be the same for all. God is capable of anything and everything so why do some feel compelled to limit what does or does not occur in heaven?

The love I have for Ginny is perhaps even stronger today than it was the day she passed. I absolutely know I will never stop loving her. A part of me is with her and a part of her is with me and that will never change. Certainly one enveloping attribute that heaven contains is Love. Like heaven, love cannot truly be measured; it has no form or substance. Though I ask some rhetorical questions within this writing, I need no answers to them. I believe, I have faith, and in time will develop a deeper trust in God. I absolutely believe that heaven will witness the reuniting of my wife and me. It's really quite simple...for my heaven must fulfill this essential need in me...a need I believe she also holds within her spirit even now.

Ginny's death brought back to me the sense of loss and separation I had not felt since 1975 when I went away to college. I remember how tough it was for both of us and how many times I just wanted to quit, walking away from further schooling so that we two could be together. Unlike then, it isn't for a period of a couple of weeks but for my remaining time on earth. Knowing this is hard to take. I struggle with my new reality most of the time. Yet she remains in me, guides me in a manner. Surely God knows this as well. His infinite love and mercy will ensure we two are one again in heaven. I just need to persevere; to proceed along my path...faith and love will do the rest.

Dear Father,
December 8, 2014

Regarding My Personal Journey (letter # 24)

A few weeks ago I received an invite to attend a special memorial service being sponsored by the funeral home we'd used. The service was yesterday. The only person I'd invited was Ginny's sister Carol. I won't get into all my reasons for not having extended such to other family members other than to say I simply did not want to create a forum for folks to express sympathy to me. I don't like sympathy or pity.

Carol and I hadn't seen each other for some time, so it was good to see her. I can tell she has struggled in trying to come to grips with Ginny's passing. The service included about 200 people; families of all the folks who had passed in 2014 and had used this particular funeral home. They had a soloist…she sang beautifully. Midway through, they had a candle lighting where member(s) of the families went up to light a candle for their loved one. It was so sad…many were for wives or husbands who passed…some though were clearly for small children, twin girls in one case. In front of us was a man with his family…he must have been in his mid-80s…he was crying over the loss of his wife. I asked Carol to go up with me…I lit a candle and they gave me a box. In the box was a glass angel ornament with Ginny's name along with DOB and DOD dates. I opened it upon returning to the pew, and told Carol that I know Ginny is in heaven, and although she's not really an angel, she is MY angel.

This concept of marital unity is explained in the words contained in C. S. Lewis' book, *Mere Christianity.* In speaking about Christian marriage, he says that Jesus referred to such as when a man and woman become of "one flesh." Lewis retranslates that phrase to be "of one organism."

This is how I feel…a part of a whole. In every sense of the meaning, Ginny and I were not one of two people in a marriage…but part of one; succinctly 1+1=1. So you see; I am incomplete without her here. I will go on, for I promised. Few folks could really understand what it is I'm saying…but I hope you have a better sense of what I mean.

Dear Father,
December 22, 2014

Regarding My Personal Journey…Life, Death, and Beliefs (letter # 25)

I like to write down my thoughts on many different matters. Doing so forces me to think about the topic in a less haphazard manner. Unfortunately it seems that many folks don't do a lot of thinking about anything. That has probably been unchanged over the ages. Some leave the thinking to others; they can only follow, never lead. All too many just seem to get caught up or so focused upon the immediate that they give little thought to the broader picture. I was prey to that many times in my life. How terribly short-sighted I was.

I want to say I made it through the 17th (would have been our 37th anniversary) and the 20th (the date I proposed to her thirty-nine years ago). Some folks seem to think that I've put things behind me…am growing stronger. Well, shows they don't really understand what I'm going through. I have been able to regain a deeper sense of spirituality, of faith. In some sense, as was the case when Ginny was here, I owe this resumption of belief to her. I'm not sure you are familiar with a tune from back in 1992…it was titled "The One" by Elton John. It is my favorite song from him. My hope is that you can listen to it sometime…it is revealing. Grief still visits me daily; but it and no one can or will ever be able to abate the love I have for her. All I do is inspired by her…she is MY ONE.

I recently caught the tail end of a movie, *Polar Express*. Not sure you're familiar with it, but a theme is emphasized in the closing scene. The young boy opens up the last gift under the tree. His younger sister hands it to him. In it is a sleigh bell. The bell's meaning is quite simply this; believing in something, even when others may argue against it based on reason and logic, is what is necessary to retain a sense of awe and inspiration. When we are young, Christmas signified both the birth of Christ and the coming of Santa. Unfortunately too much emphasis is placed on the receipt of gifts and not the true meaning of the season. The same theme is explored in other classic movies, *Miracle on 34th Street*; *It's a Wonderful Life*; *A Christmas Carol*, etc. As we enter our teens we are faced with the reality that Santa is a myth. That he doesn't exist. To many children, such is not welcomed news, but one is told to simply accept it. As we age, such a fairy tale view of life is not only down-played, it is scoffed at, resulting in taunting and often ridicule. Yet it is not folly to believe in something when fact, reason, and logic seem to indicate otherwise. I'm not talking about Santa when I say, it is difficult at times to believe but it is what we must do.

Ginny was not a worldly person. She retained an innocence, a sense of value, and of beliefs that made her so endearing. I so wish I'd told her more often how wonderful she was and how proud I was to be her husband. She was, is, and will always be the most influential person in my life. Her passing has enabled me to "see" for the first times in years—to understand things that either I'd forgotten or had let go dormant long ago. It is very hard for me to live my remaining life without her, but it is what I must do. Yet she remains with me and inspires me. What a grand love it is I hold for her and she for me. I am truly blessed and thank God for this each day we spent together.

Dear Father,
December 30, 2014

Regarding My Personal Journey…Further Reflections (letter # 26)

I'll start by saying that I had a tough day on Christmas. After forty years of Christmases together with Ginny, she was not here by my side. It was one of my worst days since her passing.

Ginny and I really wanted a big family. But that was not to be. She had a miscarriage before she had Jason, and then two more within the next three years. One pregnancy had gone into the second trimester; she lost that child right before Christmas 1988, the same year her beloved father died. I remember talking about it…trying to comfort her. In the end we decided that we would simply accept whatever occurred. We were not going to avoid having more children, nor were we going to get our hopes up again. Ginny had an uncanny ability to relate to children. I never witnessed an adult who seemingly without effort could interact with them so well. She loved all kids, and they loved her in return.

In your last letter you spoke to the concept of God's graces and He taking the initiative, not us! I guess I sort of understand. This reminds me of that philosophical question…does altruism exist? In what you say, it seems what we do isn't as relevant as the fact God begins the effort. Yet we all have a choice…we can lead rather insular lives, which I often had in the past, or we can put the needs of others before our own. Which we choose is by definition our choice, not God's.

Many, including friends and family have implied that in time I may find someone else to fill the void in my heart. While I can understand why they make such a statement, what they don't understand is that void can only be filled by her. Frankly, I don't think you or other clergy can fully comprehend why I feel the way I do in regard to Ginny. You cannot possibly know, for you are not in my position or able to truly feel the pain tied to the loss of a spouse. Most people want to be loved—to be thought of in a positive way. If they don't, something is seriously wrong with them. But my longing for her is not measurable or explainable.

Last evening I got a return call from one of the other members of my surviving spouse group that I'd attended this past May to July. I've met other surviving spouses in that group. Their stories have similar facets but each is unique. No particular love is the same. Some people see love, express love, or feel love in a manner that is not what I'd term selfless. The predominate secular view is that in order to traverse the loss of a beloved one, the individual must at some point disengage emotionally and spiritually from the deceased. That is just plain nuts in my view. To me that's like equating a mate to a physical thing…your car is destroyed in an accident, so you get a new car. Love is not that way, not true love at least. There is no equivalent, no replacement. While there are many other good women who would welcome a relationship…my need is not to supplant that which I had, but to continue that which I still possess. As I said, she is not gone, just gone from this world and this world is rather transitory at best.

Dear Father,
January 28, 2015

Regarding My Personal Journey…Soul Searching (letter 30)

I believe that character is measured by deeds, not intentions. What one does when no one is looking is in fact the true measure of character. Some people act 'good' because they know their actions are monitored or seen. Yet if unseen, the question that comes to mind is, did the person do the right thing out of love or fear? I guess that's why I don't like the phrase "fear of God." One cannot do things out of fear, for even if they are doing the right thing, the motivation is all wrong. This perhaps is what separates folks in terms of goodness vs righteousness. Doing the right thing is always preferable to doing wrong. But doing the right thing for the right reason is what matters most.

Dear Father,
February 8, 2015

Regarding My Personal Journey…Purpose (letter 31)

It is hard to accept that my life will never be the same as it once was. Who I was has changed. There is a hole in my being…where once she was here; completing me as it were…she now resides in me only in spirit. To this point, sadness is a daily companion. This is not of my choosing but it is my reality. It seems no one can help me through this…it is a solitary journey. I retain close ties to family and friends, and have added to them over the last few months. I still have most all my human faults and frailties but there is now something more.

I wish I saw what I can see today a long time ago. The fact is I allowed my world to affect aspects of me that changed me; and not for the better. I stopped believing in some things, my priorities got all mixed up, and I took for granted some people, most notably my darling wife. I thought I had some things figured out…I was wrong. Yet the clarity of my "sight" today enables me to correct my path. What a price I had to pay. I miss Ginny so very much, words fail to convey just how deeply. I still speak to her several times each day. Nightly I ask that she be allowed or enabled to feel the love I hold for her. I have no idea what happens when we die. My hope is that we retain our memories and our love. If not, then what's the point of living this mortal life?

I feel I know what I must do with the rest of my life. I do not know all the specifics, but that's okay. Why are we here if not to leave this world a better place by our existence? The answer to why we live may simply be to have a positive effect on others.

Dear Father,
February 25, 2015

Regarding My Personal Journey (letter 33)

"I am not sure exactly what heaven will be like, but I know that when we die and it comes time for God to judge us, he will not ask, "How many good things have you done in your life?" rather he will ask, "How much love did you put into what you did?" - *Mother Teresa*

I'm not sure I wholly agree with this but perhaps the point is, while the outcome may be uncertain, we can choose to always be kind. What motivates me is what I've told you, to know that Ginny would be proud of me; that's my only litmus test. Small deeds matter, even if they go unnoticed—perhaps particularly when they go unnoticed. Those who "do good" with the idea of recognition are missing the most important point.

Every day I relive the last moments Ginny and I shared; the terror in her eyes…my impotence at being able to stop what was happening. It is burned into my soul as noted in the poem. But my experience is not the message…if I make it about me there is a good chance others will not see themselves in the lessons. I don't know if this makes sense to you, but it does to me.

Dear Father,
March 6, 2015

Regarding My Personal Journey (letter 34)

In revisiting the matter of acceptance you inferred in your last letter (March 2nd) that my lack of acceptance of Ginny's passing risks becoming bitterness and anger. I've written and said it before...anger and bitterness are baggage...they are corrosive. Nothing good can occur by turning towards these emotions. In the same regard, the same can be said for hate...the antithesis of love. Someone cannot truly love if they also hold hate...the two are polar opposites. I was upset with the hospital, that's for sure...but they did not cause Ginny's illness or her death. While I contend that the person who had charge of her case lacked compassion and was not forthcoming in terms of Ginny's prognosis, perhaps the doctor had simply become apathetic after seeing so many similar cases. My sense is that many doctors routinely withhold the true nature of a patient's condition given issues of uncertainty or even litigation risk. No doubt in my heart that they bias towards saying less, not more. Some see their job as complete once a case is diagnosed as terminal. Perhaps they believe it then is up to others...social workers, clergy, and other family members to deal with the sad facts. But I feel this is wrong-minded. I would have listened, but deep down perhaps was too fearful of hearing the worst.

Ginny's passing is not about my acceptance. Today I can say I do trust in God...that trust is born of faith and faith alone. I don't blame Him, I don't blame the doctors...there is no blame. I know too that nothing empirical is going to come along and affirm my beliefs. Guess that's the hard part about believing.

If a man stands aside a road with a lantern with the purpose of warning others that the bridge is out…who he is, isn't really important…it is the message that matters. In the same way, what I have to convey to others isn't a sign that I have any more wisdom or knowledge per se, but that I can now see things that others cannot or will not. In the past I often was one as described in the proverb; "There are none so blind as those who will not see".

Each of us has to traverse this life. If we're very lucky, perhaps we do so without having to go through the sort of tragedy that many face. Yet whatever the circumstance, I believe we are obliged to make the journey without self-interest being our primary motivation.

I read all the examples you cited in both the Old and New Testaments concerning "tests" that God puts before us. Yet what sort of God is man depicting that feels it necessary to "test" his children? The story of Abraham and Isaac or the story of Job all fall into the issue of biblical dichotomy I've written about to you in the past. Testing of one's faith ascribes to God in a literal sense, a need to affirm His own divinity through His creations. I do not agree with this notion. Let's not have a falling out on this…but my beliefs, my faith, is not subject to my willingness to accept all that is written in the Bible. Sometimes, as in other writings, a figurative meaning is what is intended. And perhaps sometimes, what is written and accepted by many is simply not the case. All too often folks resist anything other than the literal meaning of words. It's no wonder in my mind that so many people are so screwed up when it comes to their faith. They need everything laid out neatly…plain as day. If not, they don't understand. Worse yet, if anyone disagrees with them they refuse to accept the person, the group, or the idea that is contrary to their own. Their intolerance becomes an overwhelming force…vitriol and condemnation spew forth and this is how hatred takes root. This reality is what I see as the Achilles heel of most religions and in many of those who say they are "God-fearing believers."

I do not claim to know that there is but one answer when it comes to matters of faith though I believe there is but one God. I do not place my beliefs, my faith, above all others. The message of Christ was for all humanity, not for a select few. When a particular religion puts itself above all others, it fails to meet God's intention. Any religion or belief that divides rather than unites defies the message of Christ. As I've noted before, I believe heaven is full of peoples from many faiths. I see no dissonance in this statement. I just happen to believe that Christianity conveys best my faith, my set of beliefs.

Dear Father,
March 14, 2015

Regarding My Personal Journey…The Big Picture (letter # 35)

Humans like things to be simple; cut and dry. But the world and life in general, does not always work that way. If one has to be told exactly what to do…then they have already failed a fundamental attribute of faith…they are not thinking on their own. Religions are somewhat analogous to this conceptually. If a person needs to be told exactly what a given religion wants them to do, then such is problematic. The answer to the question is not always the same, even under very similar circumstances. We can speak about one having a moral compass, a set of beliefs, and understanding the difference between right and wrong…but all these—while important—must be answered within a person's being…not in the form of laws, rules, mores, or even accepted practices.

Doing good in order to claim a right to salvation is something akin to a view of entitlement. We can all agree that "being good" is a good step towards salvation. Yet why is one being good? If the reason is that they suppose by doing so, they can achieve some end reward…then they have already failed. Whether it is money, skills, talents, time, or what-ever…there is no specific prescription that will assure our salvation. Just as I've commented before, doing the right thing is important…but doing the right thing for the wrong reason just doesn't cut it. I did not steal because I might get caught…or because I feared the consequence. I believe it is better to steal, then later come to grips with the sin rather than to never steal and think oneself as being good.

I have a somewhat unique vantage point, as do many who have suffered a tragic loss in their lives. Doesn't make me special, but it has made me more introspective and aware than I was in the past. My insight is a byproduct of not only what happened to me, but also my search for greater meaning/understanding. While many even in my shoes may feel this way, few take the time elaborate on such thoughts; even fewer seem inclined to share their own mistakes. I feel I have an obligation of sorts to convey some of my life experience in hopes of helping others. The reality is that my own story is largely written; the past cannot be altered.

I will close with a quote below…a friend sent it to me the other day. It is unlike most other sentiments I've found or read on the topic. I find it to be a most accurate depiction of what I'm going through. They, most all who have tried to help me, really cannot understand the path I'm on or the torment I so often feel. No one's fault; it's just the way it is. But I know I'm on the path that will lead me home to Ginny.

> *"There is nothing that can replace the absence of someone dear to us, and one should not even attempt to do so. One must simply hold out and endure it. At first that sounds very hard, but at the same time it is also a great comfort. For to the extent the emptiness truly remains unfilled, one remains connected to the other person through it. It is wrong to say that God fills the emptiness. God in no way fills it but much more leaves it precisely unfilled and thus helps us preserve—even in pain—the authentic relationship. Furthermore,*

the more beautiful and full the remembrances, the more difficult the separation. But gratitude transforms the torment of memory into silent joy. One bears what was lovely in the past not as a thorn but as a precious gift deep within, a hidden treasure of which one can always be certain." Dietrich Bonhoeffer

Dietrich Bonhoeffer was a German Lutheran theologian who lived from 1906-1945. He was hanged in 1945 just two weeks before Hitler shot himself. Unlike many other theological leaders at that time, Christian, Catholic and others, Bonhoeffer stood up against Hitler beginning in the early 1930s. I've only read snippets about him but it seems he was quite a man indeed.

Dear Father,
March 16, 2015

Regarding My Personal Journey…A Long Road (letter # 36)

Our faith is always a choice just as are so many things in life. I told you some time ago that it is a shame it took the passing of my beloved wife to really wake me up…but I am now awake. I know I have many faults… and will likely always have certain attributes…being impatient, outspoken, loquacious, critical, and at times stubborn. But I do have a few good attributes too…thankful, open, sincere, and communicative. I've been working on a couple positive attributes by trying to emulate Ginny. She had so many fine attributes; the finest woman I've ever known.

It seems to me my failure—our failure—to communicate, lies in semantics. For instance, you use the words like acceptance and will in such a way that I contend is not in my set of beliefs. I do not believe it was or is God's will that she was struck with the dreaded disease of cancer. It was not God's will that she be taken so soon in her mortal life. Yet upon being taken, I had a choice; to become as you say, bitter and angry, or to "see" the larger picture. God did love and still loves Ginny. This personal tragedy is not a test of my faith…it is a reality of this mortal world. There are so many terrible happenings that transpire each and every day. The tragic death of innocents is part of the nature of this world. It is not up to you or I to accept these…they simply are.

I read the excerpts you sent from the compendium on Catholicism. I did not find them particularly helpful or informative. Even before I read the answer to the question or definition stated in the preface, I had a sense of what would be written. Now you may see this as a sign I am not listening…but that is not true. If one begins with what one believes is a basic tenet of their faith (i.e. That Abraham's faith was manifest in his willingness to give up his beloved son Isaac), the stated outcome is always going to support the tenet. While many may see this as being fundamental…Abraham's faith was put to the test; he "believed in God" and always obeyed God. I do not believe that God intervenes in our lives in such a manner. He knows of our faith; testing proves nothing that He didn't already know. If it proves anything at all, it may prove or disprove in the eyes of man some aspect of our faith. Yet in the eyes of man, what difference does it make? If one must prove any aspect of their being, then trust is not implicit.

You or others need not prove anything to me, for doing so does not change an outcome. Some people like to prove their piety, their generosity, or some other virtue. Proving to whom becomes the question. God needs no proof…and I, well the rest of humanity and I will "see" whatever we choose to see. Someone says their generosity proves their goodness…I on the other hand say it is more likely to prove their need for recognition when their generosity is done in an overt manner. An act to prove one thing may in fact prove something else entirely.

At times perhaps I've been too emphatic in the manner I've conveyed the "biblical dichotomies" I've commented upon. Yet I've told you I am not trying to sway your own beliefs or say I am right and others are wrong. That may be at the heart of the real issue. Organized religions tend to prescribe a given set of tenets, of beliefs, of dogma, and doctrine. Those that do not accept all such are often viewed less favorably. Minimally that they are misinterpreting, but perhaps that they are heretical. What I see is what I see. My beliefs are not being held out as being "more right" than others…just that they are my beliefs. It is that way in how I see such things as Ginny being in heaven. Your reply was to rebut my contention based upon the fact that we can "know" only canonized saints are in heaven. But your belief does not change my belief. People are entitled to believe what they believe. Clearly not all are correct.

Our world is full of a myriad of recognized formal religions. Many share some basic principles of faith or goodness of righteousness… some do not. Yet if we live our faith, if we set example by our actions, I would contend it doesn't matter so much what we say but what we do and how we act. Action brings evidence of faith. Words only hold potential for the same.

The back and forth banter in our many letters has helped me greatly. My faith was once weak, but is no longer so. I fervently believe in God.

These days are very hard…been a real struggle…more so of late as the calendar vividly reminds me what was going on a year ago. It is like a movie with a tragic ending—there is nothing I can do to change the outcome. I've told you I would rather be with Ginny than here in this mortal life. I have no fear of death but recognize it is not up to me when my time comes. I remain rather selfish I'm afraid, for all I want is to be with her.

I value our relationship. You have helped me greatly. I hope we can continue to exchange our thoughts in letters. You do not need to feel that you must align my beliefs to the extent they aren't precisely in sync with those of the Church. I respect you and your beliefs. While ours are not identical, we share the most important foundation. I do hope that my life can affect others in a positive way. It is also my hope that in some small way, that what I do, what I may accomplish, will bring a smile to Ginny's face; a comfort knowing that I have kept my promise, and with it she will have a wife's pride and know that one day we two will be together forever.

Dear Father,
March 25, 2015

Regarding My Personal Journey…Translation and Meaning (letter 37)

I am not the same person today that I was a year ago. No one can remain the same after having experienced such a loss. My hope is that the changes are for the better. Clearly, Ginny's passing brought me a renewal of my faith. Even more than that, my faith has now been internalized to a degree it never was before. I rather doubt it would've happened had her passing not taken place. That is why I sometimes say that she "saved my life," yet again for if I did not have this cathartic experience, terrible as it's been, my transformation was unlikely. That doesn't mean if I'd a choice I would have chosen what occurred, but I recognize it has served as a catalyst to my spiritual renewal.

Though I've spoken to this before, I must say that the level of intolerance I see evident in the world today is astounding. So few seem prepared to "live and let live"; insisting that whatever they do, think, or believe is the only solution. Their mindset is of a zero sum game where someone is right and therefore someone is wrong. This is perhaps one of the greatest problems afflicting mankind. Still, so many of these folks profess to be Christians. It just is unfathomable that as Christians, many act as they do. Those that act in such a righteous manner surely will be judged harshly one day. I wonder how they reconcile their own lives with the gospel of Matthew 25:45; "…that which you do for the least of my brethren you do for me."

Dear Father,
March 31, 2015

Regarding My Personal Journey…Personal Beliefs and Philosophy (letter #38)

Most folks don't understand me these days. My struggle is just to get through another day. I still cannot plan beyond a day or two. At times I feel I am languishing…trapped as it were between two worlds… existing in this mortal one, but drawn to the other with my intense desire to be with Ginny. Now I can tell right now you're making the assessment that I'm being selfish again…maybe I am. I know I am not the only one to lose a spouse…but as that quote I sent you noted, there is a huge chasm; a void that remains open. I was told early on by the woman that lead the surviving spouses group that the passage of time will "soften" the effect. She was right; though it seems grieving will never completely end. At times I feel a sense of peace, yet sadness does return—the price of our deep love.

Some say miracles happen; I guess I would not dispute it. But by their very nature miracles are rare, an exception to the rule of mortal life. Life is full of surprises. You have at times attributed them to God as if He is deciding to affect a particular outcome. I don't see it that way at all. Things happen in this life that are simply unfair. We may feel they are unjust, but nonetheless they happen. I don't believe this is punishment nor is it His plan or His will that such occur. The issue as I see it is simply that they will happen and how we adapt to them, how we handle them, is what determines the type of person we are or have become.

My task is to learn…to cope…to continue. To see beyond my own personal grieving to find my remaining purpose. I could simply decide to curl up and die…and frankly if breathing and heart rate were voluntary, I'd likely already be gone. Once again I have a choice to make. It is tough to see the silver lining in what has become my life. We each must live with the decisions or actions we undertake. It is okay to have regrets; if we don't then something is wrong with us, for we all have regrets to some degree.

I don't know why it is that so many people seem to feel a need to attribute mortal events to God's handiwork. It occurs to me that perhaps in part doing so leaves them free of any accountability to their own actions. Saying it was "God's will" seems to be for many the great wildcard. To just toss up any of life's occurrences as being of His making allows us to pretend we have no culpability to affect changes in this life.

Dear Father,
April 9, 2015

Regarding My Personal Journey…Institutional Failures (letter 39)

Over the past year I've had to confront the reality of my world. I've most often done so with a sense of reflection and with an eye upon my own personal failings. This has neither been easy, nor without pain, but it has all been necessary in order for me to "see" things. I still struggle each day, for even the belief that I hold that my darling wife is with God in heaven does not lessen the reality of the past or my desire to be with her. Each of us would no doubt be thrilled to be able to undo our past errors and sins. But this life does not work that way. Time moves inexorably ahead. Nothing that has passed can be undone; we can only learn from it. As obvious as this may seem to you, the concept is tough to accept. Introspection brings this reality to light and with it comes regret, perhaps guilt, and if we are fortunate, an awareness of our humanity—of our imperfection. The latter is not an excuse; it is simply the recognition that while we possess the potential for goodness, we also possess it for our own selfish wants, needs, and desires.

To this point I've said nothing about having passed the one-year mark on April 4th. It was a very tough day. I remain connected to Ginny despite the reality she has passed. I miss her so much and would do nearly anything to be with her. Yet she asked me to continue. We never really talked about what she meant by that. But if we had, the fact is I for one didn't have a clue what that would entail. What I would have said to her then is unlikely to be what I know now. It's like a number of things that happen in life; we don't really know what we'd do until we're faced with making the decision.

Dear Father,
April 15, 2015

Regarding My Personal Journey…Comments on The Pattern of Holiness (letter 40)

I've read the attachments you'd recently sent…with particular attention upon the excerpt taken from the book *Classics of Catholic Spirituality* written by Fr. Peter Cameron. The final chapter, "The Pattern of Holiness," prompts me to comment. But before I relay my thoughts, I would like to step back in order to revisit the nature and purpose of the many letters we've exchanged since Ginny's passing.

I was not prepared to cope with Ginny's sudden and traumatic passing. In a very real way, my world was torn apart. Meaning, purpose, you name it…I was clearly a lost soul. This of course wasn't helped by the fact that I'd allowed my faith, my beliefs, and my sense of spirituality, to wane over the last dozen years. I made the mistake that perhaps many are guilty of; equating the issues I had with the Church to my relationship with God. The two are not interchangeable. The Church is an institution run by mortals who, though often well- intentioned, suffer from fallibility and an over-reliance on tradition. Our letters have helped me not only regain a sense of spirituality, but to internalize my faith to a far greater extent than ever before. Initially, I had many questions dealing with why my life had been affected in such manner. I felt a sense that what happened to my darling wife was my punishment. I believe now that punishment had nothing to do with it; frankly God had nothing to do with her passing either. Perhaps when something tragic happens the question to ask is not why, but why not?

Today I have very strong beliefs and convictions. These did not spring from rationalization or from my need to cope with my loss. Rather, these came as a result of many months of reflection and introspection supplemented by readings and my rejoining a faith community. I would be the first to admit that my beliefs are not always in alignment with the teachings of the Catholic Church. I am not saying I am right and the Church/others are wrong. What I have tried to convey is that my beliefs are not tied to dogma, doctrine, tenets, and scripture alone. I "see" aspects of biblical dichotomy between the Old and New Testament; others like you do not. My faith is not static, but has and likely will continue to evolve. While my core beliefs are deeply rooted, that doesn't mean that they won't alter over time. This dynamic nature is not unique to me. The Church itself has altered its position on a number of matters over the years.

Going back to the matter of the attachment you sent me. I read it carefully…several areas I read over and over. On reflection, I will tell you I do not accept much of what was noted regardless of the source being individuals who were later canonized as saints. The two areas that I most ardently take issue with are sections 5 and 6. My reaction to both was visceral.

Section 6 deals with *The Redemptive Role of Suffering.* Before I go on, let me quote a few areas of the section:

- Thomas à Kempis tells us that "suffering is the way to the kingdom of heaven."
- Quote from *Little Flowers*…"suffering enables us to go beyond the distress of the world in embracing the transcendent."
- Saint Francis de Sales notes "God permits violent assaults only in souls whom he desires to raise up to his own pure and surpassing love."
- Saint Catherine of Siena…"suffering and sorrow increase in proportion to love."
- Quote from *Little Flowers*…"through suffering we become what we should be."
- Thomas à Kempis is noted again saying, "Nothing that is suffered for God's sake, no matter how small, can pass without a reward"… As a result, suffering ironically stands as an invaluable source of truest joy.
- Saint Therese of Lisieux, "suffering itself becomes the greatest of joys when one sees it as the most precious of treasures."
- Brother Lawrence of the Resurrection…"God does not allow a soul entirely devoted to him to have any other pleasures than with him. Suffering serves to keep our devotion to God undivided, wholehearted, and absolute."

To be honest, it's tough to even begin to assess such thoughts. I was seriously wondering when the author was going to suggest a return of the practice of self-flagellation! As I see it, suffering exists in this world not because God wants us to suffer but because this world is a natural evolving ecosystem where humanity resides. Earthquakes, floods, famine, hurricanes, tornadoes, etc. are all part of this environment in which we live. Further, man's existence here, along with his own tendency for self-centered action gives rise to inequities in regard to resource distribution. Lastly, man's inhumanity to man is well documented throughout history. None of these sources of suffering is brought about by God's will to inflict upon individuals or mankind itself a condition that causes such pain. To imply or in fact state that it is His will that suffering exist is wrong. It strikes me that such beliefs underscore the idea that suffering is meritorious. Yet I believe we all have an obligation to minimize suffering when possible, not be resigned to accept it. This is true whether it is we that suffer, or whether it is in observing the suffering of others. Surely to work to diminish suffering in others is what God wants—not to just passively accept it.

It has been stated that God never gives us a burden greater than one we can carry; that He knows what we can handle. I might suggest the folks who believe God is the source of our trials take a look at the rising suicide rate. Clearly many do not seem to be able to handle their burdens. The reality of this life is that suffering is likely to enter a person's life at some point. I would contend that having a strong faith is a crucial element in enabling us to cope—whatever the nature of the suffering. However, that's a far cry from believing that there is inherent value to such suffering, no less a spiritual causal relationship.

Karl Marx, a mid-nineteenth century German economist, sometimes referred to as the father of communism, wrote a widely misquoted statement that dealt with what he saw as unfair apportioning of wealth.

While often cited as being overly critical of religions in general, his critique was in fact a condemnation upon economic systems that disproportionately favor the ruling class; the status quo. To the extent institutions, inclusive of governance, economic, and religious, are self-perpetuating; they most often resist change over fear that change could reduce the power/authority they now possess. His famous quote, translated in English reads as follows:

> *"Religious distress is at the same time the expression of real distress and the protest against real distress. Religion is the sigh of the oppressed creature, the heart of a heartless world, just as it is the spirit of a spiritless situation. It is the opium of the people. The abolition of religion as the illusory happiness of the people is required for their real happiness. The demand to give up the illusion about its condition is the demand to give up a condition which needs illusions."*

Marx's observation of economic injustice remains quite accurate even today, though I disagree with his overly critical assessment drawing a conclusion that religion should be abolished. Quite the contrary, I think our beliefs need to drive the life we lead. Our "faith," whatever it may be, is not a Sunday suit but must be "worn" every day of our life. If not, then our faith is shallow and therefore of little help when it comes to our ability to cope with life's travails no less our redemption and salvation.

Pope Francis has spoken on the matter of the disproportionate wealth. He is no more a communist that am I. The reality is that those that "have it all" seek first to maintain what they possess. The "what" extends beyond simply resources or wealth into all areas of life; including religion. All too often religion holds out the hope of a "better life" in the next life, to those whose current condition is devoid of hope or a sense of progress. Many faiths, including Catholicism, speak to suffering as a means to our eternal life. Excerpts from the above attachments clearly seem to suggest that the "masses" should delight in their current life. There appears to be a more than passing sense that one should accept their lot in life rather than work within society's constructs to change the mechanisms which bring about inequality. I am very pleased that Pope Francis has unabashedly made efforts to bring greater visibility upon any economic system that benefits the few to the detriment of the many. I happen to believe that capitalism is the best economic system in existence in this world, but anything carried to an extreme is problematic.

Suffering, when it is unavoidable, can enable us to understand and even share in some small way the terrible trials that Jesus Himself experienced. This mortal world will always have pain and suffering in it, yet God is not the source of the suffering. All too often that source is other humans. Tragedy too will come to many, including an unexpected or untimely death of a loved one. To prevent such tragedies God would have to intervene, but that is not His role. He does not exist to referee the fairness of this life. I would not argue that our own suffering can lead to a heightened awareness of the plight of others who suffer even greater losses, but that doesn't mean suffering should be a sought-after or preferred condition of our lives.

I find that man's rationalization of the current human condition, both from a secular and non-secular perspective, is such that it makes it easy to justify and be accepting of unnecessary suffering. Things remaining as they are, status quo, is extolled by those that have, never by those that don't. There is an implied understanding that whatever exists in society is already fair with no consideration as to whether or not the current system should be changed. To the extent that religion "plays the role" to further such misconception is problematic in my eyes. This is not what God intended; this is not what Jesus Christ preached. It has been said that all that is needed for evil to triumph over good is for good people to remain silent, to do nothing. Apathy and indifference concede the result as hopeless. This is what I was speaking to in my last letter. The Church, all churches, can and should play a vital role in raising awareness and working to support peaceful changes that better society and the conditions of the many. In the long run, we all benefit, not just those that are poor and suffering.

Section 5 deals with *The Dynamic of Detachment and Holy Indifference*. Before I comment, here also are some quotes from that section.

- Saint Augustine…"If a soul clings to things whose beauty lies outside God, it is riveted only upon sorrow."
- Unclear as to attribution…"Holy Indifference to created things remains crucial for continued growth in grace."
- Julian of Norwich…"regard as nothing all things which are created."
- Thomas à Kempis contends, "When a man reaches a point where he seeks no solace from any creature, then he begins to relish God perfectly."
- Saint Louis de Montfort notes…"Attachment to other creatures can have the effect of estranging us from God, but it is not so with our attachment to Mary."

Let's for the moment assume that much of what is being referenced deals with material objects ("created things"). If that were the case, I can clearly accept many of the statements. However, once it becomes clear that the subject is meant to include our relationships with others then I find much of this appalling. In this mortal life the one thing that matters is our love, our relationships. All the rest—power, authority, wealth, and fame mean nothing. For the writer(s) to contend that even our relationships detract from God is something I will never accept.

Perhaps the part that really irks me is the all-inclusionary statement—meaning no exceptions. I believe that the greatest blessing God ever bestowed on me was Ginny and that the greatest, most perfect gift anyone has ever given me was Ginny's gift of love to me. I cannot think of another concept that I'm more opposed to than the one espoused here as dynamic detachment. I contend this concept denigrates the one "slice of heaven" that exists in this world—love.

Most, if not all, clergy within the Catholic Church took a vow of celibacy. As such, by definition they do not KNOW what it is to love another person, specifically one's spouse. I strongly contend that God would never view a loving relationship with another mortal as detracting from love of Him. I believe quite the contrary is the case. I will never sacrifice my love for Ginny to appease the Church's sense that I divorce myself for all that is not God. My view is that God is Love, so how could God want us to ever abandon our love of another person even if they are merely mortal?

Perhaps I've misinterpreted the meaning and intent of section 5 but I don't think so. You suggested that if I had further questions that I perhaps should contact an expert you'd worked with in your past. But I don't need clarification on what I believe. It wouldn't matter if a host of "experts" were to underscore the nature of "detachment and holy indifference" as being essential to my continued spiritual growth. It wouldn't make any difference to my core beliefs or in my faith in God. In the end, I find such conjecture by man to be repugnant.

In closing, one of the other enclosures you sent contained a paragraph taken from Soren Kierkegaard's in *Provocations: Spiritual Writings of Kierkegaard*. It read:

> "It is well known that Christ consistently used the expression "follower." He never asks for admirers, worshippers, or adherents. No, he calls disciples. It is not adherents of a teaching but followers of a life that Christ is looking for."

By extension, it seems to me that as one of the three-person trinity, Jesus is speaking and acting in exactly the same manner as would His Father and the Holy Spirit. Religions all too often use metaphors of our need to bow, worship, and adore Him. But is that what God wants or expects? There is a relationship we each have with our God. That relationship is not subject to debate and definition. While we may often cite His heavenly kingdom as being our end destination, I rather doubt it is His desire that the deference we show be manifest in the same manner history tells us to interact with earthly kings. I am very happy with my renewed relationship with God and thankful for your help in getting me through some very tough times. Please don't feel a need to "correct" my beliefs or the path I'm following. I absolutely believe it will lead me back home one day.

Dear Father,
April 15, 2015

Regarding My Personal Journey…Addendum to Letter of April 15th

Father, I wanted to share with you the lyrics from a song I've played quite a bit of late. I've noted before that I listen to music daily. As you know both Ginny and I loved music. I play the many songs of our life together often. Many of which hold bittersweet memories, but that doesn't change my need to listen.

Jim Brickman's song "What We Believe In" aptly reflects the depth of emotion that I feel when it comes to Ginny's passing. The lyrics towards the end say it best "And if seeing is believing, I look into the skies and there you are, You're not that far, 'Cause love is what we believe in". The song is rather sad but then life can be too. He is a wonderful pianist and lyricist; many of his songs are on my play list. On this particular song Brickman plays the piano while Pam Tillis beautifully sings the evocative lyrics. I purchased his *Destiny* CD that contains this song back in 1999 after hearing it on the way back from a west coast business trip. The lyrics to this song speak to me in a special way. A number of times I've found myself looking up to the heavens as twilight faded and the stars came out. I always think of her and yes, I tell her not to worry, as I will get to her one day. That's my solemn promise.

Dear Father,
April 30, 2015

Regarding My Personal Journey…A Connection (letter 41)

Recently a statement was made to me in regard to Ginny being gone; but she is not. To understand the idea that Ginny is not gone, one must understand the relationship that existed and still exists between her and me. We met back in '74, quite by chance it would seem. I always wondered what prompted me to go out on a Wednesday night—a work night. It was not typical of me to do so. Frankly, it was not for her either. At the time I was seeing other gals…more than one; each was aware it was not exclusive. I'd felt burned in a relationship earlier that year and as such was intent not to invest myself with any one person. If ever there were an example of "love at first sight," it was Ginny and me. I felt that way, and I later learned that she did too. There was an immediate connection between us that is hard to explain. That connection remains despite the fact she is no longer physically here.

Relationships are not static. They grow and change over time. The change is prompted by knowledge gained in our overall life and our life with the person. While it may not come as any shock to you, this world is not very accepting of an aspect of deep relationships; namely dependency. I cannot think of an empirical reference where the use of the word dependency is made without a negative connotation. We are taught to be independent, to think and act on our own based on our experiences and knowledge. Parents will often say that their goal is to raise their children to be productive and independent members of society. The problem with this concept is that while being self-reliant is viewed as positive, its focus is upon the self.

Shortly after Ginny passed I was faced with the prospect of starting anew...of finding my way forward. I sort of figured that in time I would gravitate towards looking for a new relationship. Though we did not speak of it directly, I know Ginny thought about it based on some comments she made to me. I believe it was disconcerting to her—the thought of me being with another. If the roles were reversed, I'd feel the same. So even after a terminal prognosis was made on March 17th of 2014, this idea was never on my mind. My way of dealing with the prognosis at the time was largely denial and avoidance. What was happening and would happen to us just could not happen...but it did. Even after her March 24th hospital discharge... even when she "made me promise to continue" that day in the car as we rode home from her radiation treatment, I could not wrap my head around the implications of a future without her by my side. In truth, I do not know if either of us really understood what it meant for me to "continue." All I know is that she insisted I promise her... and so I did. In the subsequent months I began to understand what that meant. The understanding did not come all at once...but slowly it dawned on me.

In the months since her passing I've learned a lot about myself. I learned the relationship we shared, while dependent, was one of symbiotic mutualism (yeah I looked it up). Our relationship evolved into what I'd call spiritual intimacy. While relationships often ebb and flow, some things are characteristic of those that are lasting; those that are what I term "true love." I came to the conclusion that no one could ever fill the void she left. Now I know that may sound overly romantic, but it is the truth. I don't believe I could ever love another as I loved her and love her to this very day. Some people need the benefit of companionship and do not want to be alone. Yet knowing how I feel, I just don't think I will ever seek another love relationship. I know that in my mind and heart it would always be compared to the one I had with Ginny. Perhaps this sounds fatalistic, but it's not. It's just the way it is. I remain very much in love with her.

People speak in terms of "falling in love," or "being in love" and then of the reality when love's fire wanes or is extinguished entirely. While each of us has the opportunity, the potential, to find true love, we are confronted with the everyday reality that often places little value upon it. This world is primarily focused upon the self. If we focus on the self, we lose the ability to truly love another. But if we put aside, disregard our own self-interests, what can emerge is the truth of love's immutable and unwavering belief in another.

At this point I've observed that many family members and friends have expectations of me in terms of an end to my grieving. Like most things, those who hold such expectations often have little understanding of the process itself. That should come as no surprise, for how could they know, for the loss is beyond their ability to understand. Some speak to it as if grieving itself had a definitive end. A grieving person must learn to adapt, employ coping techniques just to make it day-to-day. While no one should judge that which they do not know and therefore cannot understand, people do.

I love Ginny; now as much as ever before. She is still very much a part of who I am. Love endures. I came up with a simple equation to reflect my thoughts on the matter; $1+1=1$. It makes no sense mathematically or even empirically, but the equation holds the truth of the very nature of love.

Dear Father,
May 11, 2015

Regarding My Personal Journey…The Immortal Soul (letter #42)

The topic of our immortal soul has been discussed and argued through the ages. Does man possess an immortal soul? To theologians and clerics of all faiths the response would be a resounding yes. While I was raised in a Catholic tradition—my faith in God, my core beliefs—do not result from what is contained in the Bible or from the many lessons and teachings of my youth. Rather my beliefs are derived from an internalization of the writings and teachings of my past and an introspection of my life and personal assessment of what life represents.

If we look at the world today it would be easy to conclude that there is no proof, no definitive means to convince the nonbelievers that God exists. The very nature of beliefs presupposes an understanding that proof of our immortal soul—of God—cannot be derived by any empirical evidence. This is perhaps where mankind has failed to comprehend. The nature of God, of His very existence, is not subject to proof. Otherwise faith, beliefs, would be unnecessary. However, from my perspective, proof does exist and the proof is unequivocal. The simple truth is that the existence of love is proof of God.

Over the millennia mankind has looked to locate physical objects, relics, as proof. These include the Ark of the Covenant, Noah's ark, the Holy Grail, and many other items both tied to Christianity and other faiths. Yet objects themselves do not represent the person and therefore cannot be proof of any aspect other than they existed. No relic or artifact exists that holds magical properties, though mystics often believe such was or is the case. Other than much of her jewelry given to family and close friends, I've been unable to part with Ginny's clothing or possessions. Yet I know nothing in these physical things is her, they represent only memories. What does matter, whether we're speaking of God or of the deceased person, is that believing is all that counts.

Some say that God shows Himself only by His action—that He initiates all such discovery of faith; of the existence of His being. Yet that statement defies the matter of choice. We are free to choose to believe or not believe. Some put forth evidence that miracles do occur, that the miracle IS proof. Yet from my perspective and beliefs, God seldom interferes with the goings on of this mortal world.

When I suffered the loss of my wife Ginny, my world collapsed. The truth of God's existence became apparent to me not because of what I read, was told, or of an apparition from beyond. In looking for answers as to why, I found I was incapable of knowing but could choose to believe. While religions can espouse what you should believe, they cannot determine what we each do believe.

Despite the passage of time, I continue to struggle. Sort of expect that's just the way it's going to be; at least for me. While she is no longer physically here, she remains within me. Her spirit, the connection, and the love are not gone, nor will they ever be. I will no doubt continue to make mistakes, yet I believe the path I'm on is the right one for me. These days at times a sense of peace comes. I take solace in knowing that at the end, she did not suffer long. I continue to talk to Ginny each day. Perhaps the most important thing I take with me on this remaining journey is my faith and my love; in the end we need nothing more than these.

Lessons of My Life

Since Ginny's passing I've had a lot of time to ponder many matters, to reflect, and consider my actions and decisions in life. The following represents a summary of what I've determined to be the most significant factors and influences affecting my own ability to find happiness and meaning in this life. In some cases, this represents an awareness, a realization of some things I failed to recognize sooner. I share them not as a blueprint of how you or anyone should live their life but in hope of enabling you to benefit from my mistakes and misconceptions.

- *Balance and Priority*

Without exception, everyone struggles with the need to establish and maintain some sense of balance in their life. The balance I speak of is analogous to a three-legged stool. The three legs are family, career, and self. Balancing the time demands is without exception a difficult task. We are taught to think and act independently. This is an important part of what we broadly term 'growing up'. Demands upon our time however are dynamic and not always predictable. It will be a struggle to achieve balance; even more so to maintain it.

Throughout the course of my life I struggled with finding and maintaining a sense of balance and priority. All too often I let perceived urgencies dictate my actions; at times to the detriment of my family and my marriage. While I frequently would caution others by telling them to remember that we work to live, not live to work; I consistently ignored my own advice. At times this resulted in my failure to maintain a proper sense of priority. I learned the hard way that establishing and maintaining balance and priority are essential for happiness.

To most people, "living in the present" may sound rather straight-forward yet often I seemed unable to do so. I cannot explain why it was so hard for me but in hindsight it was my Achilles heel. Perhaps it represents a facet of 'perfectionism'; always feeling as if the outcome should have been better. Generally our culture views hedonism nega-tively. It's not unusual today for some companies to silently foster an attitude where even taking one's earned vacation is frowned upon. Yet taking the time to live in and enjoy the present is absolutely essential for health and happiness. There's an adage which I'll paraphrase that says "Life is what happens when you're busy pursuing your goals". When spontaneity wanes and routine predominates, life can become dull and all too predictable. My tendency to plan everything out was misguided as doing so set expectations that reality could not match. Life rarely mirrors our expectations. All too often this brought about unnecessary stress that limited my ability to simply relax and enjoy the moment. Lastly, many things we pursue or want are just that, things. In the big picture of life, things don't matter, only relationships truly matter.

Things we may pursue (wealth, fame, and power) never lead to fulfill-ment or happiness. These often distract us from what is truly of value. We expend efforts and energies to attain them only to learn this fact. Our society places far too much emphasis upon what I'd term 'the trap-pings of success'. I do not purport to know of a better economic system than capitalism yet I believe whatever is achieved, is not a result of singular efforts. Success has many parents and the truth is that failure is seldom an orphan. I believe I understood this and seldom sought ei-ther recognition or praise; perhaps I got this right. Where I failed was in thinking I could control all facets of my life. Control is an illusion.

If I had it to do all over, I'd surely make some changes in how I lived my life. I have and will always be a passionate person. Generally such is a good attribute. Yet I commit to you I'd never again make the mistake of losing my sense of what is important and I would take the time to stop and smell those roses.

• *Faith and Belief*

Personally I have found that faith and beliefs are absolutely essential. Faith is analogous to a house while beliefs are the furnishings within. Faiths and beliefs are not the same thing. As I define here, faith and beliefs also affect our ability to interact with others without the need of proof. Beliefs enable us to accept without question or reservation another's motive and intent.

It has been established that over ninety percent of the world's population identifies with a particular faith/religion so the belief in a supreme entity is shared by the vast majority of us. Though I was raised a Roman Catholic, until this terrible loss I'd failed to truly internalize my faith.

Beliefs serve as the foundation upon which you can build anything and everything. Without beliefs, we often become distracted by the trappings of life or become cynical. My entire sense of being for most my life was geared towards empiricism and pragmatism. I lacked any real sense of spirituality. This left me wholly unprepared when tragedy entered my life. While one cannot plan for tragic events almost by definition, having an outlook that realizes such can occur holds value. As I noted earlier, I wrestled with the question "Why me?" Only after considerable reflection did I begin to understand it's not the right question. Just recently when I met with a new friend who similarly had lost the love of her life she too noted that the right question is "Why not me?" To me this was further proof that I was not alone in my grief. It took me nearly sixty years to figure out that faith can sustain us and provide some sense of solace only when we have internalized it by developing a set of core beliefs. My beliefs largely align with my Catholic faith and they have been perhaps the most important means in enabling me to cope with the loss of my darling wife.

The very nature of beliefs is in the understanding that they are subjective. To believe implies an acceptance without empirical evidence. Faith can be described in many ways; blind is an adjective I'd never use. Though our intellect may not fully comprehend all the mysteries of our faith; that is not to say it is incumbent upon us to simply accept without making the effort to understand. In this regard beliefs are similar to scientific theories. Scrutiny, investigation, and examination of their nature are warranted in order to better comprehend. Those who simply believe without thought or question are likely to miss out on an opportunity to increase the depth of their faith and development a sense of spirituality. In my opinion we are not meant to simply parrot what we are told but to delve in the matters to understand as best we can; the nature and underlying principles of life and our existence. All learning occurs, and can only occur, if we make the effort to deepen our understanding. A resolute faith in God should be the result of our efforts to internalize the meaning and then act in accordance with it. Knowing what is right however is a far cry from doing what is right.

In our life we will experience both good and bad along with the related emotions of joy and sorrow. I would urge others to avoid a mindset that what happens to us is either predestined or tied somehow to God's will. From my perspective God seldom intervenes to change or produce a particular outcome. If that were true then what purpose does free will serve? The truth is bad things do happen to good people; that's just the way it is. Bad things that happen to us or our loved ones are not a sign that God disapproves of what we've done or that He is punishing us. The same can be said in reverse; good things occurring are not a reward for our behavior.

Many people attend religious services often. I think that's a good thing. Still it is more important that we **live our faith** and not just participate in ritual symbolism. History has shown that at times institutionalized religions, with their heavy emphasis on a specific set of rules and traditions can lead us to view others who follow another faith as being wrong, misled, or even inferior. In the course of my life I've met people of many different faiths and beliefs. Some people believe THEIR faith is THE ONLY TRUE FAITH. Who is God's chosen people? My perspective is simply that my God is the God of all humanity. He (she) is not just the God of one faith or sect. I'm certain that heaven contains the souls of people of many faiths including believers of Judaism, Islam, Hindus, Christians and others. Which faith one adheres to is far less important than how they lead their lives.

Today no less than before her passing, no one would accuse me of being a religious zealot. Yet now there exists within me a sense of spirituality that pervades my life. In a way it signifies another example of how my darling wife saved my life; once again.

• *Love*

What is love? I dare say it is not what most often is portrayed in this world. Our society overall, and mass media specifically, promulgates a rather cynical and self centered view of this thing we call love. To the uninformed, love is a physical act; little more than a carnal response to our own needs. Many would contend that being "in love" is just a normal hormonal response; a temporary response to an otherwise simple biological need. Beyond being cynical, these views are shallow and are not what I'm referring to in regards to love. To differentiate it I will use the term 'true love'.

True love has certain attributes or qualities that identify it as such. First and foremost, it is **selfless.** It places the well-being of another before our own needs and desires. It is said, love is blind but that doesn't mean we cannot see clearly because of it. It means it does not rely upon one's physicality or appearance. Love gives us eyes to see another for who they truly are, faults and all, and **accept** them. We all have faults. Yet it is in the recognition of our imperfections and weaknesses that another attribute shines. Each of us will make mistakes in our relationships. Some mistakes are minor transgressions, others are not. Yet true love will manifest when recognition of our human frailties, faults, and mistakes results in **forgiveness** despite the hurt that may have been inflicted. The reality is that true love is not all that commonplace. True love enables us to reveal ourselves, to become vulnerable. There is always a risk involved; of being rejected. Yet that risk must be overcome in order for love to flourish. In essence, it shows us another of its qualities; love is **fearless.** Lastly, true love lacks superficiality, it is always sincere and honest; it is **genuine.**

True love is not destined or fated to any of us. Finding it in another is tied to circumstance and determined by our receptivity and that of a potential mate. How, where and when you find your true love is anyone's guess. To some of us it may come early, others much later, and still others may never find it.

In November 1977 as we walked to one of our last Pre Cana sessions, Ginny and I talked about the vows we'd make. Back then, at least within the Catholic Church, it was not customary to write one's own vows. Father Jim, the priest who worked with us in preparation, conceded a point and agreed to make a small modification in the ceremony. Ginny and I absolutely believed our love would transcend death. We both felt strongly that our love was eternal. On our wedding day the vows we exchanged excluded the phrase "until death do us part".

I was blessed in that I found my true love as did she. Throughout our marriage Ginny taught me the meaning of love. The grace she exhibited even in those final days underscored the depth of her commitment and her core beliefs. She never gave up; she endured all matter of effort and pain in her battle with cancer, right up to and including her tragic passing. I am so very proud of her. In my eyes and in my heart she is the very epitome of love. She made all the difference in my life and our love continues to burn brightly within me. I will never stop loving her. I will never stop believing in her or in us. I will keep the faith.

Poems

The following several pages include three poems, each inspired by and dedicated to the loving memory of my wife Ginny.

To The Love of My Life

You left that day without goodbyes exchanged,
My life stood still, all our plans rearranged.

Though months have passed since you went away,
Those images are burned in my soul of that horrid day.

Though many can only imagine such a terrible plight,
Those who have walked this path know that all days turn to night.

You and I were part of "us," for it was always "we,"
But the silence screams, for now it's only me.

So here I am; somewhere I never thought I'd be.
Trapped between two worlds but trying so hard to see.

Trying so hard to understand the how and why,
Most days it seems when I think about it, I just cry.

But for the promise made I would choose to leave,
To grant myself some welcome reprieve.

Each day the struggle continues within my soul,
But I will go on, for I must pay the toll.

No matter what comes my way you remain the love of my life,
My precious darling, my better half, my dear wife.

I can remember another time similar to this,
When you and I learned the meaning of "miss."

Unlike then, now the time will be measured in years,
So please understand the reason for all these tears.

I know you are in heaven with God above,
But know this too, for I remain so very much in love.

One day we two will again be as one,
That's a promise my dear, from His only Son.

You see my darling you will always be,
Not only an important part, but the very best of me.

Left Behind

Though more than a year has gone since that day,
I still struggle and look at my new life in a rueful way.

You had it right from the very start,
Guess it's true that I was only 'book' smart.

You often tried to tell me but I wouldn't listen,
Now as I look back it's my tears, not your eyes that glisten.

I do so wish I could change the past,
But it doesn't work that way I understand at last.

I often wonder what it is that you now see,
When from where you are you look down at me.

Our dinners were always so late each day,
I'd told myself that work demands it be this way.

But today even the dishes are all put away,
Long before the time I'd come home to you most days.

What became of the many things back then that took my time,
Turns out none of them were important compared to "Mine."

I look at so much I did versus what I could have done,
I so wish I could go back and just be with the One.

The One who was always there you see,
No matter what I did that may have hurt you and me.

Yet no matter where or how much I look for you each day,
I see only shadows of all our yesterdays.

I had let myself succumb until you were no longer the only one,
Other things I said so mattered, they had won.

I'd let the outside world take hold of me,
Turns out that was my great mistake you see.

I now have this horrid sense of being left behind,
That was never your way; I was always first in your heart & mind.

Long ago I was just like that too if you recall,
Before I took my eye off the ball.

Perhaps I'm not looking at this right,
As I search for answers every day and every night.

Perhaps it's true you never left as some might say,
But have gone ahead to prepare for the day.

When once again it's like it used to be,
The two of us together, just you and me.

If You Could Hear Me

Each day I wonder and question why,
But no one answers and so I often cry.

If you could hear me perhaps then,
Things would be different, like back when.

I'd go looking for something yet seldom find it,
That is until you'd tell me just you sit.

"Let me search for I know you,
You lack any patience, you know that's true."

If you could hear me perhaps you'd say,
"Don't worry mine there'll come a day,

When my voice returns you'll see,
Just how much you mean to me.

I know you miss me for that is clear,
On that day I'll wipe away your tears.

All that longing that came to pass,
Will come to an end at last.

In my arms you will take a rest,
You will see it's not been a test.

For I know you love me and I do you,
You continued on just as I pressed you too.

You wrote our story so others would know,
Just how wonderful a love we did sow.

I see you struggling each day, so very sad,
Please don't worry for it isn't bad.

I'm here waiting for that day,
So be patient mine you'll find a way.

Back in my arms is where you're meant to be,
I a part of you, and you a part of me.
Together again, now as one."

Epilogue

In my own life, as the years passed, I had become jaded, overly critical, and judgmental. The idealism and spontaneity of my youth had largely been displaced by pragmatism and routine. Nothing but facts mattered and having a plan was essential. Any problem could be solved given enough time and effort. Resolution and progress therefore, was tied to facts, never beliefs.

During the intervening months since Ginny's passing I've been both blessed and cursed by time; time to think, to contemplate, to reflect upon the past. I've tried to use some of that time to closely examine my life—to assess what I've done right as well as what I've done wrong. In regard to beliefs and faith, my perspective has been inexorably changed from what it was before she passed. I've concluded that having and holding true to one's beliefs is absolutely essential in maintaining a balance in one's life.

As children many of us were read stories, fairy tales. In these an event or outcome occurs that could never happen simply using reason, logic, and empirical methods. So as children we are taught to believe many things. Later we learn that many of these things are not true, not based in fact, not real; they were simply make-believe. This presents us with a dichotomy, a conflict between what we were told and what is real or the truth. The problem as I see it is that we begin to conclude that all that is factual or truthful is provable. This can and often does pervade most aspects of our lives. Not only do we suspend many of our beliefs, we may begin to lose faith and trust in one another.

It is not my intent to convince anyone that I have found THE answer based on my experiences and introspection since Ginny's passing. What I have done however is to find MY answer. Today I have strongly-held beliefs that happen to include a belief in God and in the power of love. Relationships matter, things do not. We risk losing everything if we turn our backs on the idea of believing in things that are not provable.

Some who have known me most of my life may say that I'm fairly intelligent. I don't know about that. I think I'm neither the sharpest nor dullest tool in the shed. In any case, it took the passing of my wife for me to understand some things that my wife always knew, always believed. There's a vast difference between intelligence and wisdom. Turns out the one who taught me so much, my wisest teacher, just happened to be my wife. She possessed not only beauty, compassion, and grace, but a set of core beliefs that made her an extraordinary person.

In this writing I've told you a story about a couple of people who I know well. My sincere hope is that anyone who reads this will be affected in a way that enables them to "see" with their heart rather than only their eyes. I remain a flawed person, but a significantly better person for having found the love of my life in Ginny. I absolutely know that one day she and I will be together again. So you see, this journey, the story of our life will have a very happy ending. All one must do is believe.